Pragmatics, Discourse and Text

Open Linguistics Series

The *Open Linguistics Series*, to which this book makes a significant contribution, is 'open' in two senses. First, it provides an open forum for works associated with any school of linguistics or with none. Linguistics has now emerged from a period in which many (but never all) of the most lively minds in the subject seemed to assume that transformational-generative grammar—or at least something fairly closely derived from it—would provide the main theoretical framework for linguistics for the foreseeable future. In Kuhn's terms, linguistics had appeared to some to have reached the 'paradigm' stage. Reality today is very different. More and more scholars are working to improve and expand theories that were formerly scorned for not accepting as central the particular set of concerns highlighted in the Chomskyan approach—such as Halliday's systemic theory (as exemplified in this book) Lamb's stratificational model and Pike's tagmemics—while others are developing new theories. The series is open to all approaches, then—including work in the generativist-formalist tradition.

The second sense in which the series is 'open' is that it encourages works that open out 'core' linguistics in various ways: to encompass discourse and the description of natural texts; to explore the relationship between linguistics and its neighbouring disciplines such as psychology, sociology, philosophy, artificial intelligence, and cultural and literary studies; and to apply it in fields such as education and language pathology.

Open Linguistics Series Editor
Robin F. Fawcett, University of Wales College of Cardiff

Modal Expressions in English, Michael R. Perkins
Text and Tagmeme, Kenneth L. Pike and Evelyn G. Pike
The Semiotics of Culture and Language, eds: Robin P. Fawcett, M. A. K. Halliday, Sydney M. Lamb and Adam Makkai
Into the Mother Tongue: A Case Study in Early Language Develoment, Clare Painter
Language and the Nuclear Arms Debate: Nukespeak Today, ed.: Paul Chilton
Functional Approaches to Writing: Research Perspectives, ed.: Barbara Couture
The Structure of Social Interaction: A Systemic Approach to the Semiotics of Service Eneounters, Eija Ventola
Grammar in the Construction of Texts, ed.: James Monaghan
On Meaning, A. J. Griemas, trans. by Paul Perron and Frank Collins
Biological Metaphor and Cladistic Classification: An Interdisciplinary Approach, eds.: Henry M. Hoenigswald and Linda F. Wiener
New Developments in Systemic Linguistics, Volume 1: Theory and Description, eds.: M. A. K. Halliday and Robin P. Fawcett
Volume 2: Theory and Application, eds.: Robin P. Fawcett and David Young
Eloquence and Power: The Rise of Language Standards and Standard Language, John Earl Joseph
Functions of Style, eds.: David Birch and Michael O'Toole
Registers of Written English: Situational Factors and Linguistic Features, ed.: Mohsen Ghadessy

Pragmatics, Discourse and Text
Some Systemically-inspired Approaches

Edited by
Erich H. Steiner, IAI EUROTRA-D and University of the Saarland
Robert Veltman, University of Kent, Canterbury

Ablex Publishing Corporation
Norwood, New Jersey 07648

© Erich H. Steiner and Robert Veltman 1988

All rights reserved. No part of this publication may be reproduced, stored in a retrieval system, or transmitted by any other means without the prior written permission of the copyright holder. Please direct all enquiries to the publishers.

Printed in Great Britain

Library of Congress Cataloging-in-Publication Data
CIP applied for
ISBN 0-89391-546-7

Ablex Publishing Corporation
355 Chestnut Street
Norwood, New Jersey

Contents

Foreword by Robin P. Fawcett — vii

Introduction
Erich H. Steiner and Robert Veltman — 1

Part I Meeting the challenge of 'pragmatics' — 13

1. Systemic linguistics, semantics and pragmatics
   Christopher S. Butler — 13
2. English questions: a 'significance-generating device' for building in context
   Eirian C. Davies — 28

Part II Explorations in thematic structure and information structure — 47

3. Marked themes with and without pronominal reinforcement: their meaning and distribution in discourse
   Daniel Kies — 47
4. Functional sentence perspective in the context of systemic functional grammar
   M. P. Williams — 76
5. Thematization in legislative language: the observations of Bentham and Coode in relation to the FG definition of Theme
   Frederick Bowers — 90

Part III Insights from discourse analysis — 99

6. The structure of family conversation in Yoruba English
   Femi Akindele — 99
7. From illocution to syntactic and prosodic realization in making requests
   G. Tucker — 120

Part IV The text as a product of interaction and cognition — 133

8. Grammatical metaphor: an initial analysis
   L. J. Ravelli — 133

9. Cohesion in spoken Arabic texts
   Yowell Y. Aziz 148
10. Text structure and text semantics
    J. L. Lemke 158
11. Cognitive processes in context: a systemic approach to problems in oral language use
    Jonathan Fine 171

Bibliography 181

Index 183

Foreword

When, in 1973, I organized a small workshop for those working in systemic linguistics, I had no idea that this single meeting of a score or so of invited scholars would grow to become the annual international conference that it now is, often attracting approaching two hundred participants. I had no idea, indeed, that there would be a second workshop at all. But steadily the numbers have grown, and steadily the international nature of the meetings has become established. First we added the word 'International' so that the meetings were, for example, the 'Seventh International Systemic Workshop', and this has been reflected in the places in which the meetings have been held. Three, including that of the present year, have been held in North America, and one in Australia. One interesting aspect of this internationalism is that, with the costs of travel as they are, most of the participants in each workshop come from the local continent—so that if we put together all of those who attend when they can the total number is something of the order of five hundred.

Another change is that, with some regrets, the meetings have become less workshop-like and more formal—though we still try to include workshop activities within the overall programme. And at the Fourteenth Workshop in Sydney it was decided that since the annual meetings had in effect become international congresses, this is what they should be called. So the 1988 meeting is the Fifteenth International Systemic Congress.

One advantage that this growth has brought with it is that more of the talks are presented as full papers. It has therefore become natural to think in terms of publishing selected papers from the workshops. The two people who have done most to encourage this trend are Jim Benson and Bill Greaves, of York University, Toronto, who have jointly edited papers from the ninth and twelfth workshops. The present volume, however, is the first to emerge from a workshop on the Eastern side of the Atlantic, and it is all the more welcome for that.

This volume represents another development in the workshops; they are no longer attended only by fully committed, 'insider' systemic linguists, but also by many others who are interested in applying systemic ideas or in relating their thinking to the broad framework that Michael Halliday's Systemic Functional Linguistics makes available to those who work with language. For it is pre-eminently a usable theory, and an adaptable theory; indeed, it is doubtful whether, if there were no applications for linguistics, the theory would exist at all.

This volume, then, includes some contributions that reflect current central concerns within systemic theory, and some that illustrate the way that scholars who are not committed to the full theory nonetheless find it a useful framework to which to relate their thinking. Hence the title.

Robin P. Fawcett
Radyr, July 1988

Introduction

Erich Steiner
IAI EUROTRA-D and University of the Saarland
Robert Veltman
University of Kent, Canterbury

This volume brings together a number of essays on three interwoven themes of PRAGMATICS, DISCOURSE and TEXT.

There was a time when editing such a volume would elicit an introductory statement of a defensive nature. Now, thankfully, such apologies are no longer offered. The prevailing climate recognizes that language has many LEVELS of organization and is applied to the service of a vast variety of FUNCTIONS, which theoretically increase in number with each new utterance. Whether 'levels of organization' is the appropriate term or not is a question which will be treated presently, but it is the insight of SYSTEMIC-FUNCTIONAL LINGUISTICS that the multilevelled and multifunctional aspects of languages are intimately related.

The notion of linguistic organization according to 'levels' or 'strata' or even 'components' is, probably, not more than a useful fiction, heuristically applied in order to create an illusion of hierarchy and order, not a little encouraged by the ancient but insidious concept of 'priority'. Firstly, the elements known as 'levels' operate interactively, but as the recent history of linguistics tells us, inter-level interaction is not a necessary inference that can be drawn from the notion of levels alone, when their only significant point of contact is the so-called 'trading relation' between the components of a generative grammar. Secondly, there is probably no fundamental evidence for or general value in the unidirectional character of level interaction, as embodied in stratally organized models, restricted to reflection of real-time, speaker-only communicative activity.

How, then, is it possible to portray language holistically, as a working phenomenon but sufficiently generalized to account for phenomena other than speech production? To accomplish this it is necessary to disentangle and reclassify vital elements of description, as was done, for instance, in the critique by Sinclair and Coulthard (1975) and Coulthard and Brazil (1979) of ethnomethodological treatments of conversation by applying Halliday's SCALE and CATEGORY methodology (Halliday 1961). The vital ingredients of holistic description are, as might be expected here, PRAGMATICS, DISCOURSE and TEXT. Whereas elsewhere these three have been treated as sorts of 'linguistic levels' or 'components of grammar', we wish to consider them as different but complementary aspects of dimensions of description with an ultimately identical focus. The dimensions concerned are PERSPECTIVE, PROCESS and PRODUCT.

PRAGMATICS is more a 'perspective' than a genuine level or component, as is commonly assumed, where it is contrasted usually with semantics (Leech 1983: 5–7), or grammar (Chomsky 1980: 59), or even language itself (Radford 1981: 8, 1988: 10–11). A recent review of the semantics–pragmatics relation (Lyons 1987) suggests that it suffers from ingrained inconsistency and vacuousness, with the concepts continuing to be so starkly opposed. It is therefore time that these two fundamental constructs are disassociated and allowed to breathe independently. Pragmatics is the means by which students of language come to terms with language as a PROCESS as well as language as a PRODUCT, and thus links discourse to text, for pragmatics is the perspective that is determined by language as synthesis, as a global act, rather than by analysis, which accounts for the more classical components of linguistic description. Indeed, Levinson (1979) forecasts the development of an 'analysis by synthesis' approach as a natural consequence of investigations of communication within Artificial Intelligence. Furthermore, phenomena arising in all these components—semantic, syntactic, lexical, morphological, phonological—can be accounted for pragmatically.

Take, for instance, the following text from a BBC broadcast: 'This point is reinforced by Chinua Achebe, *a Nigerian novelist*, who writes—I feel that the English language will be unable to carry the weight of my African experience'. In logic, the definite and indefinite articles in English are said not to be synonymous (Fodor *et al*. 1975), but in this context of apposition they may be, in that 'the Nigerian novelist' does not mean that Chinua Achebe is the only Nigerian novelist. On the other hand, the indefinite article carries a deprecatory sense compared with the definite article. Are the two competing phrases synonymous or not? An account of grammatical meaning from the pragmatic perspective will detail and explain all the above observations, which involve consideration of 'syntax' (apposition), 'grammar' (article system), 'semantics' (definiteness and indefiniteness) and 'lexis' (*novelist* versus *capital*, as in 'Lagos, the Nigerian capital'), as well as features traditionally characteristic of 'pragmatics' (eulogistic versus deprecatory). It may seem, then, that it is possible to treat meaning in language from one or other of two perspectives: the LOGICAL and the PRAGMATIC. However, since Grice (1975), 'logic' in language has become distinctly pragmatic in sense. Moreover, the choices made between what speakers take to be logical or literal and affective or non-literal meanings (to mention only two sets of the many relevant distinctions made) are PRAGMATIC choices. And where pragmatic choice resides, FUNCTIONAL choice does too (see Butler; Davies: this volume).

DISCOURSE comes closest of our three elements of description to what is known as a 'level': it apparently arises through a breakdown at the upper end of the RANK SCALE, where a different, non-grammatical mode of organization is called for. But it is wrong to infer that a higher organizational stratum is required simply because a HIGH-ranked UNIT cannot cope. If discourse is a 'level', then it is the level at which texts are PRODUCED and which accounts for the internal organization of texts. Since, however, we have suggested that the notion of 'level' is inappropriate for the holistic treatment of the language act, let us say what descriptive dimension discourse is associated with—discourse is language as PROCESS—and as such is associated with the classical notion of RHETORIC.

TEXT is the PRODUCT of language activity encoded in words and delivered into the world in the substance of speech, writing or signing. Spoken texts have a certain privilege in discourse studies, a view promoted within systemic-functional linguistics, since they, it is claimed, make greater demands on the resources of the grammar and the human unconscious (Halliday 1985a: xxiv). This is a compelling argument, owing much to Labov (1972), and it is of vital significance too, since it explains linguistic competence in performance, and hence in pragmatic terms, thereby liberating students of language from the paradox of the Saussurean and Chomskyan dichotomies. However, the understanding of the relationship between language and consciousness remains to be fully investigated; and, as insights into the nature of written texts increase in number and vigour, they may also prove to make extremely varied and specific demands on the system of language at all levels (see Halliday 1985a, b; Ravelli: this volume), and on important interactional mechanisms (Widdowson 1979, Sanford and Garrod 1981).

Thus from the point of view of PERSPECTIVE, PROCESS and PRODUCT, pragmatics, discourse and text, the system respectively associated with these dimensions of description, together comprise the leading edge of language, and it is to the integration of these notions that this volume is devoted. The chapters in this collection, whose individual contents were first sketched at the XIII International Systemic Workshop at the University of Kent at Canterbury in July 1986, are roughly organized according to our three guiding notions.

Having characterized the context of the major themes of this volume, some details are required of the motivations for addressing the issues raised herein. We have identified a number of significant fields of social activity and research which these motivations emerge from: rhetoric, computational linguistics and artificial intelligence, language teaching, literary stylistics and linguistics itself.

The source of interest in discourse and text studies has classically been in the field of RHETORIC, both as an academic discipline and as a profession. Current rhetoric is rediscovering linguistics as a provider of more explicit tools and explanations than are otherwise available (cf. Chilton (ed.) 1984 as one good example). We are witnessing the re-emergence of a union between rhetoric on the one hand, and grammar and philosophy on the other, in the explicit recognition of language as the prime medium of the processes which are studied by these disciplines. This merging of domains is illustrated in this volume in contributions inspired by both advances in linguistic pragmatics and functional language theory, the latter having, arguably, as its core a SYSTEMIC FUNCTIONAL GRAMMAR. Needless to say, the formal and informal methods advocated in the contributions to this volume have to be justified in a context of rhetoric, and for such a justification it is necessary to show that the application of such methods actually yields new insights in rhetorical investigations. Although a number of appropriate and far-reaching devices for such investigations have already been developed within the framework of Systemic Functional Grammar, such as register theory, cohesion and grammatical metaphor, and elsewhere, for instance, implicature (Grice 1975), relevance (Sperber and Wilson 1986) and primal versus actual content (Wilensky 1987), there is a pressing need to clarify, interrelate and apply theories and methods, as the expositions in this volume attempt to do.

Recent years have witnessed an increasing interest in CLINICAL APPLICATIONS of ideas and techniques of linguistics. Practitioners in such areas as diagnosis and therapy of schizophrenia, aphasia and disturbances in language development have been drawn into linguistic theories, and more particularly to theories of discourse and text structure (cf. Rochester and Martin 1979; Fine: this volume). In order for applications in such fields to succeed, linguistic models would be expected to come meaningfully close to reflecting the psychological reality of human language processes, or at least to model aspects of language in such a way that these models can be related successfully to processes of language and cognition. Interestingly enough, it has turned out that the Systemic model of language, which originally was not meant to be an approximation of human cognition or psychology—a 'sociological' orientation was Halliday's view of the explanatory goal of the model (Halliday 1973, 1978)—has something to offer these areas. This might also reflect back on theoretical debates within Systemic linguistics, as to how 'psychological' the model is meant to be: the chapters on pragmatics in this volume point to a possible disintegration of the barriers between these two conventionally distinct orientations—the 'psychological' and the 'sociological'. It is hoped, then, that confirmation is provided here that systemic approaches to discourse and text are a fruitful source for the clinicians' own models of language and language processes.

While it might come as something of a surprise that Systemic linguistics is of value to the clinical context, the same can hardly be said for the field of LANGUAGE TEACHING and LEARNING, which, since 'Categories of the Theory of Grammar' (Halliday 1961), has drawn heavily on the model and the descriptions that emerged from it to form the outlook and methodology of a whole generation of language teachers, particularly where English and the English speaking are concerned, but increasingly in respect of other languages and other speech communities. If Halliday (1961) marks the beginning of systemically inspired pedagogical descriptions (e.g. Scott *et al*. 1968; Muir 1972), it is from Halliday *et al*. (1964) that the more methodologically and learner-oriented impact on the language teaching procession is derived, a tradition upheld in numerous publications (e.g. Halliday 1969, 1975) and gatherings, such as the AILA World Congress in Sydney 1987. Just as Systemic theory has progressed from a primary focus on the clause to one on discourse and text, so the requirements of language teaching have become broader and more comprehensive, to the point where models of discourse and text have become an essential ingredient thereof. We hope that this volume can speak meaningfully and inspirationally to language-teaching and language-textbook-writing professions, particularly in this latter respect.

Another area in which, as in clinical therapy and treatment, Systemic theory has had a surprising and recent impact, is COMPUTATIONAL LINGUISTICS and ARTIFICIAL INTELLIGENCE. After all, it lacked extensive formalisation until only a few years ago (cf. Kasper 1987). However, any absence of mathematical rigour and foundation was, as far as the disciplines of application were concerned, compensated for by the HOLISTIC view of language inherent in the model, functionally inspired as it is (cf. Veltman 1985), which this volume as already stated wishes to emphasize. Thus research such as Winograd's SHRDLU program (Winograd 1972), the 'Nigel' project (cf. Mann's and Mathiessen's chapters in Benson and Greaves (eds) 1985, Kasper 1987 and Kempen (ed.) 1987) has developed alongside non-systemic work in the area (cf. Danlos 1987: 101ff.; Grishman 1986: 140ff.; Nirenburg (ed.) 1987). Most of the earlier systems were sentence-based, which is probably still true nowadays, but the needs for solving problems like pronominal reference, definiteness, focus, scope, theme–rheme structures, etc., is leading more and more investigators even in sentence-based systems to examine discourse and text theories. It is certainly not accidental that the full force of such problems was fully recognized not so much in analysis, but in generation. In addition, the more Computational Linguistics and Artificial Intelligence systems interact with non-linguistic knowledge bases, the more natural a text-based strategy becomes, because, essentially, in many ways the highest unit of organizing knowledge is the text, rather than the sentence. Also, and quite naturally, a realistic attempt at modelling anything even remotely resembling natural interaction between some user of a system and the system itself in the form of some discourse requires well-structured theories of human discourse in all its aspects. So there is an increasing demand from the fields of Computational Linguistics and Artificial Intelligence for text and discourse theories and we hope to indicate in this volume that Systemic Functional Grammar is a valid and fruitful source of relevant theory and methodology.

For many the study of discourse and text is synonymous with LITERARY CRITICISM, which in the absence of any cogent linguistic theory has over the decades developed its own methodology. For a considerable time now, there have been interactions between linguistics studying 'style' and literary critics (cf. Leech and Short 1981; Birch and O'Toole 1988). Generalizing very broadly, it might be claimed that whereas traditional rhetoric is an ancestor of discourse analysis, traditional literary analysis is the progenitor of text-linguistics. However, a certain amount of circumspection is worthwhile in considering the relation between linguistics and literary studies in the light of claims to the effect that linguistics has substantial insights to offer literary criticism. If it has, then it must be a linguistics with a far-reaching interest in text structures. Several contributions to this volume should be able to meet this demand (see chapters by Kies, Williams, Aziz, Bowers and Lemke in this volume).

Thus far, we have tried to map out the range of interest in text and discourse studies from outside linguistics. We now turn to 'core' linguistics itself with the aim of locating the main sources of interest there.

It is possible to divide present-day schools of linguistics into two broad categories: those which have a more philosophical background and those with a more rhetorical background (cf. Halliday 1985c). Those schools which owe more to the philosophical tradition have, in practice, not shown major interest in units 'larger' than the sentence, and this is still largely true of currently familiar, syntax-based theories, such as Government and Binding (Chomsky 1981), Lexical Functional Grammar (Bresnan (ed.) 1982) and Generalized Phrase Structure Grammar (Gazdar *et al*. 1985). But even within those theories, certain phenomena which residually resist a strict sentence-based treatment have, as it were, forced the 'philosophical' tradition in linguistics to adumbrate at least the beginnings of theories of suprasentential structures (cf. Rochemont 1986). Apart from this particular family of schools of linguistics, truth-value-oriented semantics has begun to recognize the need for theories of text and discourse (Seuren 1985), and so has speech-act-based pragmatics (cf. Butler, Davies in this volume). Those schools of linguistics whose number includes Systemic Linguistics, which have antecedents in the more rhetorical tradition, have for a considerable time worked on theories of text and discourse (cf. Brown and Yule 1983; Halliday and Hasan 1976), and it is in terms of this perspective that there will be very obvious interest in the issues addressed in the present volume.

An enumeration of the connections which we are attempting to make with the existing research tradition in Systemic Linguistics would become impossible if exhaustiveness were our goal (see Butler 1985 for a pioneering survey of this interdisciplinary potential). Systemic Linguistics, as has been indicated, enjoys a privileged position in the field of text and discourse, which has by now yielded a very complex picture of research activities, a complete survey of which lies beyond this introduction. Let us, therefore, outline some of the principal strands of investigation with which contact is made in this volume.

Halliday (1985c) shows convincingly how a FUNCTIONAL GRAMMAR inevitably impinges on a text/discourse grammar at several crucial points. It is in this area that work on issues of THEMATIC STRUCTURE (Kies, Williams, Bowers in this volume) are most directly concerned, in the same way that work on COHESION (cf. Aziz in this volume) has a bearing on the issues raised by Halliday and Hasan (1976).

Fawcett *et al*. (forthcoming) successfully extend system network methodology to the area of discourse structure, a direction reflected in Tucker's chapter on SERVICE ENCOUNTER discourse, a continuation of a fruitful line of research inspired by Ventola's studies (Ventola 1982). While much is owed in discourse analysis to the Labovian and ethnomethodological tradition, the novel departures undertaken from the critical perspective of Systemic Linguistics, as in Sinclair and Coulthard (1975), Coulthard and Brazil (1979), and, more recently, Berry (1987) have a decisive influence on this significant field, which has special appeal beyond linguistics.

Mann and Thompson (1987) and Mathiessen and Thompson (1987) have recently begun to develop 'Rhetorical Structure Theory', which in many ways links up directly with Halliday's (1985a) accounts of the CLAUSE COMPLEX, and with ongoing work in text generation outside Systemic Linguistics. Although this particular strand of research is not represented in the present volume, it is hoped that some of the ideas generated here will be of interest to future developments in Rhetorical Structure Theory as well.

In an obvious way many of the contributions to this volume will merge with the direction within Systemic Functional Grammar which treats language as a special form of activity, whether by positing realizational relationships of language to 'activity structures' (Lemke in this volume), or to models of human goal-directed action (Steiner 1984, 1988; Mohan 1986, 1987). The interface between such models and language, quite clearly, will in the end never be the sentence or the clause, but rather text and discourse, viewed from a pragmatic perspective. The same, it should be said, applies to models of genre structure developed in the work of Hasan, Martin and others.

We have now arrived at a point at which the chapters in this volume fit very directly into currently existing research traditions. We have, as it were, gradually focused in on our present work from discussion of leading themes of pragmatics, discourse and text, to the significance of these factors for the worlds within and beyond language, with special regard to their interaction with Systemic Linguistics, and Systemic Semantics in particular. At first sight, this might have the sole function of outlining something like the intended readership of the book. However, our intention in preparing the reader in this way is a more fundamental one. It seems to be important, at certain points in the development of lines of research as well as in the development in the work of an individual, to become aware of the external and internal motivations for the activities one is engaged in. This is partly necessary to provide means of critical evaluation. Yet it seems to be even more necessary in order to determine one's decisions as to how and in what directions future research is to go—and this is part of the function that we would like such a volume as the present one to have. Taking stock of what we have, let us critically assess the intrinsic interest it has for people with a legitimate interest in the field, and let us, against the background of these assessments, determine the future directions of work in that field. If this book is able to make a contribution to these processes, it would, in our view, have served a useful purpose.

Before closing this introductory section, an outline of the contributions to this volume is offered.

Systemic Linguistics nowadays has a considerable scope: from phonology through grammar, lexis, the semantics of the clause, to the form and the semantics of text and discourse. It is perhaps fair to say that while many people continue to work in the former 'core' areas of the grammar and semantics of the clause, more and more emphasis is given to developing models of discourse and text structure. It is in this context that the present selection of papers from the XIII International Systemic Workshop should be seen.

Part 1 illustrates how Systemic Linguistics and Pragmatics are influencing each other. While Butler discusses the question of the mutual influence of these two fields on a theoretical level, Davies illustrates in detail how the formalization of certain aspects of a 'Systemic Pragmatics' leads to the well-constrained generation of research hypothesis. Both chapters indicate avenues of future research which will certainly be followed within Systemic Linguistics.

Part 2 explores Systemic concepts in the areas of thematic structure and information structure of the clause. It is shown how these aspects of clause structure contribute to the semantic structure of text and discourse.

Kies illustrates in his corpus study how precisely certain types of Marked Theme are dependent on the speaker's decisions on text level, rather than on sentence level alone. He also provides a valuable comparison of Systemic and other approaches to the particular types of marked theme which he is investigating.

Williams in his chapter confronts the Systemic notions of thematic structure and information structure with more recent developments in the Prague school approach, as well as with Sperber and Wilson's widely discussed ideas on 'relevance' in sentences and texts. This, one may feel, is something which has been due for some time in Systemic Linguistics, and it is to be hoped that other Systemicists may follow the general line of investigation advocated by Williams.

Bowers takes Systemic ideas on thematic structures, showing how the linguistic properties covered by these ideas were recognized long ago as being highly relevant to understanding in the realm of legislative language. He thus creates for us one of these very important moments in which we as linguists realize that linguistics is not something which should be done as 'arts for art's sake', yet as something which has relevance and responsibility towards the people using language.

Part 3 explores discourse analysis dimensions of texts. Akindele highlights certain crucial aspects of the structure of family conversation in Yoruba English. He explores the relationship between socio-semantic notions like 'control' and 'dominance' and their manifestations in the structure of discourse. In doing so, he makes some very valuable contributions to the problem of the theoretical relationship between the levels of socio-semantics and discourse, a line of research which is very active currently within Systemic Linguistics and elsewhere.

Tucker takes us one step further in his chapter: while Akindele investigates patterns of social dominance as independent variables, taking discourse patterns as dependent variables—i.e. he studies the linguistic realization of socio-semantic patterns on the linguistic level of Discourse—Tucker takes discourse structures as given and studies their realization in syntax and intonation. As far as the type of phenomena investigated is concerned, Tucker, on a general level, also links up with Davies's chapter; only his orientation is more towards Discourse Analysis, while Davies's is more towards Pragmatics—both tendencies are, in fact, well documented in current Systemic Work. Both chapters illustrate the growing awareness of Systemic Linguists that models and concepts of the 'higher' levels of the theory have to be related to the realizational statements in order to become fully meaningful within the theory.

Part 4 illustrates how the apparent opposition between 'interaction' and 'cognition' in the general orientation of Systemicists towards 'Semantics' is beginning to break down in the light of the task of accounting for the structure of text and discourse in a fuller way than before. Ravelli explores certain types of grammatical metaphor which are receiving more and more attention from Systemicists, at least since Halliday's (1985a) *An Introduction to Functional Grammar*.

Aziz illustrates how language-specific means of cohesion have to be seen as encoding the same functions across texts in relatively unrelated languages. Lemke represents the 'interaction'-oriented side, developing certain aspects of a theory of social semiotics to the point where the opposition between 'interaction' and 'cognition' becomes almost meaningless, thus illustrating one possible way of uniting these dialectical opposites. In his account of structural vs. thematic meaning, he reflects the difference between a functional and a representational orientation in semantics. He demonstrates that both only appear as radically different, whereas in reality they are merely two aspects of one phenomenon, 'text meaning'.

Fine's chapter fits in very well with that of Lemke, even if he is looking at cognition and some of its neurophysiological correlates. If Lemke sets out to represent the 'interaction' pole of the opposition, Fine represents the 'cognition' pole. Being Systemicists, though, they both use their different starting points to pursue a path that leads to the eventual breaking down of the original opposition.

The XIIIth. International Systemic Workshop commemorated by chance the passing of 25 years since Halliday's 'Categories of the theory of grammar' was first published. As we have already indicated in respect of language teaching and learning, Halliday's original statement has been far-reaching and influential, to say the least. One reason for its robustness is its proven ability to serve as a 'core' of adapting knowledge of language and its relation to its environment, whether or not the paper itself or the notions therein are explicitly referred to in these developments. Evidence of this ever-lengthening temporal and intellectual link is, we hope, to be found in these discussions of pragmatics, discourse and text.

BIBLIOGRAPHY

Benson J. D. and Greaves, W. S. (eds) (1985), *Systemic Perspectives on Discourse, Vol. 1*, Norwood, NJ, Ablex.
Berry, M. (1987), 'Is teacher an unanalysed concept?', in Halliday and Fawcett (eds), 21–63.
Birch, D. and O'Toole, M. (1988), *Functions of Style*, London, Frances Pinter.
Bresnan, J. (ed.) (1982), *The Mental Representation of Grammatical Relations*, Cambridge, Mass., MIT Press.
Brown, G. and Yule, G. (1983), *Discourse Analysis*, Cambridge, Cambridge University Press.
Butler C. S. (1985), *Systemic Linguistics: Theory and Applications*, London, Batsford.
Chilton, P. (ed.) (1984), *Language and the Nuclear Arms Debate*, London, Frances Pinter.

Chomsky, N. (1980), *Rules and Representations*, Oxford, Blackwell.
—— (1981), *Lectures on Government and Binding*, Dordrecht, Foris.
Coulthard, R. M. and Brazil, D. (1979), *Exchange Structure English Language* Research Monograph No. 5, Birmingham, Birmingham University Press.
Danlos, L. (1987), *The Linguistic Basis of Text Generation*, Cambridge, Cambridge University Press.
Fawcett, R. P., van der Mije, A. and Van Wissen, C. (forthcoming), 'Towards a systemic flowchart model for local discourse structure', in R. P. Fawcett, and D. Young (eds), *New Developments in Systemic Linguistics, Vol. 2*, London, Frances Pinter.
Fodor, J. D., Fodor, J. A. and Garrett, M. F. (1975), 'The psychological unreality of semantic representations', *Linguistic Inquiry*, 6, 515–31.
Gazdar, G., Klein, E. H., Pullum, G. K. and Sag, I. A. (1985), *Generalized Phrase Structure Grammar*, Oxford, Blackwell.
Grice, H. P. (1975), 'Logic and conversation', Harvard William James Lectures 1967, in Cole, P. and Morgan J. L. (eds), *Syntax and Semantics, Vol. 3, Speech Acts*, New York, Academic Press, 41–58.
Grimes, J. E. (1975), *The Thread of Discourse*, The Hague, Mouton.
Grishman, R. (1986), *Computational Linguistics*, Cambridge, Cambridge University Press.
Halliday, M. A. K. (1961), 'Categories of the theory of grammar', *Word*, 17, 241–92.
—— (1969), 'Relevant models of language', *Educational Review*, 22, 26–37, reprinted in Halliday (1973), 9–21.
—— (1973), *Explorations in the Functions of Language*, London, Edward Arnold.
—— (1975), *Learning How to Mean*, London, Edward Arnold.
—— (1978), *Language as Social Semiotic: The Social Interpretation of Language and Meaning*, London, Edward Arnold.
—— (1985a), *An Introduction to Functional Grammar*, London, Edward Arnold.
—— (1985b), *Spoken and Written Language*, Victoria, Deakin University Press.
—— (1985c), 'Systemic background', in Benson and Greaves (eds), 1–15.
Halliday, M. A. K. and Hasan, R. (1976), *Cohesion in English*, London, Longman.
Halliday, M. A. K. and Fawcett, R. P. (eds) (1987), *New Developments in Systemic Linguistics, Vol. 1*, London, Frances Pinter.
Halliday, M. A. K., McKintosh, A. and Strevens, P. (1964), *The Linguistic Sciences and Language Teaching*, London, Longman.
Kasper, R. (1987), 'Feature structures: a logical theory with application to language analysis', Ph.D. thesis, University of Michigan.
Kempen, G. (ed.) (1987), *Natural Language Generation*, Dordrecht, Martinus Nijhoff.
Labov, W. (1972), *Sociolinguistic Patterns*, Philadelphia, University of Pennsylvania Press.
Leech, G. (1983), *Principles of Pragmatics*, London, Longman.
Leech, G. and Short, M. (1981), *Style in Fiction: A Linguistic Introduction to English Fictional Prose*, London, Longman.
Levinson, S. C. (1979), 'The essential inadequacies of speech act models of dialogue', in Parett, H., Sbisà, M. and Verscheuren, J. (eds), *Possibilities and Limitations of Pragmatics*, Amsterdam, John Benjamins, 473–92.
Lyons, J. (1987), 'Semantics', in Lyons, J., Coates, R., Deuchar, M. and Gazdar G. (eds), *New Horizons in Linguistics, Vol. 2*, London, Penguin, 152–78.
Mann, W. C. (1985), 'An introduction to the Nigel text generation computer program', in Benson and Greaves (eds), 84–95.
Mann, W. C. and Matthiessen, C. M. I. M. (1985), 'A demonstration of the Nigel text generation computer program', in Benson and Greaves (eds), 50–83.

Mann, W. C. and Thompson, S. A. (1987), 'Rhetorical structure theory: description and construction of text structures', in Kempen (ed.), 85–97.

Mathiessen, C. M. I. M. (1985), 'The systemic framework in text generation: Nigel', in Benson and Greaves (eds), 96–118.

Matthiessen, C. M. I. M. and Thompson, S. A. (1987), 'The structure of discourse and subordination', in Haiman and Thompson, S. A. (eds), *Clause Combining in Discourse and Grammar*, Amsterdam, John Benjamins.

Mohan, B. (1986) *Language and Content*. Reading, Mass: Addison-Wesley.

—— (1987) 'The structure of situation and the analysis of text', in Steele, R. and Threadgold, T. (eds) *Language Topics: Essays in Honour of Michael Halliday, Vol. 2*, Amsterdam: John Benjamins, 507–22.

Muir, J. (1972), *A Modern Approach to English Grammar*, London, Batsford.

Nirenburg, S. (ed.) (1987), *Machine Translation*, Cambridge, Cambridge University Press.

Radford, A. (1981), *Transformational Syntax*, Cambridge, Cambridge University Press.

—— (1988), *Transformational Grammar*, Cambridge, Cambridge University Press.

Rochemont, M. (1986), *Focus in Generative Grammar*, Amsterdam, John Benjamins.

Rochester, S. and Martin, J. R. (1979), *Crazy Talk: A Study of the Discourse of Schizophrenic Speakers*, New York, Plenum Press.

Sanford, A. J. and Garrod, S. C. (1981), *Understanding Written Language: Explorations of Comprehension beyond the Sentence*, Chichester, Wiley.

Scott, F. S. *et al.* (1968), *English Grammar: A Linguistic Study of its Classes and Structures*, Auckland, Heinemann.

Seuren, P. A. M. (1985), *Discourse Semantics*, Oxford, Blackwell.

Sinclair, J. M. and Coulthard, R. M. (1975), *Towards an Analysis of Discourse*, London, Oxford University Press.

Sperber, D. and Wilson, D. M. (1986), *Relevance: Communication and Cognition*, Oxford, Basil Blackwell.

Steiner, E. (1984), 'The concept of "context" and the theory of "action"', in Chilton (ed.), 215–30.

—— (1987), 'Language as a form of goal-directed action: the analysis of a moral dilemma', in Benson, J. D. and Greaves, W. S. (eds), *Systemic Functional Approaches on Discourse*, Norwood, NJ, Ablex, 211–39.

—— (1988), 'Language as a form of goal-directed action: the analysis of a moral dilemma', in Benson, J. D. and Greaves, W. S. (eds), *Systemic Functional Approaches on Discourse*, Norwood, N. J.: Ablex, 211–39.

Veltman, R. (1985) 'Comparison and intensification: an ideal but problematic domain for systemic-functional theory', in Benson and Greaves (eds), 187–212.

Ventola, E. (1982), 'Contrasting schematic structures in service encounters', University of Sydney, mimeo.

Widowson, H. G. (1979), 'The realisation of rules in written discourse', *Recherches et Échanges*, 4, 2, 1–20.

Wilensky, R. (1987), 'Primal content and actual content: an antidote to literal meaning', University of California, Berkeley, mimeo.

Winograd, T. (1972), *Understanding Natural Language*, Edinburgh, Edinburgh University Press.

Part I
Meeting the challenge of 'pragmatics'

1 Systemic linguistics, semantics and pragmatics

Christopher S. Butler
Department of Linguistics, University of Nottingham, UK

1.0 INTRODUCTION

Halliday (1978: 108) poses the following question as a central concern of systemic functional linguistics:

How do people decode the highly condensed utterances of everyday speech, and how do they use the social system for doing so?

To many linguists, especially those outside the systemic tradition, this would be taken to imply a major overlap between the kinds of phenomena investigated in systemic linguistics and in pragmatics. One would at least expect that work in systemic linguistics would illuminate work in pragmatics, and vice versa. And yet the now substantial literature on pragmatics is all but ignored in the work of Halliday and most other systemic linguists; furthermore, there are few references to systemic work in publications on pragmatics.

The aim of this chapter is first to investigate why there is this lack of communication between the two groups of linguists, and then to suggest ways in which systemicists could benefit from close study of the pragmatics literature, and also advantages which could be gained in pragmatics by taking a systemic description as semantic input.

1.1 WHY THE LACK OF DIALOGUE?

Most of the linguists whose work constitutes what might be thought of as 'mainstream' pragmatics were schooled within the Chomskyan approach to language. Although many have become dissatisfied with some of the limitations of Chomskyan grammars, certain assumptions deriving from that approach are still prevalent: an emphasis on explanatory power, economy and elegance; the view that formalization is necessary, at least in the end; and often an assumption that semantics is essentially truth-conditional. The assumptions made in Halliday's work are very different: there is an emphasis on WHY language is as it is, and this functional bias tends to reduce the value accorded to economy of generalization and to elegance; Halliday holds (1985: 78, fn.) that 'semantics has nothing to do with truth'; and he regards formalization as not absolutely necessary for most purposes, and as potentially dangerous.

Halliday would thus probably regard most work in pragmatics as embodying assumptions which are contrary to his own. He contrasts the psychologically and philosophically oriented 'intra-organism' approach of the Chomskyans with his own sociologically oriented 'inter-organism' view of language. For instance, he insists (1978: 38) that systemic grammar has no room for a distinction between competence and performance, but rather operates with the notion of a language potential and its actualization. Even Hymes's (1971) 'communicative competence' is rejected (Halliday 1978: 38) as being an intra-organism approach to an essentially inter-organism phenomenon. And yet it is quite clear, both from the quotation with which this chapter began, and from more extended consideration of Halliday's work, that there are in fact major overlaps between his concerns and those of pragmaticians. The basic difference between the two approaches is one of emphasis: systemic grammars tend to concentrate on the sociological factors influencing language, whereas pragmatics brings in the more psychological and philosophical influences, while, it could be argued, not necessarily neglecting the sociological. There is no inherent conflict here: indeed, one systemic linguist has already suggested a synthesis of the sociological and the psychological (see Fawcett 1980).

There are, I think, further reasons for the lack of dialogue. Systemicists have tended to publish in rather obscure places, this tendency being reinforced, if not created, by the lack of interest shown in things systemic by the major journals. And yet one cannot entirely blame the journals for this: most of them have on their editorial boards linguists for whom the principles of explicitness and falsifiability are sacred, and these are qualities which much work in systemic linguistics has so far lacked (for discussion see Berry 1982; Butler 1985a).

1.2 LEECH'S CRITICISMS OF HALLIDAY

One pragmatician who has taken some account of Halliday's work in the development of his own model is Leech (1980, 1983). Since I believe that at least some of Leech's criticisms of Halliday are justified, I shall examine them in some detail in this section.

Leech (1983: 56–7) recognizes the importance, not only of the cognitive or ideational kind of meaning which formed the core of semantic theorizing for many years, but also of the interpersonal and textual elements in language. Indeed, he relates them to four functions (argumentative, descriptive, signalling, expressive) derived from the work of Popper. Where Leech and Halliday differ is in their view of the relationship between these 'functions' and the grammars of languages. Halliday's claim (see e.g. 1978: 45–50) is that all three functions (which he now calls 'metafunctions') are central to the organization of the grammar itself, in that they correspond to three relatively independent blocks of systemic options. Halliday's metafunctions are thus very different from the purely extrinsic functions postulated by Bühler (1934) and Jakobson (1960). Halliday regards the three functions as being equally important, although he also states that for some purposes it might be advantageous to concentrate on one. Leech, on the other hand, regards this view as over-grammaticalization of what properly belongs within pragmatics. For him, only the ideational component belongs in the grammar (which subsumes the syntax, morphology, semantics and phonology of a language), the interpersonal and textual components constituting what Leech terms 'general pragmatics'. Leech points out that Halliday himself (1973: 38–9) has admitted that '. . . the ideational function [. . .] is a major component of meaning in the language system which is basic to more or less all uses of language', and that he has claimed (1979: 66–70) that only the ideational (or rather, the 'experiential' part of it, rather than the 'logical' sub-function involved in co-ordination, subordination, etc.) is realized by the type of constituent structure generally seen as the concern of grammar, interpersonal meanings being realized by prosodic structures and textual meanings by culminative structures according special status to elements at unit boundaries. Leech (1983: 58) interprets this as indicating that

Halliday seems to be moving closer to a conception of language in which the ideational component is grammatical in an orthodox sense (dealing in constituent structures, rules and systems), as distinct from the interpersonal and textual components, which are more pragmatic in conception.

Leech's reasons for holding the above view are basically that ideational phenomena can be handled in terms of DISCRETE RULES of a CONVENTIONAL kind, whereas interpersonal and textual phenomena are better dealt with in terms of PRINCIPLES of a NON-CONVENTIONAL kind, involving CONTINUOUS, INDETERMINATE values.

Halliday would, I think, be unhappy with Leech's association of the ideational component with 'rules' and the other two components with 'principles', for two reasons. I find neither reason convincing, but both are important as indicating the kind of difficulty which many non-systemicists would have when trying to get to grips with work in systemic linguistics.

Firstly, Halliday (1984) prefers to avoid the use of the term 'rule', associating it with TG-style grammars which concentrate on the specification of syntagmatic structures. Since the mid-1960s, Halliday's own models have been based on the claim that the fundamental relationships within the grammar are the PARADIGMATIC ones captured in system networks, the syntagmatic structures being derived from these by realization processes (see e.g. Halliday 1966a). Because of this paradigmatic orientation (which I shall later suggest is an important aspect of systemic grammars as far as their possible use to pragmaticians is concerned), Halliday considers that the concept of 'resource' is more appropriate for systemic models than that of rule: 'In investigating language and the social system, it is important [. . .] to interpret language not as a set of rules but as a *resource*' (Halliday 1978: 192, original emphasis).

The assumption that paradigmatic phenomena cannot be adequately discussed in terms of rules is, however, without foundation. System networks are themselves sets of rules, since they predict in an explicit manner which features can be combined in a selection expression representing a stretch of language, and which are barred from doing so.

Secondly, Halliday (1980: 70) opposes 'rules' to 'tendencies', so implying that rules are necessarily all-or-none. Certainly systemic linguistics, with its emphasis on the study of language in relation to its social context, must make do with a much lower degree of idealization than could be tolerated in a less context-oriented approach, and this means that statements of a probabilistic kind must often be made. But it is by now well established that even the 'core' areas of syntax, semantics and phonology are often 'fuzzy' (see e.g. Bolinger 1961; Quirk 1965; Ross 1973; Labov 1973; Leech and Coates 1980; Channell 1980, 1983). We do not need to abandon the notion of rule because of this; rather, we need to build in the concept of PROTOTYPICAL CATEGORIES (see e.g. Rosch 1977; Lakoff 1977; Leech 1981) to which we can relate more peripheral examples.

The issue of conventionality versus non-conventionality is, I think, more crucial to the debate. Leech, correctly in my view, claims that rules define mappings which are conventional in that they are not predictable or deducible from non-linguistic entities. On the other hand, principles, characterizing the pragmatics, are non-conventional, being motivated by, and predictable from, the goals and motives of participants in the interaction. We may, according to Leech, be able to give some explanation of why some grammatical rules are as they are, in terms of metagrammatical statements which may refer to pragmatic principles, but these will not precisely predict the form of the rules. Leech's (1983) book is devoted to a discussion of the interpersonal rhetoric, including Grice's (1975) Co-operative Principle and other principles of politeness and irony, and of the textual rhetoric, consisting of principles concerned with processibility, clarity, economy and expressivity. Leech demonstrates the derivability of these from goals and motives, and claims that they represent universal aspects of human behaviour, which interact with constraints imposed by conditions local to particular cultures and settings.

I shall now turn briefly to the evidence relating to Halliday's contrary view that interpersonal and textual as well as ideational phenomena form an integral part of the grammar. Detailed arguments are available elsewhere (see Martin 1984; Butler 1985a, 1985b), so I shall merely list what I see as the main problems facing the metafunctional hypothesis:

(i) Although Halliday claims that the blocks of systems in different metafunctions are relatively independent, it is easy to find examples where choices from one putative metafunction do affect choices from another, and these are not just peripheral phenomena, but are concerned with central aspects of the grammar such as transitivity, mood and modalization.

(ii) The claim of 'relative independence' for blocks of networks is not stated explicitly enough for us to be able to falsify it.
(iii) The hypothesis is, in any case, testable only if criteria for the construction of system networks are explicit (which they are not) and free of functional bias (which is unproven and debatable). It is significant that different accounts of the same area of the grammar, even by one and the same linguist, frequently present different networks (see e.g. Halliday 1968: 206, 1969: 84).
(iv) There are still disagreements between systemic linguists as to how many metafunctions should be postulated (see Fawcett 1980).
(v) Evidence for metafunctional organization has been discussed mainly in relation to the rank of clause, but the indications are that it is even weaker at other ranks.
(vi) Halliday (1979) has suggested that evidence is also available from the relationship between semantic choice and situation type, in that it is claimed that ideational choices are influenced mainly by the field of discourse, interpersonal choices by tenor, and textual choices by mode. Such evidence is, however, weakened by the difficulties involved in providing clear definitions of the situation-type categories, and by the co-determination of single types of discourse meaning apparently postulated by Hasan (1978).
(vii) As we saw earlier, Halliday (1979) has also suggested that the three metafunctions have different types of typical realization: constituency structures for ideational meanings, prosodic structures for interpersonal meanings, and culminative structures for textual meanings. But as with the claim about the internal 'relative independence' of networks in different metafunctions, it is easy to think of central counterexamples (e.g. mood in English is realized largely by the presence and/or ordering of constituents). Furthermore, Halliday has said that these correlations may not hold, or at least not so clearly, for languages other than English.

Despite these difficulties, it would not be wise to conclude that Leech is correct in claiming that only ideational phenomena belong in the grammar. Mood and modality are, according to Halliday, interpersonal, and yet they are subject to rules of the type which Leech regards as grammatical: indeed, he himself has discussed them at some length in semantic terms (Leech 1983: 114 ff.; Leech and Coates 1980; Coates and Leech 1980). There is no doubt that phenomena of this kind must be accounted for within the grammar. Similarly, distinctions of constituent ordering which realize Halliday's textual theme choices must also be dealt with, since there are syntactic restrictions on what can be thematized in particular types of clause (see Hudson 1976: 100 ff.). What Leech specifically objects to is not the inclusion of such phenomena within the grammar (though his bald statement that only ideational meanings belong there would seem to be contrary to such inclusion), but rather Halliday's treatment of ILLOCUTIONARY FORCE and TONALITY/TONICITY as 'grammatical'.

It is not surprising, in view of his inter-organism, function-based approach, that Halliday prefers to talk of 'speech function' rather than of illocutionary force. He has postulated (Halliday 1984) that options in speech function (basically statement, question, command, offer) realize options available for 'moves' in dialogue (essentially the giving or demanding of information or goods-and-services), and are themselves realized by lexicogrammatical mood options (basically declarative, interrogative, imperative). Again, I have discussed this proposal and Martin's (1981) version of it in detail elsewhere (Butler 1986, 1987), and so shall focus only on those aspects of it which relate to Leech's criticisms.

One major problem is that system networks, by their very nature, force us to handle choices in terms of neat oppositions. I argued earlier that system networks represent sets of rules, and can deal with fuzziness by making use of the concept of prototype. But this will not help us here: as Leech points out, any purely taxonomic classification of speech acts will present too rigid a view of communication, since an utterance can have more than one force/function at once (a situation which is not allowed by Halliday's networks), and any single label oversimplifies the essentially indeterminate and negotiable nature of speech acts. Leech's view is in fact in line with Halliday's own general view of language as fluid, adaptable and negotiable, so it is rather surprising that Halliday has taken the more rigid position.

Fawcett (1980: 98 ff.), when attempting to construct semantic networks for illocutionary force, avoids the most serious of these problems by excluding from consideration what he calls 'intended deduction', and referring to Grice and others for accounts of this area. Fawcett's position is thus closer than Halliday's to Leech's and to my own, though I have argued elsewhere (Butler, 1987) that his model still attempts to account semantically for distinctions which are better dealt with in pragmatic terms.

A second problem is concerned with the relationships between levels in Halliday's model. He claims that there are 'congruent' realizations of sets of features at one level by sets of features at the next lower level: for instance, the combination [initiating: demanding; information] at the highest, 'social contextual' level is congruently realized by the feature set [initiate; demand: question], and this in turn is congruently realized at the lexicogrammatical level as [indicative: interrogative]. Halliday recognizes that there are many non-congruent realizations, and treats these in terms of 'grammatical metaphor'; the discussion (e.g. in Halliday 1985: 342–5) is, however, rather sketchy. More importantly, Halliday provides no account of WHY a speaker might choose a non-congruent rather than a congruent realization. He would presumably want to relate this at least partly to tenor of discourse; such links are intuitively reasonable, and we should try to obtain evidence for them. But we also need to know about the principles by which such choices can be arrived at, and by which non-congruent choices can be interpreted. This, I suggest, requires the importation of principles such as those discussed by Grice, Leech, and Sperber and Wilson (1986). Halliday actually seems very sceptical of the possibility of studying the how and the why of such choices, when he comments (1985: 345) that '. . . there is no way of tracking the process whereby a speaker or writer has arrived at a particular mode of expression in the discourse'. Pragmaticians such as Grice, Leech, Sperber and Wilson would certainly regard this as unduly pessimistic.

Let us now turn to the area of tonality and tonicity. Halliday (1963a, 1963b, 1966b, 1967, 1970, 1985) sees intonational choices themselves as constituting phonological systems, but considers that they realize choices in information distribution, speech function and attitude which were originally regarded as grammatical, and are now viewed as semantic. Leech comments on Halliday's appeal to the concept of markedness in this area, and points out that the unmarked choice, chosen by default, could be seen pragmatically as one which is made according to a certain textual maxim when no competing maxims override it. Wherever we decide to locate these distinctions, we still need to account for WHY certain information-distribution patterns occur in certain circumstances, how speakers decide what to present as 'given' or 'new' information, and how speakers are able to decode the informational status of particular parts of the utterance. Halliday's work offers no general principles to guide us here.

I conclude, then, that Leech's criticisms of Halliday's approach are basically justified, as far as illocutionary force and information distribution are concerned, though certain phenomena related to the interpersonal and textual aspects of language will have to be accounted for within the grammar. My own position on illocutionary force is quite close to that of Eirian Davies, whose work on different orders of significance in the area of mood and its import, represented in this volume by her chapter on interrogatives, also builds in the notion of a context-free semantics and further contextually based levels of interpretation of the semantics.

1.3 SOME OTHER AREAS WHERE SYSTEMIC LINGUISTS NEED TO TAKE NOTE OF PRAGMATICS

My discussion so far suggests that in areas to which systemic linguists have given some attention, pragmatic principles of some kind are needed. The question which now arises is whether there are any areas of pragmatics which are important to the goals of systemic grammar, and yet have been insufficiently or inadequately discussed in the systemic literature. In my view, there are two such areas: IMPLICATURE and PRESUPPOSITION.

1.3.1 Implicature

A crucial aspect of 'how people decode the highly condensed utterances of everyday speech' is how connections can be made between utterances whose propositional contents are not related in a simple way. Consider the following:

A. Why isn't Jim back yet?
B. There's a blue Renault parked outside Judy's house.

How is A able to decode the fact that B's reply counts as an attempt to explain why Jim has not arrived, in view of the lack of shared propositional content? It is not enough simply to regard this as some kind of 'metaphorical' mode of expression: we have to be able to say why some replies are more appropriate and so more easily decoded than others, and by what principles the decoding can occur. Such explanations appear to require some kind of 'relevance maxim', but there is little in the systemic literature to suggest that such things are regarded as important (though see the brief comment in Fawcett 1980: 101-2, alluded to earlier).

Systemic models also fail to account for other kinds of implicature. Take the following:

Sue has four children.

The most usual (default, unmarked) interpretation of this would be that Sue has only four children. Does this therefore mean that *four* means 'four and only four'? Surely not:

A. You have to have at least four children to get the super-allowance.
B. Oh, don't worry, Sue has four children all right – there's a whole house full of them all running about.

So what does a systemic grammar do? Must we say that *four* is ambiguous as between the meaning 'just four' and 'at least four', according to the context? This is a most unwelcome expedient, since it means that all numbers have two meanings, and we have no way of saying why this is. It is surely much better to say that a number has just one meaning, but that there is a generalized quantity implicature (see e.g. Levinson 1983: 132ff.) deriving from the scalar nature of the number system: using a weaker term from such a scale (in this case a lower number) implicates that the speaker has no evidence to support the use of a stronger term (higher number). The notion of implicature here provides a powerful explanation which is generalizable to a variety of other scales.

Finally, let us look briefly at manner implicatures:

Mary is a nurse and Graham is a teacher.
Graham is a teacher and Mary is a nurse.

Bill went in and sat down.
?Bill sat down and went in.

Why is there (approximate) equivalence between the first pair of sentences but not the second? Does *and* have two different meanings: just additiveness in the first case, but temporal sequence in the second? Again, we can achieve greater explanatory power if we regard *and* as unisemantic, and invoke the notion of implicature: the orderliness submaxim of Grice's maxim of manner enjoins us to make language reflect the order of events whenever there is no good reason to do otherwise.

In summary, then, I wish to claim that systemic grammars need to build in principles/maxims similar to those of Grice and Leech, or to produce some alternative which is equally powerful in explaining how the communicative function of apparently obscure utterances can be understood.

1.3.2 Presupposition

There is still a good deal of uncertainty about the nature of presupposition (how to define it, whether it is semantic or pragmatic, and so on), and this is not the place to go into these arguments. Whatever the answers may turn out to be, presupposition is clearly an important area for anyone who wants to explain how people manage to decode meanings. Halliday does in fact attempt to account for some of the phenomena which most linguists handle in terms of presupposition. For example, the distinction between factive and non-factive mental process verbs is handled by postulating a distinction between the 'projection' of 'ideas' and of 'facts' (Halliday 1985: 244–5). Halliday's examples follow:

||| Mark Anthony | thought || that Caesar was dead |||
||| Mark Anthony | regretted [[that Caesar was dead]]

The first is seen as projection of an idea by the main clause, which has a cognition type of process; Halliday points out that the *that* clause cannot be preceded by *the fact*, or replaced by a nominal group *Caesar's death*, but that it can be replaced by direct speech. In the second example, we have a fact rather than an idea; in consequence, we can add *the fact*, or replace the clause by a nominal group, but not by direct speech. Furthermore, the main verb is said to be one of affect, rather than one of cognition. For Halliday, these differences are paralleled by differences in grammatical structure: the first sentence shows hypotaxis, the second embedding. Other types of mental process illustrating the factive/non-factive distinction are dealt with in the same way. Halliday does not, however, relate these phenomena to others which share the property of constancy of the implied information under negation. For instance, the following can also be taken to imply that Caesar was dead, though admittedly the argument has been challenged:

Mark Anthony did not regret that Caesar was dead.

How, for example, would Halliday's approach handle the similarity in this respect between *regret* and *manage* (to do something) or *stop* (doing something)? And what of the large range of other phenomena gathered together by Kartunnen (see Levinson 1983: 181–4) under the heading of 'presuppositional triggers'?

1.4 HOW CAN PRAGMATICS BENEFIT FROM SYSTEMIC GRAMMARS?

My comments so far have been rather negative towards systemic grammars. There are, however, certain areas of interest to pragmaticians in which systemically based models have arguably made greater advances than other models. There are also some basic properties of systemic grammars which, if the evidence for some of their claims can be strengthened, give them considerable advantages as input to a pragmatic component.

1.4.1 Areas where systemic grammars have made important advances

1.4.1.1 *Deixis*

Levinson (1983: 62) lists five types of deixis: person, place, time, discourse and social deixis. Accounts of all these areas can be found in the systemic literature, and the fact that all are concerned with anchoring of the speech event in the here-and-now of the speaker is emphasized. Only a brief treatment can be given here.

Person deixis

Halliday (1978: 132, 1985: 168–9) treats this as an interpersonal aspect of nominal group structure. It should be noted, though, that because of the English focus of much of his writing, the extensive use of verbal inflection to mark person in many languages is not discussed.

Place deixis

Demonstratives are regarded as part of a more extensive deictic system within the nominal group, and there is considerable discussion of the dimensions of meaning involved (see e.g. Halliday 1985: 160 ff.). The demonstratives are also related to adverbs such as *here*, *there*, though again there is little recognition of the very complex systems present in some languages.

Time deixis

Halliday recognizes the deictic nature of tense—indeed, he goes further, and relates both tense and modality to the category of finiteness, and sees this as the verbal equivalent of the deictic element in the nominal group, in that both provide an orientation for the group in terms of 'the speaker now' (see Halliday 1985: 176). This is a good example of an interesting generalization made by Halliday but missed by other writers on this area. His account of tense is, however, marred by his insistence that what most linguists regard as aspect belongs to the tense system: the progressive is seen as a 'secondary present', obscuring the fact that it marks the internal temporal constituency of the event, not its temporal location (see Comrie 1985).

Discourse deixis

By this is meant the use of expressions to refer to some portion of the discourse in which those expressions are themselves situated. It is here that systemic linguists have made their most important contribution to the study of deixis. Halliday and Hasan (1976) is a detailed treatment of this area, whose worth is recognized even by its critics. There are nevertheless some problems with this account: see Morgan and Sellner (1980), Huddleston (1978), Brown and Yule (1983) and the summary in Butler (1985a: 179–88). More recent systemic work can be found in Halliday and Hasan (1980, 1985), and Hasan (1984a).

Social deixis

This refers to the use of linguistic expressions to encode aspects of the identity of, and relationships between, participants in the discourse, including terms of address, honorifics, and so on. There is rather little on this in the systemic literature, but the interesting work of Poynton (1984) on vocatives is worthy of mention.

1.4.1.2 Conversational structure

This is an area in which systemic linguists have made large and important contributions. Two main types of approach can be recognized: those which treat speech functions within discourse as semantic (Halliday 1984, 1985; Fawcett 1980; Martin 1981); and those which discuss discourse patterning in terms of a rank scale of act, move, exchange, transaction, interaction, which is viewed as separate from the grammar itself (see Sinclair and Coulthard 1975 for the original proposals). The Halliday approach was outlined earlier in this chapter, where I attempted to indicate some of the problems. For a more detailed discussion of various accounts in relation to a piece of attested discourse, see Butler (1986). The 'semantic' approach has given rise to developments in which discourse structure is related to register and genre (see e.g. Martin 1985; Hasan 1978, 1984b; Ventola 1979, 1983, 1984, 1987).

1.4.2 Advantages of systemic models as input to a pragmatic component

In this section, I want to suggest that the most fundamental characteristics of present-day systemic grammars are such as to make them potentially extremely attractive as the input to a pragmatic component in an overall model of language. I shall discuss three such characteristics: the semantic orientation of systemic grammars, the primacy accorded to paradigmatic organization, and the attempt to relate situation types to meanings.

1.4.2.1 *Semantic orientation*

As Leech (1983: 12) notes, pragmatics interacts with the grammar primarily through the semantics. Since Halliday's (1966a: 62–3) suggestion that 'underlying grammar is "semantically significant" grammar' and that system networks represent 'that part of the grammar which is as it were "closest to" the semantics', his grammars have become increasingly semanticized, so that the latest models treat the semantics as their core and generative base. We might expect that such models will form a more suitable basis for the operation of pragmatic principles than, say, transformational generative grammars, which, despite the attempts made by generative semanticists in the late 1960s and 1970s, are now again fairly firmly centred on the syntax. The dangers of trying to link essentially pragmatic categorizations directly to form are evident from the attempt by Sinclair and Coulthard (1975: 32) to specify rules for the interpretation of modalized interrogatives as directive speech acts. One of the conditions is that the sentence should contain one of the modals *can*, *could*, *will*, *would*. Since Sinclair and Coulthard relate interpretations directly to the FORM of the modals, they are unable to explain why these particular modal forms, and not, for instance, *may*, *might*, *must* are used in directives with interrogative form. In order to do this, reference needs to be made to the MEANINGS of the modals, as I have demonstrated elsewhere (Butler 1987, in press).

1.4.2.2 *The primacy of paradigmatic relations*

As we saw earlier, from the mid-1960s one of the main claims of systemic grammars has been that paradigmatic relations, formalized as system networks, represent the fundamental aspects of linguistic patterning, syntagmatic relations being derivable from systemic choices by realization processes. This is one of the main respects in which systemic grammars differ from transformational generative grammars, which have always been largely syntagmatic in their emphasis. Pragmatics is largely concerned with the relationships between different ways of saying things, and between these different ways and the factors conditioning the choices. It is obvious that a model which treats paradigmatic relations as primary is better suited, as a basis for pragmatic interpretation, than one which gives priority to structures.

1.4.2.3 *The putative relationship between situation type and meaning choice*

Leech (1983: 10) explicitly distinguishes between 'general pragmatics', which he describes as 'the study of the general conditions of the communicative use of language', and 'socio-pragmatics', in which is studied the variability in the operation of these universal principles with 'local' conditions. Leech's own work is deliberately restricted to general pragmatics, and so excludes, for example, the effect of register factors on how pragmatic principles are put to use. For instance, when discussing politeness, he is concerned only with the 'absolute politeness' of sentence types, and excludes politeness relative to context. While this is a valid means of restricting the area for initial study, it makes the scope of general pragmatics rather narrow, since it means that we shall not be able to predict how interactants in a particular discourse, created in a particular type of social situation, will interpret each other's utterances. For instance, it means that we shall not be able to predict when an 'inherently polite' sentence may be interpreted as too polite for the context, and so ironic or indirectly impolite. Here, systemic linguistics can potentially offer a remedy. IF we can obtain much firmer evidence for the validity of the situation-type categories of field, tenor and mode, and IF we can demonstrate convincingly that the semantic choices within the grammar, suitably restricted as outlined in this chapter, are functionally organized and correlate with situation-type factors in the way Halliday suggests, THEN we shall be able to extend Leech's model so that it accounts for social appropriateness relative to context. But I must emphasize that in my view such a research programme depends crucially on the extent to which the categories employed are well motivated.

1.5 CONCLUSION

In summary, I want to make two claims. Firstly, I believe that systemic linguists need to re-examine very carefully their proposals for functional grammars, paying particular attention to the obtaining of solid evidence for the functional organization of the semantics, for the situation-type categories of field, tenor and mode, and for the relationship between the two. We should also investigate the possibility of integration with a pragmatic component which would take over some of what is now, in my opinion unsatisfactorily, dealt with in the semantics. Secondly, systemic models already build in two fundamental characteristics (semantic orientation and the priority of paradigmatic relations) which make them more suitable than other models as the input to a pragmatic component. They will offer even more if the problems raised in this chapter can be resolved.

BIBLIOGRAPHY

Bailey, C.-J. and Shuy, R. W. (eds) (1973), *New Ways of Analysing Variation in English*, Washington, DC, Georgetown University Press.
Berry, M. (1982), 'Review of Halliday 1978', *Nottingham Linguistic Circular*, 11, 64–94.
Bolinger, D. L. (1961), *Generality, Gradience, and the All-or-None*, The Hague, Mouton.
Brown, G. and Yule, G. (1983), *Discourse Analysis*, Cambridge, Cambridge University Press.
Bühler, K. (1934), *Sprachtheorie: die Darstellungsfunktion der Sprache*, Jena, Fischer.
Butler, C. S. (1985a), *Systemic Linguistics: Theory and Applications*, London, Batsford.
—— (1985b), 'Function in systemic linguistics', *Linguistic Journal of Korea*, 10, No. 1, 23–57.
—— (1986), 'What has systemic functional linguistics contributed to our understanding of spoken text?', in *Proceedings of the 1984 Working Conference on Language in Education*, Brisbane, Brisbane College of Advanced Technology.
—— (1987), 'Communicative function and semantics', in Halliday, M. A. K. and Fawcett, R. P. (eds), *New Developments in Systemic Linguistics, Vol. 1: Theory and Description*, London, Frances Pinter, 212–29.
—— (in press) 'Politeness and the semantics of modalised directives', in Benson, J. D., Cummings, M. and Greaves, W. S. (eds), *Linguistics in a Systemic Perspective*, Amsterdam, Benjamins.
Channell, J. (1980), 'More on approximations: a reply to Wachtel', *Journal of Pragmatics*, 4, 461–76.
—— (1983), *Vague Language Use: Some Vague Expressions in English*, unpublished Ph.D. thesis, University of York, UK.
Coates, J. and Leech, G. (1980), 'The meanings of the modals in modern British and American English', *York Papers in Linguistics*, 8, 23–34.
Comrie, B. (1985), *Tense*, Cambridge, Cambridge University Press.
Fawcett, R. P. (1980), *Cognitive Linguistics and Social Interaction: Towards an Integrated Model of a Systemic Functional Grammar and the Other Components of a Communicating Mind*, Heidelberg, Julius Groos Verlag, and Exeter, University of Exeter.
Grice, H. P. (1975), 'Logic and conversation' (Harvard William Jones Lectures 1967),

in Cole, P. and Morgan, J. L. (eds), *Syntax and Semantics, Vol. 3: Speech Acts*, New York, Academic Press, 41–58.
Halliday, M. A. K. (1963a), 'The tones of English', *Archivum Linguisticum*, 15, 1–28.
—— (1963b), 'Intonation and English grammar', *Transactions of the Philological Society*, 143–69.
—— (1966a), 'Some notes on "deep" grammar', *Journal of Linguistics*, 2, 57–67.
—— (1966b), 'Intonation systems in English', in McIntosh, A. and Halliday, M. A. K. (eds), *Patterns of Language: Papers in General, Descriptive and Applied Linguistics*, London, Longman, 111–33.
—— (1967), *Intonation and Grammar in British English*, Janua Linguarum Series Practica 48, The Hague, Mouton.
—— (1968), 'Notes on transitivity and theme in English, Part 3', *Journal of Linguistics*, 4, 179–215.
—— (1970), *A Course in Spoken English: Intonation*, Oxford, Oxford University Press.
—— (1973), *Explorations in the Functions of Language*, London, Edward Arnold.
—— (1978), *Language as Social Semiotic*, London, Edward Arnold.
—— (1979), 'Modes of realisation and modes of expression: types of grammatical structure and their determination by different semantic functions', in Allerton, D. J. Carney, E. and Holdcroft, D. (eds), *Function and Context in Linguistic Analysis: Essays Offered to William Haas*, Cambridge, Cambridge University Press, 57–79.
—— (1984), 'Language as code and language as behaviour: a systemic-functional interpretation of the nature and ontogenesis of dialogue', in Fawcett, R. P., Halliday, M. A. K., Lamb, S. M. and Makkai, A. (eds), *The Semiotics of Culture and Language, Vol. 1: Language as Social Semiotic*, London, Frances Pinter, 3–35.
—— (1985), *Introduction to Functional Grammar*, London, Edward Arnold.
Halliday, M. A. K. and Hasan, R. (1976), *Cohesion in English*, London, Longman.
—— (1980), *Text and Context: Aspects of Language in a Social-Semiotic Perspective*, Sophia Linguistica VI, Tokyo, Sophia University Press.
—— (1985), *Language, Text and Context: Aspects of Language in a Social-Semiotic Perspective*, Victoria, Deakin University.
Hasan, R. (1978) 'Text in the systemic-functional model', in Dressler, W. U. (ed.), *Current Trends in Textlinguistics*, Berlin and New York, de Gruyter, 228–46.
—— (1984a), 'Coherence and cohesive harmony', in Flood, J. (ed.), *Understanding Reading Comprehension*, Newark, Delaware, International Reading Association, 181–219.
—— (1984b), 'The nursery tale as a genre', *Nottingham Linguistic Circular*, 13, 71–102.
Huddleston, R. D. (1978), 'Review of Halliday and Hasan 1976', *Lingua*, 45, 333–54.
Hudson, R. A. (1976), *Arguments for a Non-Transformational Grammar*, Chicago and London, University of Chicago Press.
Hymes, D. H. (1971), *On Communicative Competence*, Philadelphia, University of Pennsylvania Press.
Jakobson, R. (1960), 'Closing statement: linguistics and poetics', in Sebeok, T. A. (ed.), *Style in Language*, Cambridge, Mass., MIT Press, 350–77.
Labov, W. (1973), 'The boundaries of words and their meanings', in Bailey and Shuy (eds) (1973: 340–73).
Lakoff, G. (1977), 'Linguistic Gestalts', in *Proceedings of the Thirteenth Annual Meeting of the Chicago Linguistic Society*, Chicago, Chicago Linguistic Society, 236–87.
Leech, G. (1980), *Explorations in Semantics and Pragmatics*, Amsterdam, John Benjamins.
—— (1981), *Semantics*, 2nd edn., Harmondsworth, Penguin.
—— (1983), *Principles of Pragmatics*, London, Longman.
Leech, G. and Coates, J. (1980), 'Semantic indeterminacy and the modals', in

Greenbaum, S., Leech, G. and Svartvik, J. (eds), *Studies in English Linguistics: For Randolph Quirk*, London, Longman, 79–90.
Levinson, S. (1983), *Pragmatics*, Cambridge, Cambridge University Press.
Martin, J. R. (1984), 'Functional components in a grammar; a review of deployable recognition criteria', *Nottingham Linguistic Circular*, 13, 35–70.
—— (1985), 'Process and text: two aspects of human semiosis', in Benson, J. D. and Greaves, W. S. (eds) (1985), *Systemic Perspectives on Discourse, Vol. 1: Selected Theoretical Papers from the 9th International Systemic Workshop*, Norwood, NJ, Ablex, 248–74.
Morgan, J. L. and Sellner, M. B. (1980), 'Discourse and literary theory', in Spiro, R. J., Bruce, B. C. and Brewer, W. F. (eds), *Theoretical Issues in Reading Comprehension*, Hillsdale, NJ, Lawrence Erlbaum, 165–200.
Poynton, C. (1984), 'Forms and functions: names as vocatives', *Nottingham Linguistic Circular*, 13, 1–34.
Quirk, R. (1965), 'Descriptive statement and serial relationship', *Language*, 41, 205–17.
Rosch, E. (1977), 'Human categorization', in Warren, N. (ed.), *Advances in Cross-Cultural Psychology, Vol. 1*, New York, Academic Press, 1–49.
Ross, J. R. (1973), 'A fake NP squish', in Bailey and Shuy (eds) (1983: 96–140).
Sinclair, J. McH. and Coulthard, R. M. (1975), *Towards an Analysis of Discourse: The English Used by Teachers and Pupils*, London, Oxford University Press.
Sperber, D. and Wilson, D. (1986), *Relevance*, Oxford, Blackwell.
Ventola, E. (1979), 'The structure of casual conversation in English', *Journal of Pragmatics*, 3, 267–98.
—— (1983), 'Contrasting schematic structures in service encounters', *Applied Linguistics*, 4, No. 3, 242–58.
—— (1984), 'The dynamics of genre', *Nottingham Linguistic Circular*, 13, 103–23.
—— (1987), *The Structure of Social Interaction: A Systemic Approach to the Semiotics of Service Encounters*, London, Frances Pinter.

2 English questions: a 'significance-generating device' for building in context*

Eirian C. Davies
Department of English, Royal Holloway and Bedford New College, University of London, UK

Anyone who examines occurrences of polar ('yes/no') interrogatives in a range of texts cannot fail to be struck with the multiplicity of uses to which they seem to be put. They can be used to exclaim (especially when negative), to suggest, to undermine another's assumptions, to rally, to reprove, to advise, to formulate a shared problem of uncertainty, to test, to give a 'cue' to another to speak, and so on. The great variety of different illocutionary forces which can be achieved in uttering sentences of this type has been much remarked on in the literature for some time, especially by those engaged in the analysis of conversation; for example, Schegloff (1977), Sinclair (1980). It was this characteristic, as shared by the other basic sentence types, which led Austin to avoid the study of 'primary' or 'implicit' performatives in his development of the concept of illocutionary force in the first place (1962: 32-3).

Various approaches to this problem of what we might call 'pragmatic multivalency' have been explored, including a large body of work on indirect speech acts (e.g. Searle 1979), Gordon and Lakoff's (1975) suggestion of 'conversational postulates', Sinclair and Coulthard's (1975) approach in terms of three levels (partly echoed in Quirk *et al.* (1985: 803-5), and Halliday's (1985: 319-45) proposals concerning 'grammatical metaphor' (for which last see the discussion in Butler, this volume). In two previous studies (Davies 1979, 1985), I have put forward some other suggestions for a means of approaching this conundrum; and it is these that I hope to explore further here. I shall confine the discussion largely to positive polar ('yes/no') interrogatives (PPIs).

In principle, there seems to be a choice between two basic alternatives in approaching the problem, which could be roughly formulated as follows: 'we have a single sentence type in the syntax, and a multiplicity of different pragmatic effects produced by utterances of sentences of this type in different contexts: therefore, we must either allow for multiple 'meanings' of the sentence type; or, we must infer a single 'meaning' such that, in combination

---

* I am grateful to the Council of Royal Holloway and Bedford New College for the grant of a sabbatical term's leave in which to pursue the research on which this chapter is based.

with different contexts, it yields the different effects observed. There is in fact a third option: we could say that the sentence type itself has no 'meaning', different effects achieved in using it being entirely accountable for by differences in contexts of utterance. If we are tempted to this third 'solution' in relation to the interrogative, we should, for consistency, also have to adopt it for the declarative, which is equally multivalent in this way. If we do that, then we are claiming implicitly that it will not make a meaningful difference which of these two sentence types is used, in any given context whatever.[1] That is, if there is no such thing as a meaning of the sentence type, associated distinctively with syntactic form, then declarative and interrogative will be consistently in free variation, wherever either is used. I shall take it as axiomatic that this not the case; and that any proposal which has this claim as a consequence is thereby falsified.

On this basis, our options reduce to the initial alternatives: multiple/single meaning(s) for the syntactic construction (i.e. sentence type). Here, if we accept that different sentence types 'have' different meanings, we will need to make suggestions about what these meanings are: that is, we will need to postulate a grammatical semantics which need not coincide with the pragmatic effects produced in utterance. This is most clearly so if we adopt the single meaning hypothesis; but, a point which is sometimes overlooked, it applies equally if we opt for the multiple meanings approach, if we are not to readmit 'syntactic meaninglessness', by the back door.

Both alternatives raise problems, and neither is immediately attractive. The first seems to lack an element of 'control': how are we to circumscribe the range of 'meanings' associated with a given sentence type? The second seems often to fly in the face of the facts, and poses very considerable problems when we tackle the challenge of making proposals for just what that single meaning might be.

One test which will help us discriminate between the two hypotheses is that of 'pragmatic ambiguity'. That is, if we can attest an instance in which utterance of a given sentence type may convey two different pragmatic effects in exactly the same context, then the multiple meanings hypothesis (MMH) is substantiated for that sentence type, and the single meaning hypothesis (SMH) is falsified. In such a case, given that context is kept constant, the only source of a perceived ambiguity is in the semantics. This means that the issue has often been discussed in terms of semantic ambiguity; but the crucial point is that the only 'hard' test of semantic ambiguity lies in this limiting case where, because context is kept exactly constant, it cannot be held to play any part in accounting for differences between the more than one 'meanings' perceived. If we are dealing with the utterance of a sentence, these 'meanings' are pragmatic effects; so here we have the case where pragmatic ambiguity implies semantic ambiguity. It would not be unfair to claim that Firthian linguistics as a whole has held reservations about the notion of 'ambiguity in context' (pragmatic ambiguity); and that it is for this reason that it has laid less stress than have other models on the importance of the concept of ambiguity in general.

The converse does not apply: if we cannot yet attest a case of pragmatic ambiguity for any of the sentence types under review, this does not falsify the MMH nor prove the SMH; but it leaves the former open to question, and encourages investigation of the latter. Both hypotheses relate to the semantics of linguistic form. It will be helpful at this stage to attempt to be more precise about terminology, since 'meaning' is widely used in a number of different and potentially conflicting senses. I suggest the term 'significance' for the 'meaningfulness' of an utterance of a given sentence type in a given context: its pragmatic effect. 'Meaning' can then be reserved for the semantics of linguistic form.

As already implied in our discussion of pragmatic ambiguity, the choice between the MMH and SMH cannot be considered in isolation from the problem of what role is played by contextual factors in producing what we are now calling 'significance'. The case we have postulated for pragmatic ambiguity is one where contextual factors contribute nothing to variation in significance, since there is more than one pragmatic effect while context is held constant. What we have here is a single sentence type, a single context, and two kinds of significance; and we have attributed two meanings to the sentence type as a result. Let us explore this approach further, and examine some further cases, set out in a comparable fashion.

If we could attest a case where utterances of two different sentence types in exactly the same context produced the same significance, we would have to view this as prima facie evidence for 'syntactic meaninglessness'. That is, if this kind of 'syntactic synonymy' were found to obtain over a wide range of different contexts, we would normally conclude that the two sentence types concerned were not meaningfully distinct. The next step, then, would be to examine utterances of the same two sentence types in a second context. Suppose we found that, here, utterances of each sentence type produced its own distinctive significance, and that each of these was in turn distinct from the shared significance which utterance of either produced in the first context. This would disprove 'syntactic meaninglessness' for the two constructions concerned; but it would also raise more complex considerations.

Let us take the positive and negative polar interrogatives as two separate sentence types, and consider, for example, a context in which a first-time grandmother is showing photos of her new grandson to her favourite sister.[2] In this context it is made clear, independently of the sentence used, that both participants hold that he is a sweet baby. In such a case we might judge that the significance of the utterance, by either participant of,

(1) Is he a sweetie.

would differ little, if at all, from the significance of an utterance of

(2) Isn't he a sweetie.

Both would count as an enthusiastic affirmation of the proposition that *he is a sweetie*.

On the other hand, if we consider a context in which both participants have an open mind with respect to the proposition at issue, for example, one in which two scientists are discussing whether or not there might be vegetation on Mars, we may find a radical alteration with respect to significance, for utterances of both sentence types. Suppose one of them says,

(3) Is there life in extra-terrestrial space? (this is the general question we need to address).

We might say of this that it would count as 'posing' a question in neutral terms; whereas, in the same circumstances, an utterance of

(4) Isn't there life in extra-terrestrial space?

would convey an opinion, and be, to some extent, conducive to 'yes'. Neither of these utterances would count as an enthusiastic affirmation of the proposition that *there is life in extra-terrestrial space* in such a context; and so both would differ in significance from the utterances of (1) and (2) in the first context. But they also differ from one another, in the second context.

We are now dealing with two different sentence types, two different contexts and three different kinds of significance. From the first context we must conclude that, as utterance of two different sentence types produces one and the same significance, it is not the syntactic construction type alone which determines significance, since this is varied but significance remains constant. From the second context, where utterance of each different sentence type gives a significance distinct from utterance of the other, we must conclude that it is not contextual features alone which determine significance, since these are held constant and yet variation occurs.

However, equally, difference in sentence type corresponds with change in significance in the second context; so it seems that syntactic distinctions CAN be associated with variation in significance, even if not uniquely determining it. Further, if we take either sentence type separately, we have a case where the significance of its utterance varies between the first and second context, suggesting that the same is true for contextual features and changes in significance. We have found that syntactic distinctions do not ALWAYS correspond with variation in significance, from considering the first context. We can test for whether or not contextual distinctions ALWAYS do so by looking for a case (for either sentence type) where its utterance has the same significance in both of two different contexts.

Suppose we take utterances of

(5) Can you afford it?

(i) in a context where the speaker otherwise indicates that it seems to him that this might not be the case, but does not have grounds for definitely holding that it is not so, and also, (ii) in a context where he shows, perhaps by a more openly disapproving manner, that he does definitely hold that 'no'. Suppose that in both cases it is clear from the Addressee's behaviour that she definitely holds that 'yes'. It could be argued that the significance of an utterance of (5) would be pretty much equivalent in both cases.

If this, or another example, can be accepted as showing non-variation of significance across contextual differences, we will need to conclude that neither syntactic form nor contextual features consistently co-vary with the significance of utterances of sentence types.

However, even if this is so, we will not have shown that a COMBINATION of syntactic form and contextual features does not so co-vary. This is one argument for investigating the ways in which they might combine.

The notion that it might be a combination of linguistic and contextual features which accounts for significance has a number of consequences. First, and most importantly, it demands that the kind of meaning which we postulate for syntactic form is such that it CAN be combined with contextual features. The proposal below for an account of the (force-) semantics of sentences types in terms of propositional attitudes represents one attempt to meet this requirement. Secondly, there are different consequences for the MMH and SMH. Broadly, it makes the MMH more difficult to sustain, for the problem of limiting and specifying a list of the multiple meanings associated with a given sentence type, in a principled way, becomes more acute. Also, the MMH becomes less attractive. If we are seeking to account for a one-to-many relation between sentence type and categories of significance by means of suggesting different combinations of features in the linguistic semantics with those in context, we should at any rate start with a single bundle of semantic features per sentence type, and see if that will suffice. Since we are now postulating an alternative account of 'pragmatic multivalency', which relies exclusively neither on linguistic semantics nor on contextual features, we do not need to allow for 'multiple meanings', that is semantic ambiguity, unless we encounter pragmatic ambiguity in texts. I would want to claim that, from several points of view, the SMH is more within the general spirit of a Firthian and Systemic approach to language than is the MMH.

The attraction of the 'multiple meaning hypothesis' is that it appears to account for the facts without strain. Its weakness is that it is potentially vacuous, amounting to no more than a description of contextual features, with a hidden implication of syntactic meaninglessness as a consequence.

The problems involved in attempting to validate the 'single meaning hypothesis' are often more evident than its attractions to those whose chief orientation is empirical. Primarily, it appears NOT to account for the facts. Nevertheless, it has engaged considerable energy and attention (cf. the discussion in Levinson 1983: 263–74 of work on the 'literal force hypothesis'; also Bolinger 1977). The main attraction of this approach lies in the fact that it makes a strong claim for the meaningfulness of linguistic form. It also imposes a stern discipline: for it demands that we offer a specification of exactly WHAT it is that each distinct sentence type can be said to 'mean'. Whatever this is will have to be shown to be capable of in some way yielding the multiplicity of different pragmatic effects with which we began.

There are a number of ways of attempting to meet these challenges. Let us take 'WHAT it means' first. Here, one approach would be to look for the 'highest common denominator' of meaning: that which is present in all occurrences of the sentence type in whatever context, and abstract this out as its 'single meaning'. A very interesting example of this approach is given in Bolinger (1977) with respect to the English imperative. His conclusion is that the only common factor of meaning associated with this sentence type in all contexts is 'plus hypothetical'; but, in fact, even this can be denied, and we are again left with syntactic meaninglessness.³ Alternatively, if we postulated a 'rich' meaning for the imperative, as in Searle (1969, 1979), there are many cases, as Bolinger convincingly shows, where several of the claimed features appear to be inoperative in context. In order both to (i) account for the variety of Bolinger's data, AND (ii) avoid the conclusion that syntactic form is meaningless, we need to postulate some mechanism which will allow features in the semantics to be 'changed', or even 'cancelled out' by related features in context. This in turn will involve postulating that the SAME KIND of features are operative in BOTH these different levels: semantics and context.

If we could find a 'highest common denominator' element of meaning for a given sentence type, AND if we could find cases of utterance of this sentence type where its 'meaningfulness' could be FULLY accounted for by just that HCD, then we might be justified in terming this the 'literal' meaning of the construction: otherwise, the term is not helpful.⁴ An analysis such as Searle's (1969) account does not fulfil the first of these conditions; one such as Bolinger's (1977) treatment does not fulfil the second. Halliday's concept of 'grammatical metaphor', which has something in common with Givón's (1979) discussion of 'grammaticalization', relies on a notion very close to 'literal meaning' (1985: 342–5); but the examples he gives tend not to satisfy either condition. This is for the good reason that he takes, in effect, what is the most 'central' kind of 'meaningfulness' of the construction type as basic: that significance with which we intuitively feel it is most often found in use.

In the remainder of this chapter I want to explore the 'single meaning hypothesis'; but not as a candidate for 'literal meaning'. That is, I should like to return to the notion that, in order to account for the pragmatic forces of sentence types, we need to allow for some process whereby a semantic feature associated with a type may be cancelled, or otherwise altered, by a related contextual feature in a given situation of utterance. This approach allows for a semantics of sentence types which is distinct from pragmatics, not by virtue of being assessed in terms of features (variables) of different KINDS, but because it may have different 'values' on variables of the SAME kinds. It permits that the semantic specification of any given sentence type may ALWAYS be different from the pragmatic effect produced by utterances of sentences of this type, in any context whatever. That is, it allows for a semantics which is never directly perceivable, because it is never directly encountered. Such a notion is by no means foreign to systemic linguistics. If we are prepared to accept that 'having meaning' for Halliday is equivalent to 'having' what I am here calling 'significance', then it is entirely in harmony with the claim that any linguistic expression is meaningless out of context. The present proposal merely involves extending the view that the semantics of linguistic form does not, ON ITS OWN, supply that which we respond to as communicatively competent interpreters of texts, to its natural conclusion.

Let us return to 'basics' for a moment, and examine what kind of activity we are engaging in when we analyse utterances of sentence types for their pragmatic (force-)effect. What we encounter in the text is a sentence type in a context, where 'context' is taken to cover both linguistic ('co-text') and non-linguistic environment. What we respond to, as communicatively competent users of the language, is their combination: it is to this that we have developed and refined our capacities for interpretation and discrimination throughout our lives, both as producers and receivers. It is this 'significance' which will come first to mind, and leave the deepest impression, as much to us as linguists as to us, and others, as interactionally well-functioning human beings. There is a strong case for supposing that, even as analysts, we do not so much 'infer' the significance of an utterance as START with it. If this is so, then the challenge for the linguist is to avoid STAYING with it. That is, I would argue, our intuitions about the meaningfulness of sentence types are largely intuitions about significance, and we need to work out what role semantics plays in these, as a separately stateable component: our 'given' is a composite value.

The problem for linguistics is to CONNECT significance with linguistic form in a principled and systematic way; and it is hardly possible to overstate the importance of this for the standing of the discipline. If it cannot ultimately succeed, linguistics has nothing more to offer than techniques for discriminating between well- and ill-formed strings: it provides no basis for preferring one well-formed string to another, either in the same or different circumstances. And pragmatics on this basis would be a mixture of (micro-level) sociology and a semi-systematized branch of literary criticism.

I want to proceed on this basis: that the significance of utterances constitutes the raw data of our investigation, and that the problem posed is to relate this systematically to categories of linguistic form. I shall attempt to formulate proposals on a narrow front, namely that of 'force-effects' only, taking the 'single meaning hypothesis' (SMH). In its 'strong' form, which I shall adopt, the SMH involves the claim that there is a one-to-one relation between each syntactically identified sentence type and a uniquely associated semantic specification.

It follows from the SMH in this form that (1) and (2) above have different semantic specifications (SeSs) for 'force'; and so for (3) and (4); but that the (force-)SeS for (1) is the same as that for (3), and so also for (2) and (4). The examples (1) and (2) were taken to illustrate that two different SeSs may be 'neutralized' in a given context, in the sense that utterance of the sentence type associated with either will produce a roughly equivalent pragmatic effect. It would seem that an adequate framework of analysis must be able to account both for this and for what we have taken to be axiomatic: namely, that such neutralization does not occur in all contexts for any two sentence types. That is, it will need to be based on a testable hypothesis about the principles governing combination of features in the semantics with those in context. We should be looking for a framework which allows us to formulate answers to both the questions: (i) how does context act to modify the semantics of sentence types?; and (ii) how does the utterance of a given sentence type act to change context?

I have elsewhere (1979: 27–8, 37–8, 187–8; 1985) proposed one such hypothesis, which will be somewhat modified and extended in what follows. It can be expressed in the form of rules, which constitute the 'Significance-generating device' of my title. This hypothesis is based on a feature of the general approach mentioned above: namely, that semantics and context are analysed in the SAME terms. (In the partial proposals which follow, these will be restricted to propositional attitudes.) This in turn rests on a distinction fundamental to sociological role theory (and to the use made of interactional roles in Davies 1979): namely, that between a role, as such, and any given individual who occupies it on a particular occasion. My suggestion is that the linguistic semantics of sentence types ('force-semantics') may be expressed in terms of propositional attitudes ascribed to the speech roles of S(peaker) and A(ddressee); and that the relevant features of context may be expressed in terms of propositional attitudes ascribed to particular individuals occupying those roles on a given occasion of utterance. A framework of this kind allows us to provide without difficulty for cases of 'blatant insincerity', of the kind found in some 'rhetorical questions', such as, for example,

(6) Are we electors?

addressed to a black audience by a black orator in South Africa today, where the point of the utterance is to draw attention to the fact that neither holds that 'yes'. These can be accounted for as instances where the semantics and context clash, thereby generating a significance which differs from the value of either of them alone. In this way, we can be freed from the underlying assumption of a narrowly conceived 'appropriateness' which has done much to bedevil speech-act theory.

We have allowed, above, that the SeS of a given sentence type may be different from the pragmatic effect produced by uttering a sentence of this type in any context whatever. If pragmatic effect (=significance) is derived from the combination of SeS and the relevant contextual features (in the contextual specification—CoS), this seems in theory too wide an allowance. If SeS and CoS are to be stated in terms of the same variables, then there will always be one theoretically possible CoS which is the same as the given SeS; and, at least in that one case, SeS will also be the same as significance. This does not in fact invalidate the earlier formulation, since it may still be the case that no utterances of the associated sentence type in a context of that 'matching' type will be encountered in texts.

It is not, then, a consequence of the proposed approach that semantics and context need (ever) coincide. This enables us to discriminate different kinds, and degrees, of appropriateness, rather than being confined to regarding all cases where semantics and context fail to match as some sort of problem-posing 'exception'. We are released from what Levinson (1983: 263) refers to as the 'literal force hypothesis', whether in its 'rich' version, as in Searle's (1969, 1979) approach, or in a parsimonious variant such as Bolinger's (1977) common denominator treatment of the meaning of the imperative. Nevertheless, we have retained the single meaning hypothesis.

The proposals for semantic, and contextual, specifications which follow are two-part in each case. That is, they take the form of statements of propositional attitudes ascribed BOTH to the role of Speaker AND to that of Addressee for the semantics, and to BOTH (groups of) individuals occupying these respective roles for context. Some background on the motivation for making a double ascription of this kind is available in an earlier study of modal declaratives with predictive *may(not)/might(n't)* (Davies in press); but I hope that further justifications for doing so will emerge in the course of the ensuing discussion. Briefly, these have to do with an element of 'discourse meaning' and 'discourse significance'. That is, I follow Halliday (1970, *et passim*) in accepting multiple components of meaning in the semantics. 'Force-semantics' here has much in common with his 'interpersonal component' (e.g. 1970: 159–60), but is seen as closely interrelated with a semantics of 'connectedness' or 'coherence', which I suggest calling 'discourse meaning'. This would seem to fall most naturally under his 'textual component' (1970: 143). No attempt is made to consider features of 'ideational meaning': the proposals below are artificially limited in this respect, and therefore offer a partial account only (cf. Davies 1979: 31–4).

A formal statement of the proposed framework of analysis is given in the notes to this discussion. In the main body of the text I want to consider its potential usefulness informally, along the following lines. First I shall outline the list of propositional attitudes in terms of which it is proposed to state the SeSs of (indicative) sentence types. CoSs will be stated in terms of this same list. Proposals for the SeSs of four sentence types in these terms will be put forward. SeS:CoS combination rules will be outlined and applied, and the results considered. At this point, we shall have what amounts to a body of testable predictions to evaluate.

List of propositional attitudes:[5]
('p' is any proposition; 'Alpha' denotes a variable whose values are names: in semantic specifications, these will be names of roles (Speaker/Addressee); in contextual specifications, these will be names of particular individuals.)

The list can be given, for the purposes of discussion, in terms of the following informal glosses:

(1) 'Alpha holds that yes.'
(2) 'Alpha holds that no.'
(3) 'Alpha doesn't hold that yes.'
(4) 'Alpha doesn't hold that no.'
(5) 'Alpha has an open mind.'
(6) 'Alpha reserves a definite view.' ('Alpha holds one or other (mutually exclusive) definite view; but WHICH this is not given.')
(7) 'Alpha is neutral.' ('Alpha has some propositional attitude towards p; but WHICH this is is not given.' p is a member of the universe of discourse.)

Semantic specification of four (non-modal) sentence types (expressed informally):

(i) Positive declarative (PD): 'S holds that yes; A has an open mind.'
(ii) Negative declarative (ND): 'S holds that no; A doesn't hold that no.'[6]

(iii) Positive polar ('yes/no') interrogative (PPI): 'S has an open mind; A is neutral.'
(iv) Negative polar ('yes/no') interrogative (NPI): 'S doesn't hold that no; A reserves a definite view.'

Contextual specifications:
These are seen as varying independently of any SeS. Further, each element in a CoS is seen as potentially varying independently of the other. Given our list of seven propositional attitudes above, this means that a total of 7 ★ 7 different CoSs may be derived from it. That is, for each SeS, we are initially considering forty-nine different CoSs with which it may combine, through utterance of the sentence type concerned. In practice, neutralization occurs: the relations between the propositional attitudes proposed are such that each of the SeSs in (i)–(iv) above is predicted to yield the same significance in more than one CoS. In this respect, the combination rules act reductively.

Combination rules ('Significance-generating device'):
The general status of this component in the model has been outlined and, to some extent, developed elsewhere (Davies 1979, 1985). The approach it represents can be summarized briefly as follows (partly recapitulating on the discussion above). We are adopting the single meaning hypothesis. If we take the unique SeS of a sentence type, the problem is to account for pragmatic multivalency in terms of force. The hypothesis is that our data consist of the perceived significance of utterances of sentence types in context. We therefore need to propose some account of how interaction between the two (i.e. the semantics of sentence types and contextual factors) can be shown to take place, so as to yield pragmatic multivalency of linguistic form. Combination rules represent one proposal for such an account. The proposed combination rules (CRs) have the general form:

'X operator Y = V'

where 'operator' may be either the sign for addition ('+'), or that for multiplication ('★').

Combination rules are recursively applicable. In a first application, 'X' is a variable ranging over semantic specifications, 'Y' is a variable ranging over contextual specifications, and 'V' is a variable ranging over categories of FIRST order significance. On a second application, 'X' is a variable ranging over categories of FIRST order significance (FOS), 'Y' is a variable ranging over a further set of contextual features, and 'V' ranges over categories of SECOND order significance. And so, in a parallel way, for further applications, and 'higher' orders of significance. In this fashion, the SGD offers a means of systematically stating different degrees and kinds of 'indirectness', by providing for the 'building in' of different 'layers' of contextual factors at different stages. In what follows, we shall not attempt to go beyond FIRST order significance.

Within this general framework, the detailed application of the approach will need to take into account the bipartite nature of the SeSs and CoSs. That is, for each combination of a SeS and a CoS, two CRs will apply: one to the Speaker value in SeS, linking it to the individual 'occupant value' in CoS, and the other to the Addressee value, linking that to its related occupant value in CoS. In this way, statements of first order significance will also be bipartite. My proposal is that the CR which applies to the Speaker value in semantics has the '+' operator; and that which applies to Addressee has '★'. I shall call these, respectively, the 'sum' and 'product' rules. Then, given the formal framework used,[5] Speaker:occupant combinations are treated in terms of the union of sets; and Addressee:occupant combinations in terms of the intersections of sets.

The motivation for this distinction is to do with the origin(s) of ascription, and relates to underlying practicalities. It is a PERSON who ascribes propositional attitudes, to himself, and also to others. In the case of the individual who occupies S, he may make it evident in the context of utterance that he holds one propositional attitude, but, nevertheless, simultaneously explicitly claim that he holds a different attitude by virtue of uttering a given sentence type with a 'clashing' S value in its semantics, as in, for example, (1) and (2) above. Here, the origin of both conflicting ascriptions is the same person. The significance of his utterance, with respect to its first element, derives from his ascribing two views to himself; and this can be captured in the FOS statement by giving both views: their 'sum'.

With respect to A values, the position is different. I would argue that an A value represents a 'projection' made by the person occupying the S role. That is, by virtue of uttering a sentence of a given type, the person at S 'makes public'/'presents for attention' the A value in its associated semantics as his estimate of another's view.[7] But here, the view indicated in context originates from a different person: the occupant of the A role himself. It is the area of overlap (or the lack of it) between these two ascriptions which is important for significance. This represents the extent to which the person at S explicitly accepts, or rejects, the self-presentation of the person at A. ('Non-matching' here may convey subtle forms of implicit disagreement or correction.) Overlap is obtained in FOS by using '★' as operator in the combination rule, to yield a product: the intersection of sets. Given the A value proposed above for the SeS of positive interrogatives, use of the product rule has the effect of ensuring that the FOS value is the same as that in CoS, for this second element, throughout.

We have, then, a form of statement for categories of FOS which consists of two elements, arrived at respectively by the application of the sum CR for S, and the product CR for A, with CoS. We may use these to derive two further measures within significance: (a) the sum of the two elements in first order significance will give a set membership statement for p which is non-controversial for all 'parties' in both semantics and context; and (b) their product will yield a measure of agreement/disagreement, giving type and degree of 'core consensus'.

Predictions:

We are now in a position to consider the output of the SGD, given the preceding framework. This consists in predicted categories of first order (force-)significance, which can be evaluated by reference to textual evidence. That is, for example, the SGD makes specific predictions about the different kinds and degrees of conduciveness conveyed by positive and negative polar interrogatives in varying contexts. Further, it predicts 'neutralizations': cases in which (i) a given sentence type will have the same significance in more than one context, and (ii) cases where two (or more) different sentence types will have the same significance in one given context (but not in others). It also predicts an exact number of different kinds of first order significance for any given sentence type, taking the list of propositional attitudes above for the specification of both semantics and context. (On the current proposals, this number is significantly lower for the negative, as opposed to the positive, polar interrogative: eight, as compared with twenty-eight.) Predictions of these kinds are 'hard', in the sense that they can be tested against the evidence of both texts and intuitions: they offer several opportunities for falsification.

The proposals for SeSs listed in (i)–(iv) above, in conjunction with the suggested combination rules, have been tested for neutralization predictions in as far as time has allowed. The interpretations of (1)–(6) above, in the contexts sketched, are as predicted by this model. What follows below is a list of illustrations of the categories of FIRST order significance which these proposals predict for the positive polar interrogative. Both examples and contexts are largely constructed or informally 'remembered'.

I would fully agree with Levinson (1983) that the only genuinely satisfactory evidence of the significance of utterances in texts is provided by the reactions of other participants at the time. What I have to offer below falls far short of this ideal, but is provided largely by way of a spur to further thought and criticism, and as an orientation for genuine textual investigations.

The illustration of FOS categories are arranged in groups, on the basis of CoS values for the individual at Speaker. Ordering within each group follows a repeated pattern, according to CoS values for the individual at Addressee, as follows:

This individual: 'is neutral'/'has an open mind'/'reserves a definite view'/ 'holds that yes'/'doesn't hold that no'/'holds that no'/'doesn't hold that yes'. (Labels for the categories are mnemonics only.)

Illustrations:

Group I: The individual at Speaker has an 'open mind'

(7) Child to passer-by:) *Is it four o'clock?* (No clocks in sight; not discernible whether or not the passer-by is wearing a watch.) (7) uttered in this context would probably count as a 'question' in any ordinary sense of that term. We might call it an 'Open Inquiry'.

(8) *Is there life on other planets?* ('that's the question'). One scientist to another: neither of them holds that there definitely is, or that there definitely is not. 'Poser' (cf. (3) above).

(9) *Is it raining?* said by someone sitting in a room with the curtains drawn to someone who has just come back from looking outside. (cf. (9a) *Is it tidy now?* said by small boy to his mother, who has told him to make his bedroom tidy before he can go out. He is not sure what (minimum) will count as 'being tidy'; she can be expected to hold a definite view. Also, perhaps, (9b) *Do you like being at university?* Friend at home to someone on their first visit back. The friend has an open mind, but the student is in a position to hold a definite view on the matter.) 'Interrogation'.

(10) *Is Julie going to the party in those jeans?* Father to mother, who has just said 'Have a good time' and waved goodbye to their teenage daughter, as she left the house with a friend at about the right time for going to the party concerned. 'Silly question'? i.e. seems clear in the context (his wife's behaviour on their daughter's departure) that the mother holds that 'yes'. On the other hand, Julie sometimes dresses up for parties; and she is sometimes late going to them. Her father is not sure, 'Query' (possible undertones of *shouldn't be*).

(11) *Have you got your key?* said as a matter of routine to someone who sometimes forgets his key, but continues to have faith in his own memory. 'Check' (reminder).

(12) *Have you got a few minutes?* John to Bill, who seems on the point of leaving the common room. If it's three minutes before two o'clock and classes start at two, it would seem from Bill's behaviour (preparing to go) that he holds that 'no'. John doesn't know Bill's timetable (not every one has a class at two that day). Even so, 'silly question'? Comparable to (10): 'Query' (possibly with undertones of *should have*).

(13) *Is it upstairs?* said to John who is looking downstairs for a book he can't find. 'Check' (suggestion).

Groups II and III: 'Biased'
Group II: Bias to 'yes'
(Individual at Speaker 'holds that yes', or, 'does not hold that not'.)

(14) *Is the union's pay claim fair?* said by union official to non-member whose view is not derivable from context ('undisclosed/neutral'). 'Leading question: from yes'.

(15) *Am I hungry!* said to someone with an open mind on the matter. cf. (15a) *Do you look great!* to someone unsure about their appearance; and (15b) *is he a winner!* to someone who doesn't know 'him'. 'Declamation'.

(16) *Are things here in good shape now?* said by Mabel, a political agent, about the local party office which she has just reorganized, to the parliamentary candidate for whom she is working. 'Tester' (for positive).

(17) *Was that a lucky one!* Andrew to Alice: they have just caught the last train home, but only because it left two minutes late. 'Exclamation' (voicing

consensus view). (cf. (17') *Wasn't that a lucky one!*, and discussion of (1) and (2) above.)

(18) *Are you worried about hair loss?* In advertisement by manufacturer of hair-restoring lotion in magazine with a middle-aged male readership. 'Compatible Insinuation' (that yes).

(19) *Now, is this the right street?* Roger to Maggie: they are on their way to visit Bill in his home. There are indications from preceding discourse that Roger is sure that they are in the street in which Bill lives, and that Maggie is sure they are not. Bill's house is one of a very few in the area which are painted bright purple. They turn a corner and Roger sees a purple house. 'Claim' (overriding opposite view).

(20) *Has he hurt himself?* to normally fond mother who is taking no notice of her yelling child, who has just had a minor fall. 'Contrastive ('corrective'?) Insinuation' (that yes).

Group III: Bias to 'no'
(Individual at Speaker 'holds that no', or 'does not hold that yes'.)

(21) *Is it right to accept a union-negotiated pay rise without belonging to the union?* said by union member trying to recruit new colleagues whose view is not derivable in context ('undisclosed/neutral'). 'Leading question: from no.'

(22) *Have we passed that house before?* Jack to Jill. They are having a long country walk in an area which is familiar to Jack, but not to Jill. Jill is feeling completely lost and is beginning to panic and think they will never find the way back to their car again. She claims they have just been going round in a circle for the last hour. Jack, trying to reassure her, says: [Look at that house.] *Have we passed that house before?* But it is clear in context that all the houses they've passed look pretty much the same to Jill, and she isn't sure whether they have, or have not. We might call (22) a 'Claim' (but one which does not work successfully).

(23) *Is that boiler safe?* Jane to plumber: she has smelt ominous fumes coming from the kitchen boiler, and has called in a plumber to give expert advice. 'Tester' (for negative).

(24) *Can you afford it?* Aunt to extravagant but impoverished niece, who seems on the point of buying herself an expensive new dress without worrying about the price. 'Contrastive ('corrective') Insinuation' (that no). cf. discussion of (5) above.

(25) *Are your shoes all right for muddy fields?* Polite hostess to visitor who seems unperturbed about going for country walk in high heels. 'Contrastive ('corrective') Insinuation' (that no).

(26) *Are we downhearted?* Rallying cry to enthusiastic audience. 'Rhetorical question' (conducive to no). cf. Firth (1957: 10).

(27) *Is your hair as thick as it was?* In advertisement by manufacturer of hair tonic in a magazine with a middle-aged male readership. 'Compatible Insinuation' (that no).

Group IV: Enigmatic individual at Speaker

(28) *Is Berlin the capital of the Federal Republic of Germany?* Quiz master to contestant. 'Exam question.'
(29) *Are there any points of comparison between Browning's poetry and that of Donne?* Tutor to student who has read the works of both poets.'Prod.'
(30) *Is 'In Memoriam' Tennyson's greatest work?* Tutor to student who has read all Tennyson's works. 'Probe.'
(31) *Are the activities of the City of London good for the British economy?* Polite radio interviewer, addressing the Chairman of the Stock Exchange. 'Cue' (for reasons why yes).
(32) *Is Hopkins a difficult poet?* Tutor to student who is struggling rather with the poet's language. 'Opening' (for yes).
(33) *Is the government's present policy likely to succeed?* Polite radio interviewer, addressing the Leader of the Opposition. 'Cue' (for reasons why no).
(34) *Is the ending satisfactory?* Tutor to student who has expressed uncritical enthusiasm for *The Mill on the Floss*. 'Quiz.'

Commentary:
Given the SeS proposed for positive interrogatives, one effect of the combination rules is to yield a smaller number of categories of FOS than there are different CoSs. Where the significance of uttering a PPI is predicted to be the same in more than one CoS, I have illustrated with only one of such contexts (values for the individual at S). These cases are given below, as 'internal neutralizations'.

Neutralizations: 'internal'
The analysis predicts that the pragmatic effect of uttering a PPI will be the same in the following cases:

(i) across contexts where the individual at Speaker indicates that he holds that yes, or does not hold that no;
(ii) across contexts where the individual at Speaker indicates that he holds that no, or does not hold that yes.
(iii) across contexts where the individual at Speaker indicates that he is either 'neutral' or 'reserves a definite view'.

Neutralizations: 'external'
The analysis predicts that the significance of uttering a positive polar interrogative will be equivalent to that of uttering a negative polar interrogative where both the individual at S and the individual at A show independently that they hold that 'yes'.

This chapter is intended as a spur to discussion. It may serve to arouse some potentially fruitful disagreement.

NOTES

1. This 'syntactic meaninglessness' hypothesis would be falsified by finding any one context in which all the sentence types under review had distinct pragmatic effects.
2. This is a context for which I have recorded conversational data.
3. For example, an utterance of

    All right then, blame me.

    in a context where it was only too clear that this was what the Addressee was already doing, would provide an instance where the imperative was non-hypothetical in context. (cf. Davies 1985: 241).
4. cf Wilensky (1987) who, arguing on different grounds and data, comes to a similar conclusion.
5. The list of propositional attitudes employed can be expressed more strictly as follows:

    1. p is a member of the set of propositions which alpha holds to be the case.
    2. p is a member of the set of propositions which alpha holds not to be the case.
    3. p is a member of the set of propositions which alpha does not hold to be the case.
    4. p is a member of the set of propositions which alpha does not hold not to be the case.
    5. p is a member of the set of propositions which alpha does not hold to be the case, AND p is a member of the set of propositions which alpha does not hold not to be the case.
    6. p is EITHER a member of the set of propositions which alpha holds to be the case OR a member of the set of propositions which alpha holds to be not the case; but not of both, and not of neither.
    7. p is a member of any one of the sets in (1)–(4).

Let:

{B} be the set of propositions which alpha holds to be the case;
{D} be the set of propositions which alpha holds not to be the case;
{I} be the set of propositions which alpha does not hold to be the case;
{J} be the set of propositions which alpha does not hold not to be the case;
{W} be the intersection of {I} and {J};
{Z} be the union of {B} and {D};
{U} be the union of {I} and {J}.

Then,

{J} includes {B};
{I} includes {D};
{J} includes {W};
{I} includes {W};

The Unions of sets can be expressed as follows:

{J} + {B} = {J}
{J} + {W} = {J}
{B} + {W} = {J}.

{I} + {D} = {I}
{I} + {W} = {I}
{D} + {W} = {I}.

$$\{J\} + \{D\} = \{U\}$$
$$\{I\} + \{B\} = \{U\}$$
$$\{W\} + \{Z\} = \{U\}$$
$$\{J\} + \{Z\} = \{U\}$$
$$\{I\} + \{Z\} = \{U\}.$$

$$\{B\} + \{D\} = \{Z\}.$$

$\{U\}$ + any other set = $\{U\}$.

These are the outputs of the 'sum' combination rule.

The intersections of sets can be expressed as follows:

$$\{J\} \star \{B\} = \{B\}$$
$$\{J\} \star \{W\} = \{W\}.$$

$$\{I\} \star \{D\} = \{D\}$$

$$\{I\} \star \{W\} = \{W\}.$$

$$\{J\} \star \{I\} = \{W\}.$$

$$\{J\} \star \{Z\} = \{B\}$$
$$\{I\} \star \{Z\} = \{D\}.$$

$$\{Z\} \star \{B\} = \{B\}$$
$$\{Z\} \star \{D\} = \{D\}.$$

$\{U\} \star$ any other set = that other set.

These are the outputs of the 'product' combination rule. For an approach in terms of a four valued product logic, which is comparable in also assigning values to both Speaker and Addressee, cf. Hoepelman (1983).

6. Arguments which support these analyses for the positive and negative declarative are given in Davies (in press). On the negative declarative, cf. Givón (1978).
7. cf. Davies (in press).

BIBLIOGRAPHY

Austin, J. L. (1962), *How to do things with words*, Oxford, Clarendon Press.
Bolinger, D. (1977), 'Is the imperative an infinitive?', in Bolinger, D. (ed.), *Meaning and Form*, London, Longman, 152–82.
Davies, E. C. (1979), *On the Semantics of Syntax: Mood and Condition in English*, London: Croom Helm.
—— (1985), 'On types of meaningfulness in discourse', in Benson, J. D. and Greaves, W. S. (eds), *Systemic Perspectives on Discourse, Vol. 1*, Norwood, NJ, Ablex, 229–47.
—— (in press), 'On different possibilities in the syntax of English', in Benson, J., Cummings, M. and Greaves, W. (eds), *Linguistics in a Systemic Perspective*, Amsterdam, Benjamins.
Firth, J. R. (1957), 'A synopsis of linguistic theory 1930–1955', in Firth, J. R. (ed.), *Studies in Linguistic Analysis*, Oxford, Blackwell, 1–32.
Givón, T. (1978), 'Negation in language: pragmatics, function, ontology', in Cole, P. (ed.), *Syntax and Semantics 9: Pragmatics*, New York, Academic Press, 69–112.
—— (1979), 'From discourse to syntax: grammar as a processing strategy', in Givón, T. (ed.), *Syntax and Semantics 12: Discourse and Syntax*, New York, Academic Press, 81–114.

Gordon, D. and Lakoff, G. (1975), 'Conversational postulates', in Cole, P. and Morgan J. L. (eds), *Syntax and Semantics*, *vol. 3: Speech Acts*, New York, Academic Press, 83–106.

Halliday, M. A. K. (1970), 'Language structure and language function', in Lyons, J. (ed.), *New Horizons in Linguistics*, Harmondsworth, Penguin, 140–65.

—— (1985), *Introduction to Functional Grammar*, London, Edward Arnold.

Hoepelman, J. (1983), 'On questions', in Kiefer, F. (ed.), *Questions and Answers*, Dordrecht, Holland, Reidel, 191–227.

Levinson, S. C. (1983), *Pragmatics*, Cambridge, Cambridge University Press.

Quirk, R., Greenbaum, S., Leech, G. and Svartvik, J. (1985), *A Comprehensive Grammar of the English Language*, New York, Longman.

Schegloff, E. (1977), 'On some questions and ambiguities in conversation', in Dressler, W. (ed.), *Trends in Textlinguistics*, New York and Berlin, de Gruyter.

Searle, J. R. (1969), *Speech Acts*, Cambridge, Cambridge University Press.

—— (1979), *Expressions and Meaning*, Cambridge, Cambridge University Press.

Sinclair, J. McH. (1980), 'Discourse in relation to language structure and semiotics', in Greenbaum, S., Leech, G. and Svartvik, J. (eds), *Studies in English Linguistics: For Randolph Quirk*, London, Longman, 110–24.

Sinclair, J. McH. and Coulthard, M. (1975), *Towards an Analysis of Discourse*, London, Oxford University Press.

Wilensky, R. (1987), 'Primal content and actual content: an antidote to literal meaning', Report No. UCB/CSD 87/365, Berkeley, Calif., University of California, Computer Science Division (EECS).

Part II
Explorations in thematic structure and information structure

3 Marked Themes with and without pronominal reinforcement: their meaning and distribution in discourse*

Daniel Kies
College of DuPage, Illinois, USA

3.0 INTRODUCTION

After studying a corpus of spoken texts (the unedited transcripts of two television interview programs, *The MacNeil/Lehrer Report* and *Donahue*), one discovers that sentences employing a marked theme without pronominal reinforcement ('topicalized' structures), e.g., *John Smith I haven't seen for ages*, and sentences employing a marked theme with pronominal reinforcement ('left dislocated' structures), e.g., *John Smith I haven't seen him for ages*, serve a variety of distinct communicative functions in discourse. Further study reveals that those marked structures are distinctive syntactically, semantically, pragmatically, and distributionally. The findings allow one to hypothesize a direct relationship between the communicative functions and the syntactic forms of sentences employing marked themes with or without pronominal reinforcement.

The meanings, uses and distribution of MARKED THEMES (as they are called in Halliday 1985, or THEMATIC FRONTING as they are called in Quirk *et al*. 1985, or TOPICALIZATIONS and LEFT DISLOCATIONS as they are called in the transformational-generative literature) have not yet been fully examined. Often these sentence types are characterized as EMPHATIC, but the pre-theoretic, intuitive notion of emphasis has never been fully explicated. The purpose of this study is to explicate the intuitive notion of emphasis associated with marked themes, particularly pronominally reinforced marked themes (PRMTs) and unreinforced marked themes (UMTs). To do that, one must fully explicate

---

* A version of this chapter was presented at the XIIIth International Systemic Workshop at the University of Kent at Canterbury, 16–18 July 1986. I am grateful to the many Workshop participants who shared their insightful comments with me. I am especially indebted to Erich Steiner, Robert Veltman, Richard Cureton, Jessica Wirth, Edith Moravcsik, Fred Eckman, Peter Fries, Ivan Lowe, Minoji Akimoto and Anne-Marie Simon-Vandenbergen, all of whom commented thoughtfully on drafts.

— the syntactic and semantic properties of marked themes, which define the notion of 'topic';
— the pragmatic functions of marked themes, which follow from the semantic properties; and
— the discourse distributional properties of marked themes, which illustrate the differences between PRMTs and UMTs in this study.

If successful, this study can be seen as a plea for corpus studies of linguistic phenomena, because only through corpus studies is one able to discover the distributional differences between various marked themes.

3.1 Pronominally reinforced marked themes (PRMTs) and unreinforced marked themes (UMTs) defined.[1]

Sentences with UMTs and PRMTs, as in (1) and (2) respectively, appear to be marked correspondences of unmarked sentence types.[2]

(1) The basic idea we do in fact accept. [MacNeil/Lehrer transcript No. 1287][3]
(2) The child that has the temper tantrum in the store, fine, let 'em have the temper tantrum because they can't have the cookies. [Donahue transcript No. 10059]

The UMT of sentence (1) is characterized by the sentence initial appearance of a noun phrase that has a grammatical function other than subject. Usually the sentence initial noun phrase is the direct or indirect object of the clause; less commonly it is the object of a preposition. Sentence (3) is the unmarked corresponding form to the UMT structure in (1).

(3) We do in fact accept the basic idea.

The characteristics of the PRMT of sentence (2) not only include the sentence initial appearance of a noun phrase that has a grammatical function within the clause, but also the appearance of a co-referential pronoun within the sentence, 'sharing' the grammatical function of the sentence initial constituent and 'holding' the grammatical position of the sentence initial constituent within the clause. In (2), the sentence initial constituent *The child that has the temper tantrum in the store* is co-referential with the pronoun *them* (reduced to *'em*) appearing in the following clause. The pronoun shares the grammatical function of the sentence initial noun phrase and holds the grammatical position of the sentence initial noun phrase. The corresponding unmarked form is (4).

(4) Fine, let the child that has the temper tantrum in the store have the temper tantrum because they can't have the cookies.

Additionally, it is possible to distinguish UMT structures from PRMT structures with a number of METALINGUISTIC MARKERS, such as, *As for*, *Concerning*, *Speaking of/about*, *About*, or *But with*. Only PRMTs allow such metalinguistic markers, cf. (5):

(5) a. * {As for / Concerning / About / Speaking of/about / But with} the basic idea we do in fact accept.

b. {As for / Concerning / About / Speaking of/about / But with} the basic idea we do in fact accept it.

3.2 A REVIEW OF THE LITERATURE

At the risk of oversimplifying the issues, one could divide the literature into three camps. First, there are those who see marked themes as surface structure reorderings for stylistic/rhetorical purposes, e.g. Chomsky (1965) and Katz (1972). Secondly, there are those who are interested in the pragmatic effects/functions of marked themes, e.g. Green (1980), Quirk *et al.* (1972, 1985), and Chafe (1976). Thirdly, there are linguists who are interested in the semantics of sentences with non-canonical word order, e.g. Ross (1967), Firbas (1964), Halliday (1967, 1985), Gundel (1977), and Rodman (1974). Finally there are two studies, Green (1982) and Lyons (1977), that are concerned with the semantics of word order inversions. Both studies are mainly of interest here because they make comments based on inadequate corpus studies and faulty intuitions. Thus these two studies demonstrate the need for careful corpus study.

3.2.1 Stylistic reordering

In the standard theory of transformational-generative grammar, Chomsky dismissed sentences like (1) and (2) as stylistic variants of more basic sentences. Chomsky (1965: 126–7) asserts that

> grammatical transformations do not seem to be an appropriate device for expressing the full range of possibilities for stylistic inversion ... the rules of stylistic reordering ... are not so much rules of grammar as rules of performance ... with no apparent bearing, for the moment, on the theory of grammatical structure.

Further, in a footnote to those remarks, it is clear that UMTs, and presumably PRMTs, fall into this area of stylistic reordering:

> Notice, for example, that Case is usually determined by the position of the Noun in surface structure rather than in deep structure, although the surface structures given by stylistic reordering do not affect Case ... stylistic inversion of the type we have just been discussing gives such forms as 'him I really like,' 'him I would definitely not try to antagonize'. [Chomsky 1965: 221–2]

By labelling sentences with UMTs and PRMTs as stylistic phenomena of language performance, Chomsky was one of the first transformational grammarians to ignore these forms as essentially MEANINGLESS, hence uninteresting.

It is important, however, to recognize a distinction between the kind of stylistic variation that is determined by the speakers' communicative intent, their social status and role, and their situation or context at the time they speak, and the kind of stylistic variation that is undetermined by such factors. The first kind of stylistic variation is consciously controlled more easily. For example, the social status and participant roles of two interlocutors influence their choice of diction and degree of formality. The second kind of stylistic variation is not consciously controlled easily. Word order and the location of main stress (which is affected by stylistic reorderings) are examples of that second kind of stylistic variation. So if by 'stylistic', Chomsky understands the variation resulting from free choices made by the speaker, it seems strange to call word order and placement of main stress stylistic phenomena. It seems more appropriate to treat those examples of the second kind of stylistic variation as grammatical, not performance, phenomena. Nevertheless, the notion of stylistic reordering survives.

Katz (1972: 417–34), for example, argues for the basic correctness of the standard theory of transformational grammar and proposes a separate 'rhetorical' component to account for the effects of stylistic inversions.

3.2.2 Pragmatic studies

Other grammarians focus on the pragmatic functions served by inversions in general, cf. Green (1980), Quirk *et al.* (1972), and Chafe (1976). These studies explore the usefulness of non-canonical word order for textual cohesion, contrastiveness, euphony, and ease of language processing. As fruitful as pragmatics is to the understanding of how people actually use language, there are some linguists who are uncomfortable using pragmatic principles as an explanatory force in linguistics for two reasons. First, pragmatic principles of language organization are not very rigorous as scientific principles; i.e. they do not make completely accurate predictions about word order. Pragmatic principles discuss GRAMMATICAL TENDENCIES, which are the result of one discourse function or another. Pragmatic principles are not GRAMMATICAL RULES. For example, Rodman (1974), Green (1980), Quirk *et al.* (1972), and others have often noted the tendency for 'heavy' clausal constituents to appear clause finally—the euphonic function of 'end-weight'. Yet, in (6) below, the 'heavy' subject does not necessarily occur later in the clause for reasons of euphony (or as the transformationalists would say, 'trigger right dislocation'), even in impromptu speech.

(6) ... the Victorian husband whose wife didn't know what job he had downtown was probably well in control in the bedroom. [Donahue transcript No. 07269]

Likewise, the principle of end-weight, which Rodman (1974) and Quirk *et al.* (1972) employ to explain the function of right dislocation and extraposition, will not explain the presence of 'heavy' clause initial constituents as in (7).

(7) Finally, and then I'll stop, we had a bunch of prominent people, largely former Republicans or Republicans—Arthur Burns and Paul McCracken and George Shultz and William Simon—who formed a committee to fight inflation, and issued a report just a couple of months ago. And the only tax cut they advocated was a very small initial tax cut on business. NO PERSONAL CUTS, NO ACROSS-THE-BOARD TAX CUTS, NO KEMP-ROTH, THEY SAID, IN ORDER SCRUPULOUSLY TO AVOID REKINDLING THE FIRE OF INFLATION. [MacNeil/Lehrer transcript No. 1284] [author's emphasis]

In the UMT in (7), one might expect the principle of end-weight to 'disallow' the heavy marked theme sentence initially for the sake of euphony. Yet the principle of end-weight does not apply, making the entire issue of pragmatic explanations suspicious for some.

The second problem with pragmatic principles as explanatory concepts in syntax involves the nature of explanation in the philosophy of science. Any explanation of syntactic phenomena that appeals to explanatory principles or concepts beyond the realm of syntax is suspect unless there is compelling evidence to justify the validity of the explanatory principle and the relevance of the explanatory principle to the syntactic phenomena in question. Hence, many grammarians are reluctant to accept explanations of non-canonical word order as 'emphatic', 'focusing', or 'highlighting' constructions without some elaboration of the concepts. Bever (1975: 601) expressed similar sentiment when he wrote:

I have taken care to argue that each specific linguistic phenomenon is interpreted as due to independently motivated aspects of speech perception. I have attempted to avoid vague references to properties such as 'mental effort', 'informativeness', 'importance', 'focus', 'empathy', and so on. I do not mean that these terms are empty in principle: however, they are empty at the moment, and consequently have no clear explanatory force.

Nevertheless, neither criticism of pragmatic studies is insurmountable. The first criticism fails to take into account the interaction of various pragmatic principles functioning for different purposes in discourse. In the case of example (7), the connective function of the marked theme overrides the euphonic function of end-weight. Thus the heavy constituent *No personal cuts, no across-the-board tax cuts, no Kemp-Roth* provides textual cohesion with *the only tax cut they advocated*, which appears in the previous clause. It seems reasonable to expect that in particular discourse situations some pragmatic principles would be more highly valued than others, and so in the context of example (7) the connective function of the marked theme seems more important for effective, efficient communication than the euphonic function of the principle of end-weight.

The second criticism is just the kind of admonition one would expect whenever one proposes any explanatory principle. The pragmatic functions of UMTs and PRMTs, discussed in section 3.4, must be justified on independent grounds. An examination of the syntactic and semantic properties of UMTs and PRMTs, in section 3.3, provides the independent motivation for the pragmatic functions of presentation, connection and contrast.

Still, as a final cautionary note, one should be careful not to overgeneralize any one pragmatic function as the sole reason for the existence of a particular type of sentence. Such overgeneralizations could lead the sceptical to doubt the explanatory force of pragmatic principles.

Chafe (1976: 49–50), for example, argues that the notion of 'contrastiveness' alone captures the meaningful differences between sentences employing marked themes with and without pronominal reinforcement and their corresponding unmarked forms. Chafe believes that sentences with UMTs and PRMTs are marked to show only a contrast in focus so that when speakers utter *The play John saw yesterday* or *As for the play John saw it yesterday*, they appear to make more explicit that *the play* is one item of many that John may have done or saw yesterday. However, given a corpus containing both UMTs and PRMTs, one discovers that contrast of focus is not as general as Chafe believes, cf. the UMT in (8) and the PRMT in (9):

(8) *Lehrer*:
There's no question in your mind that this is discrimination, and that you accept the idea—Newman's basic argument about comparable work. Is that true?
Norton:
THE BASIC IDEA WE DO IN FACT ACCEPT. [MacNeil/Lehrer transcript No. 1287] [author's emphasis]

(9) *Audience*:
Do men readily seek the advice of a psychiatrist when they're impotent?
Dr. Weisberg:
No. No, men are very ashamed about being impotent and they're not going to go to a psychiatrist. And particularly the older man who thinks that psychiatrists are crazy and so why do I have to do that, but they also feel that—they're so ashamed because it's a part of aging. They can justify it, they can say, well, I'm 55, 60, 65, 70 years old. It's part of life not to have more sex. MY FATHER, MY GRANDFATHER, THEY ALL TOLD ME, so I'm not going to go to a doctor about it. [Donahue transcript No. 07269] [author's emphasis]

The UMT in (8) has a connective function. The UMT, *The basic idea*, provides lexical cohesion with an earlier clause, *you accept the idea—Newman's basic argument*. The connective function of the UMT is aided by the repetition of the lexical items.

The PRMT in (9) has a presentative function. The PRMT, *My father, my grandfather*, presents the necessary 'universe-of-discourse' to interpret correctly the pronoun *they* in the main clause of the sentence. In other words, the PRMT presents the TOPIC of that clause. Notice that there is no explicit or implicit contrast between the UMT in (8) or the PRMT in (9) given their respective contexts.

3.2.3 Semantic studies

Finally, there are those grammarians who search for meaningful differences between sentences that seem to exhibit only a 'stylistic' reordering of constituents, cf. Ross (1967), Firbas (1964), Halliday (1967, 1985), Gundel (1977),

Rodman (1974), Gary (1976), and Bolinger (1977). The principle governing these studies maintains that differences in syntactic forms express differences, though perhaps subtle, in meaning. Bolinger (1977: 4) states the principle of one form-one meaning most explicitly:

> Obviously the idea that even in syntax one could have identity with difference could not have gained currency without some empirical support. The classical case is that of the passive voice. If some differences of meaning are ignored, it is possible to say that *John ate the spinach* and *The spinach was eaten by John* are the same. They report the same event in the real world. The same entities are present and they are in the same relationship of actor and patient. But if truth value were the only criterion of identity in syntax we would have to say—as some have recently been trying to say—that *John sold the house to Mary* and *Mary bought the house from John* are just as much the same as the active-passive pair ... Linguistic meaning covers a great deal more than reports of events in the real world. It expresses ... such things as what is the central part of the message as against the peripheral part, what our attitudes are toward the person we are speaking to, how we feel about the reliability of our message, how we situate ourselves in the events we report, and many other things that make our messages not merely a recital of facts but a complex of facts and comments about facts and situations.

Ross (1967) argues that sentences with UMTs and PRMTs should be derived transformationally from more basic forms exhibiting canonical word order. His formulations of the Topicalization and Left Dislocation rules have remained fundamentally unchanged in much of the transformational literature. Through Ross, sentences with UMTs and PRMTs became a small part of a larger debate in transformational generative grammar. Some grammarians wished to relate transformationally all the reorderings of an underlying representation expressed in the surface representations of a language. Other grammarians wished to constrain the power of transformations, dealing with subjects like stylistic reordering of constituents by some other component of the grammar. However, Ross's thesis did not explain the value of sentences with UMTs or PRMTs. In 1967, assuming that transformations were meaning preserving, linguists argued that the one function and *raison d'être* of a transformation was to link different levels in a derivation for the purpose of relating in the theory sentences that speakers find related in the language. Thus the meaningful differences between the next to last clause in (10) and (11), for example, were considered negligible, often described only as 'emphatic' although the exact nature of the emphasis in (11) was never culled out.

(10) ... they treat me like a regular, normal kid, and that's the way I like it because I don't think I'm a star and OTHER PEOPLE, GIRLS ON THE STREET, ASK ME FOR MY AUTOGRAPH and I give it to them.

(11) ... they treat me like a regular, normal kid, and that's the way I like it because I don't think I'm a star and OTHER PEOPLE, GIRLS ON THE STREET, THEY ASK ME FOR MY AUTOGRAPH and I give it to them.

More recently, some grammarians have appealed to the distribution of 'old' and 'new' information in the clause, e.g. Firbas (1964). However, a general principle that says topics are 'old' information and that 'old' information precedes 'new' information conflicts with examples like (12) where the

PRMT, presumably the topical element, is 'new' information in the conversation.

(12) *Mr. Donahue*:
You know what knocked me out in the shows we've done with Masters & Johnson, and others, is that it's easy to change people with therapy. I mean, not every last patient, but I was astounded at the fact that this isn't all that complicated, is it?
Dr. Kaplan:
Well, we used to think that anybody who has any sexual difficulty was suffering from something deep, and you couldn't fix it so easily, or repair it. But a good number of people can be helped rapidly, another number cannot. And something—A problem like this gentleman talked about so openly might just be a normal pattern for him, and that couple would feel better if that woman knew it was his normal pattern, she might find it much easier to accept than if she thought, 'Oh, it's I'm not pretty enough.'
Mr. Donahue:
I'll never forget Dr. Masters' response to my question. I said, 'How can you, with a lifetime, and if a person is grown up and sex is bad and the puritanical, and you don't like your body, and it's evil, and, you know, and then God is watching us. With all of that, how can you possibly, in a session, remove all those outside programmings from childhood and take it out of the soul of a person?' And he looked me right in the eye and he said, 'Like taking candy from a baby.'
Audience: (laughter)
Dr. Kaplan: (laughter)
Mr. Donahue:
Now, I don't know whether he was showing off—But the point is that it isn't—
Dr. Kaplan:
Well, there's only one cause of sexual problems, really only one, and you've mentioned lots of them, but that's anxiety about sex. The moment of making love, if you feel some anxiety, that will ruin all the reflexes and all the appetite. But that anxiety can be very minor and simple, and will cause the same mischief as some anxiety that has a very deep root, and to be a good diagnostician you have to tell, you know, THE CAR, WELL YOU JUST HIT IT WITH A HAMMER, PING, AND IT GOES GOING AGAIN, AND THE OTHER ONE THAT NEEDS TO BE TAKEN APART. They look the same. They both don't run. [Donahue transcript No. 03120] [author's emphasis]

In one sense, the PRMTs in (12), *the car* and *the other one* (also referring to a car), are 'new' information in that there was no previous mention of cars earlier in the conversation. Yet the PRMTs are presumably the topics of their respective clauses. But notice that the PRMTs in (12) are in another sense 'old' information in that the reference to cars is an analogy to an earlier comment, in which Dr. Kaplan said *a good number of people can be helped rapidly, another number cannot*. So it seems that any simple distinction between 'old' and 'new' information is not completely adequate to account for the data.

Another problem with a simple distinction between 'old' and 'new' information arises in contexts involving contrastive stress. Recall Chafe's examples of contrastive stress, *The play John saw yesterday* and *As for the play John saw it yesterday*. Chafe (1976) argued that the marked, sentence initial constituent *the play* was in contrast to other items that John may have done or saw yesterday. If the other items were mentioned earlier in the discourse, say, *the play, the film, the photograph*, then the mention of *the play* in the marked sentence is 'old' information. But there is another sense in which the UMT or PRMT is 'new' information. If one understands by 'new' information that which is unpredictable, then the contrastive use of *the play* in the marked sentences reveals a use of *the play* as 'new' information since its occurrence could not be predicted with any great accuracy from all the other members of the contrastive set.

Such a situation arises in (13) where two items, *robots* and *human workers*, are contrasted in the discourse.

(13) *Lehrer*:
 The General Electric Company, for instance, has automation plans that could eventually result in replacing half of its 37,000 employees with robots. Robot advocates say that they are more efficient, cheaper and, yes, more productive than human workers. And if the U.S. is to stay competitive in international markets, particularly against Japan, THEN ROBOTS IT MUST BE. [MacNeil/Lehrer transcript No. 1286] [author's emphasis]

In one sense the mention of *robots* in the marked sentence *then robots it must be* is 'old' information since it was already mentioned in context. In another sense, *robots* is 'new' information since it cannot be predicted which member of the contrastive set will be selected. Conceivably, Lehrer might just as well have said ... *then human workers it must not be*.[4]

Other linguists have appealed to concepts like 'theme' or 'topic', cf. Halliday (1967, 1985) and Gundel (1977). Halliday (1967) characterizes theme structurally as the first position in the clause. Gundel argues that it is ridiculous to characterize a sentence like *Probably he'll be home tomorrow* as speaking about *probably* or probability. Therefore, she modifies Halliday's definition such that the topic of the clause is usually the left-most noun phrase. Halliday (1985), however, presents an extensive overview of thematic structures, making a number of distinctions that undercut Gundel's criticism, such as the distinction between the definition of theme and its realization in the English clause (1985: 39) or the distinction between simple and multiple themes (1985: 53 ff.).

Nevertheless, it is not at all clear what Gundel's structural definitions of topic adds to the understanding of the differences between the italicized clauses in (10) and (11) above. Her definition will pick out *other people* as the topic in both (10) and (11), and nothing more is learned about the use or meaning of the PRMT used in (11). Halliday (1985: 38–67), on the other hand, elaborately details the semantics of theme and demonstrates precisely how thematic structure is incorporated with other systems in any language.

Although Rodman (1974) provides some of the most thorough analyses of the syntax of sentences with UMTs and PRMTs, he does not provide a complete account of the functions or distribution of those sentences. Rodman was primarily concerned with arguing for a base-generated analysis of 'left dislocation' and a transformational analysis of 'topicalization'. He was not concerned with discourse functions or distribution; hence he missed a number of facts about those sentence types.

3.2.4 Green (1982) and Lyons (1977)

Finally, there are two studies that are interesting here only because they demonstrate the need for careful corpus studies. Green and Lyons have argued that sentences with UMTs or PRMTs are of little interest since they are so infrequent in natural speech, cf. Green (1982: 123): '... in natural speech inversions of most types are few and far between ... So I abandoned natural speech as a primary source of inversions for syntactic study'. For this study there were 21 transcripts representing 21 hours of impromptu speech. In those 21 hours of speech, there were 43 examples of PRMTs (averaging 2 PRMTs per hour of speech) and 36 examples of UMTs (averaging 1.7 UMTs per hour of speech). The transcripts also contain a large number of other non-canonically ordered sentences, including inverted pseudo-cleft sentences, verb phrase inversion, adverbial preposing, and right dislocations.

Similarly Lyons (1977: 506) claims that 'Utterances like (6) [*John Smith I haven't seen for ages*] are relatively uncommon in Modern English; and they are even more uncommon perhaps when the grammatical subject is something other than a personal pronoun'. The examples in (14), however, are all sentences with UMTs in which the grammatical subject is something other than a personal pronoun.

(14) a. That sort of thing, this [= traditional psychiatry] is not. [Donahue transcript No. 09249]
 b. and that [= the proposition of an oversupply of physicians], I think, no one can question. [MacNeil/Lehrer transcript No. 802]
 c. And if the U.S. is to stay competitive in international markets, particularly against Japan, then robots it must be. [MacNeil/Lehrer transcript No. 1286]
 d. Wonderful it is that we have a society which resolves these matters in the courts instead of in a less rational way. [MacNeil/Lehrer transcript No. 1287]

There are two points one should learn from this short overview of contemporary linguistic treatments of non-canonical word order generally, and sentences with UMTs and PRMTs specifically. First, it seems certain that one's intuitive judgements about the frequency and meaning of unusual forms often reveals more about one's linguistic biases than about one's linguistic behaviour. That argues for the importance of corpus studies to observe sentence constructions IN DISCOURSE, since it is there that their full range of functions can be studied.⁵ Secondly, when one does collect a body of data, one learns that there is a meaningful difference between the sentences employing UMTs or PRMTs and their canonically ordered correspondences, which is discussed in sections 3.3–3.5.

3.3 SYNTACTIC AND SEMANTIC PROPERTIES OF SENTENCES WITH UMTs AND PRMTs

In this section, one will discover how certain syntactic properties of structures with UMTs and PRMTs indicate that UMTs and PRMTs are PRESUPPOSED, not asserted. The notion of presupposition that applies here follows from the fact that every statement can be seen as supplying an answer to an explicit or implicit question. And marked sentence structures also provide an answer to an explicit or implicit question that carries with it certain determinable presuppositions. For example, the statement.

(15) John saw the pláy yesterday

(with main stress on *play*) answers the question

(16) What did John see yesterday?

So (15) presupposes that John saw something yesterday and it asserts that the variable (realized by an indefinite pronoun *something* in the presupposition) was *the play*.

Similarly, negation provides another test for determining the presuppositions of a statement. Intonation and definiteness also provide tests for presupposed constituents.

3.3.1 The question test for assertion/presupposition

In (17) the question presupposes that John enjoys tea in the morning, but what is unknown (and what is asserted in the answer) is the kind of tea most enjoyed in the morning.

(17) What kind of tea does John most enjoy in the morning?
    a. John can drink English breakfast tea every morning.
    b. ?English breakfast tea John can drink every morning.
    c. *English breakfast tea, John can drink it every morning.

The unacceptability of (17b)⁶ and (17c) shows that UMTs and PRMTs are not asserted. Instead UMTs and PRMTs are presupposed within their clauses.

3.3.2 The negation test for assertion/presupposition

Chafe (1976: 49) argues that (18a)–(18c) are functionally identical: 'The so-called topic [in (18a) and (18b)] is simply a focus of contrast that has for some reason or other been placed near the beginning of the sentence'.

(18) a. The pláy, John saw it yésterday.
   b. As for the pláy, John saw it yésterday.
   c. Rónald made the hamburgers.

What (18a–18c) share in common is contrastive focus, indicated by the focal stress on the sentence-initial noun phrase. But (18a)–(18c) are not equivalent. It is impossible to include the UMT or PRMT under the scope of negation, cf. (19a)–(19c).

(19) a. *It is not the case that the pláy John saw it yésterday.
   b. *It is not the case that as for the pláy, John saw it yésterday.
   c. It is not the case that Rónald made the hamburgers.

However (20) is perfectly acceptable.

(20) As for the pláy, it is not the case that John saw it yésterday.

Example (19c) shows that *Rónald* can be included within the scope of negation, but (19b) and (20) show that PRMTs cannot. The crucial difference is that *Rónald* in (18c) is asserted, but *the pláy* in (18a)–(18b) is not. Additionally, it should be noted that the sentence initial constituents in (18a)–(18c) are new information in the sense that it cannot be predicted, and is not known, which member of the contrastive set will be selected to contrast with the other members of the set. So the difference in meaning must be the presuppositional nature of the UMTs and PRMTs.

3.3.3 Intonationally marked structures and presupposition

Another difference between structures with UMTs or PRMTs and their canonically ordered corresponding forms is intonational. Besides syntactic markedness, structures with UMTs or PRMTs are intonationally marked in that they 'break' a clause, with a single tone unit, into a clause with two tone units. The two tone units double the number of constituents that receive stress within a clause. Compare the 'neutral' intonation of (21), which has main stress on the last major class constituent, and the marked intonation of (22a)–(22b), which breaks (21) into two tone units.

(21) John ate the pízza.

(22) a. The pízza John áte.
   b. The pízza John áte it.

Intonationally marked structures often serve to evoke a set of items that Jackendoff (1972: 246) calls the 'presuppositional set'. Thus a person who says

(23) Jóhn ate the pizza.[7]

would usually presuppose *Someone ate the pizza*. The presuppositional set of the intonationally marked item *Jóhn* is all the values that could be substituted for the variable *someone* in the presupposition. Membership in the presuppositional set is defined contextually and situationally by the information shared by, and in the consciousness of, the interlocutors, cf. Chafe (1974). The presuppositional set makes a coherent and well-defined set of items in the discourse, amenable to discussion: this also suggests that topics are presupposed constituents.

So the intonational marking of UMTs and PRMTs suggests that those constituents are presupposed, not asserted, and that they are the topics of their clauses.

Also note that selecting one member of a presuppositional set amounts to contrasting one set member against the others. Thus many grammarians have called intonational marking 'contrastive stress'.[8]

3.3.4 UMTs and PRMTs realized by definite and indefinite noun phrases (NPs)

The examples in (24) and (25) show that NPs with indefinite reference do not occur sentence initially as readily as definite NPs.

(24) a. John shot the lion.
b. The lion John shot.
c. The lion, John shot him.
d. {As for / About / Speaking of/about} the lion, John shot him.

(25) a. John shot a lion. [with indefinite reference]
b. *A lion John shot.
c. *A lion, John shot him.
d. * {As for / About / Speaking of/about} a lion, John shot him.

The sentences in (26) provide more examples of unacceptable UMTs and PRMTs, which are also indefinite NPs.

(26) a. *Someone, he's coming.
b. *Someone Tom likes.
c. *A woman, he saw her.
d. *Everybody, they're doing it.
e. *Anyone, I didn't see.
f. *Many men, Mary would like to marry them.
g. *Many men Mary would like to marry.

The crucial semantic difference between the acceptable and the unacceptable sentences in (24), (25) and (26) is the notion of presupposition. Singular definite referring expressions, plurals and generic NPs make existential presuppositions. They presuppose the existence of, and succeed in identifying, the object about which something could be said. In other words, those NPs are potentially topics of a discourse. The indefinite NPs above do not have existential presuppositions, do not presuppose the existence of an object about which something could be said, and therefore are not topics.

Given the syntactic analysis presented here, one can now explain the ungrammaticality of indefinite NPs as UMTs or PRMTs. The data from the question test, the negation test and the intonational properties of sentences with UMTs or PRMTs suggest that UMTs and PRMTs are not semantically equivalent to their corresponding constituents in canonically ordered structures. UMTs and PRMTs are presupposed while their correspondences in canonically ordered structures may be asserted.

Further, presupposed constituents, as mentioned above, make reference to or identity objects about which something could be said. Presupposition is then a necessary condition for topichood. If indefinite NPs that do not presuppose the existence of anything are in a structure requiring presupposed constituents (the UMT or PRMT, for example), then this analysis would predict unacceptability, and that is precisely what one finds in (26).[9]

3.4 THE PRAGMATIC FUNCTIONS OF STRUCTURES WITH UMTs AND PRMTs

As one can see from the contextualized examples to follow in section 3.5, many UMTs and PRMTs are anaphoric in that they are co-referential with expressions that occur earlier in context. Structures with UMTs or PRMTs then certainly can have a connective function. And as discussed in section 3.3.3 above, UMTs and PRMTs can exhibit a contrastive function by virtue of evoking a 'presuppositional set'. Additionally though, sentences with UMTs or PRMTs serve a presentational function (to borrow a term from Hetzron 1975).

Note that all of the pragmatic functions discussed here are independently justified by the syntactic and semantic facts outlined in section 3.3. None of the pragmatic functions here is open to the attacks levelled against some other pragmatic studies of word order.

3.4.1 Presentational function

What are the pragmatic implications of the previous syntactic analysis? The examples in section 3.3 demonstrate the presuppositional nature of UMTs and PRMTs. Presupposed constituents represent entities that the speaker assumes to be shared knowledge among all discourse participants. And something could be said of those constituents upon whose existence speakers and their audiences co-operatively agree. Thus, topic could be defined as an entity whose existence is agreed upon by speakers and their audiences. More loosely, one might characterize the topic as a presentational device that 'sets a spatial, temporal or individual framework . . . which limits the applicability of the main predication to a certain restricted domain' (Chafe 1976: 50). Similar observations are scattered throughout the literature. Firbas (1964: 268) speaks of the 'local setting of the sentence'; Friedman (1976) defines the topic as an NP that is 'creating a *scene*'.

The presentational or stage-setting function of UMTs and PRMTs is necessary because speakers may substitute 'new' lexical items for 'old' lexical items that appeared earlier in context. The motivation for the substitution is either elegant variation or analogy. In either case, the sentence with a UMT or PRMT helps to 'change the scene' or 'present a new scene' and thereby provides for easier understanding.

The sentences with PRMTs in (12) above are examples of a change in lexical items for analogy. Recall that in (12) two PRMTs, *the car* and *the other one* [= another car], are analogous with two different populations mentioned earlier in the discourse, *a good number of people can be helped rapidly, another number cannot*. The PRMTs help to set the scene so that the clauses comprising the analogy are more easily understood.

A good example of a PRMT to set the stage with a piece of elegant variation is in (32) in section 3.5.1. There one speaker re-establishes an earlier topic, *the Moral Majority*, by using elegant variation in the form of *the evangelicals*.

3.4.2 Connective function

It has already been established that UMTs and PRMTs are presupposed. And language users may assume that presupposed items have been established earlier in the discourse, either contextually or situationally. Given the presuppositional nature of UMTs and PRMTs and assuming they are established earlier in discourse, the connective function of UMTs and PRMTs follows.

For example the UMTs in (27) and (28) are both presupposed and both refer to asserted constituents in the immediately preceding clause.

(27) *Wallop*:
They don't pay income taxes. Wyoming's never had one.
Bumpers:
Well, if they'd had one, I'm sure—
Lehrer:
What about sales taxes?
Wallop:
SALES TAXES WE DO. But we do have schools to build, and we are putting out approximately 80 percent of what we collect in Wyoming into impact aid, housing aid, or community aid. [MacNeil/Lehrer transcript No. 1285] [author's emphasis]

(28) *Dr. Dobkin*:
Well, it's getting confusing for us. As a young physician when I started medical school ten years ago, the gospel was there were too few doctors and the more that could be trained and the faster, the better. It's certainly clear now that there are still major deficiencies in terms of health services, and in many cases it seems that there is an oversupply of services or an overavailability in other areas. And assuming an imbalance—AND THAT, I THINK, NO ONE CAN QUESTION—the problem now is, I think, again the issue has been put in terms of economics... [MacNeil/Lehrer transcript No. 802] [author's emphasis]

Often the connective function of structures with UMTs and PRMTs is reinforced by other devices that also provide textual cohesion. In (27) there is an exact lexical repetition, one cohesive device. In (29) lexical repetition, grammatical parallelism (the repetition of a grammatical structure through a text) and the UMTs all provide cohesion.

(29) *Audience*:
Yes. I feel it depends on the type of—or the type of naughtiness that they've done as to the type of punishment. SOME THINGS I DO THINK YOU HAVE TO SPANK 'EM ON THE BUTT A LITTLE BIT. SOME THINGS YOU CAN SEND THEM TO A ROOM AND SET THEM ON A CHAIR. OTHER THINGS YOU CAN YELL AT AND THEY'LL PROVE IT. [Donahue transcript No. 10059] [author's emphasis]

At the lexical level there is the cohesive repetition of *some*, *things*, *you* and *can*. At the syntactic level there is repeated use of UMTs (itself forming a grammatically parallel pattern here), and there is the grammatical parallelism in clause structure. All three clauses with UMTs share the form:

UMT	subject	auxiliary	main verb
Some things	*you*	*have to*	*spank*
Some things	*you*	*can*	*send*
Other things	*you*	*can*	*yell*

3.4.3 Contrastive function

The contrastive function of constructions with UMTs and PRMTs has already been discussed in section 3.3.3. The contrastiveness of UMTs and PRMTs arises through intonational marking, which in turn evokes a presuppositional set. The UMT or PRMT is but one member of the presuppositional set, and selecting one member of a set amounts to contrasting it against all other members of the set. It is through the semantic properties of presuppositional sets that structures with UMTs and PRMTs achieve their contrastive function. Indeed, the contrastiveness of structures with UMTs and PRMTs is so common and well known that Chafe (1976: 50) believed contrastiveness was the major, if not sole, purpose of UMTs and PRMTs.

Two examples of this contrastive function are (13) in section 3.2.3 and (33) in section 3.5.2. In (13) the contrastiveness of *then robots it must be* arises through the mention earlier in the discourse of two items that comprise the presuppositional set for this UMT, *human workers* and *robots*. In (33) the sentence with a UMT *That sort of thing* [= traditional psychiatry], *this* [= surrogate therapy] *is not*, contrasts two items, both of which comprise the presuppositional set of the UMT and both of which are mentioned earlier in the discourse.[10]

3.5 THE DISTRIBUTIONAL DIFFERENCES BETWEEN STRUCTURES WITH UMTS AND PRMTS

After examining the corpus, one can make two general statements about constructions with UMTs and PRMTs, which directly relate to their distribution in discourse:

A. Contextualized examples of PRMTs in (30)–(32) show that PRMTs RE-ESTABLISH an earlier discourse topic.
B. Contextualized examples of UMTs in (33)–(35) show that UMTs MAINTAIN a current discourse topic.

These two generalizations of the functional differences between UMTs and PRMTs can be captured by the notion of consciousness. Speakers use a PRMT when they believe the presupposed constituent is no longer in the immediate consciousness of their audience. UMTs are used when speakers assume that the presupposed constituent is in the immediate consciousness of the audience. The notion of consciousness was first introduced by Chafe (1974: 111–12):

> Language ... is used primarily to increase the amount of knowledge that is shared by separate minds ... What a speaker shares with his addressee must be part of what is in the speaker's consciousness at the time ... The speaker must make assumptions as to what the addressee is conscious of, and transmit his own material accordingly.

Earlier studies of PRMTs—Rodman (1974), Givón (1979), and Duranti and Ochs (1979)—have noted the power of this sentence type to re-establish an 'old' discourse topic that seems to have been lost as the conversation shifts naturally from one topic to the next. As mentioned in section 3.4.1, part of the presentational function of PRMTs is restricted to 're-establishing on the scene' topics of conversation that are, in the speaker's judgement, no longer in the audience's immediate consciousness. In other words, the less vividly 'on stage' an idea is, the more necessary a PRMT becomes. This is part of the function of a PRMT, and this function helps to explain its discourse function of 'topic recoverability', as Givón (1979: 56–65) calls it.

Examples (30) and (32) below show how speakers shift from the present topic to an 'older' topic, older in the sense that the PRMT was a topic earlier in the conversation. Examples (33) and (35), by contrast, show that the function of UMTs is restricted to settings where the discourse topic is already established, a given, in the immediate consciousness of the speakers and audience.

3.5.1 Examples of PRMTs

(3) *Lehrer*:
  I see. Well, is it possible for you to define in Western terms what a free trade union movement under this agreement might look like in Poland?
  Szostak:
  Well, it's sort of—they will be given their demands. How many of these

demands will be given, we do not know. To what degree, is another question yet to be resolved. However, they are still—will have to fall in line with the main umbrella organization.
Lehrer:
I see.
Szostak:
So in other words, they are giving enough latitude to go so far, but there is a stopping point. While here in the United States, A FREE TRADE UNION— YOU CAN JUST GO AND DO ANYTHING YOU WANT. [MacNeil/Lehrer transcript No. 1283] [author's emphasis]

In this example, the progression of the topic through the discourse can be schematized as illustrated in Figure 3.1. In the course of describing the trade union's movement in Poland, the initial topic of conversation, Szostak touches upon two related subtopics, the union's demands and the Polish government's umbrella organization. The PRMT re-establishes an 'old' discourse topic, which seems to have been lost as the conversation shifts naturally from one topic to another.

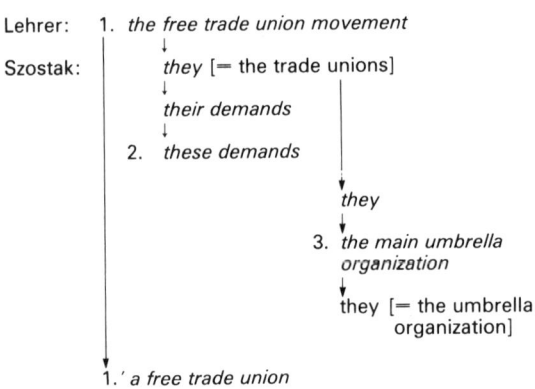

Figure 3.1

Another shift to an 'older' discourse topic through a PRMT appears in the following example.

(31) *MacNeil*:
Ms. Curry, if major concessions are granted to the Polish workers and tolerated by the Soviet Union, what will the effect be on the neighboring East European countries?
Curry:
I think first of all you have to keep in mind that the Soviets must have agreed to whatever concessions were made. These weren't made alone by the Polish leadership. And secondly, that the other worker in Eastern Europe, although economically they're getting to be in the same position as the Polish workers, they're still better off than the Poles. And these

concessions, these political concessions are not going to bring economic prosperity to Poland, at least in the short run. So, I think the Czechs are going to remember what happened in '68. That's not something they've forgotten. The Hungarians are fairly well off economically. I don't think they're gonna be concerned about threatening their economic well-being. The East Germans are a fairly repressed society, so the options for East German workers are far more limited than for Poles, who've always been a very different country than anywhere else in Eastern Europe.
MacNeil:
So, in short, you don't see a wave of imitation following this incident in Poland?
Curry: No, I don't see a wave of imitation.
MacNeil: Mr. Szostak, do you?
Szoztak:
Yes, I see a selective imitation with possibly Czechoslovkia [*sic*], Rumania. BUT WITH EAST GERMANY, IT'S A DIFFERENT SITUATION, because the Soviet Union has witnessed the ravages of war with Germany, and I think the Soviet Union would think twice before it loosens the reins in East Germany. This is why East Germans are so repressive. HOWEVER, THE OTHER COUNTRIES THAT I'VE MENTIONED, THEY WILL SEE WHAT THE MODEL IN POLAND IS, and they will gradually acquiesce, because there's no need for violence, and I think their feeling is, 'If the Soviet Union agrees to Poland, they will agree to us.' BUT EAST GERMANY—THAT'S A DIFFERENT SITUATION, because definitely for its own security protection, she wants to keep East Germany totally independent of the western part of Germany. [MacNeil/Lehrer transcript No. 1283] [author's emphasis]

Schematically the topical progression here is depicted in Figure 3.2. Again, one can see PRMTs re-establish earlier discourse topics. The first of three PRMTs re-establishes a sub-topic, *East Germany*, and the second PRMT re-establishes the topic *other East European countries*, which has been lost in the discussion. Then as the topic shifts again from *other countries* back to *East Germany*, yet another PRMT is used.

(32) *Hunter-Gault*:
Mr. Falwell, what do you say to Congressman Drinan's assertion that you don't have the real majority that you think you have, or that you say you have?
Falwell:
Well, first of all, the name Moral Majority doesn't imply that every American agrees. A December Gallup poll indicated that 84 percent of all Americans believe the Ten Commandments are valid for today. That doesn't mean they can all quote them. And certainly we don't all live up to what we believe in. That's why we go to church and serve God and pray and so on. But it does mean that intellectually a majority of Americans still believe—and I think that probably the percentage that believed in 1776—in the traditional family and basic moral values, all the things that this country was built upon, a nation under God. Therefore,

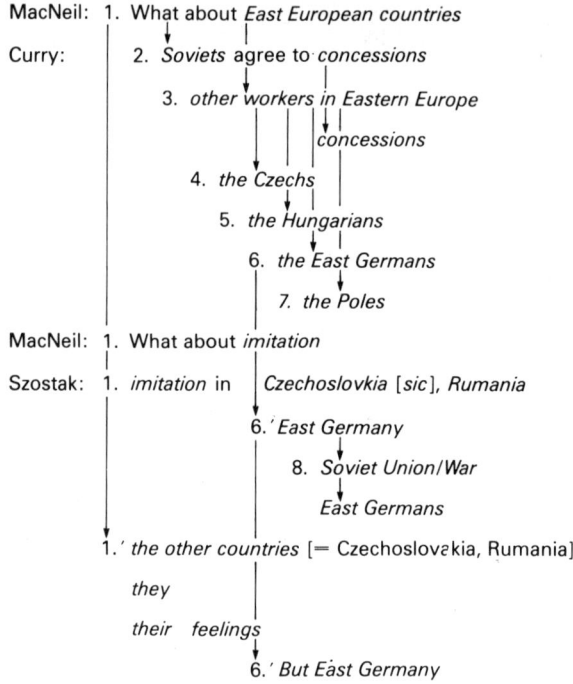

Figure 3.2

the people haven't gone bad. Leadership has. And instead of having government of the people, by the people, for the people, we now have a government in spite of the people—and Father Drinan is a typical example of that—ignoring what the majority of the people, and his own church, all God-fearing people want, and that is a return to moral sanity in this country, and a strengthening of the military fiber and fabric of this country so the citizenry can once again be safe from the attack of some aggressor somewhere, in particular the Soviet Union. To me, I say there is a majority out there, a vast overwhelming majority. But politicians have successfully come home to their constituency waving a bible in one hand and a flag in the other, saying 'I'm a conservative,' going right back to Washington, and along with the Ted Kennedy's and the Father Drinans, have voted anti-family, anti-morality, anti-strong national defense consistently every time. And I say that is the very height of hypocrisy.
Drinan:
Sir, I have never cast a vote against the family. I taught family law for a dozen years——
Falwell:
You have voted federal funding for abortion, and that is anti-family.
Hunter-Gault:

Congressman Drinan, are there any areas within that list of things that Mr. Falwell has just outlined that you can possibly agree with? I mean, is it possible for a liberal to—of your persuasion to agree with any of those things that he has laid out?
Drinan:
Of course. Christianity dictates fundamentally that we should do everything that we can to avoid war, and that's why it's appalling THAT THE EVANGELICALS, THE ONES THAT WE'RE DISCUSSING TONIGHT AT LEAST, THEY ARE OPPOSED TO SALT II. And it seems to me inconceivable that they wouldn't want to make this step forward to disarmament. Secondly, all Christians and all people of religious faith would say we have to do all that we can to feed the Third World. Now, there's people, millions of people, who are starving, and I see nothing in the evangelicals that we're discussing, nothing that would say America has to increase its foreign aid. [MacNeil/Lehrer transcript No. 1280] [author's emphasis]

Here the topical progression can be seen in Figure 3.3. The PRMT again re-establishes the earlier topic of conversation. Notice how Falwell progresses through a number of related sub-topics and Drinan's use of the PRMT re-establishes a topic long removed from the immediately preceding topic, *war*.

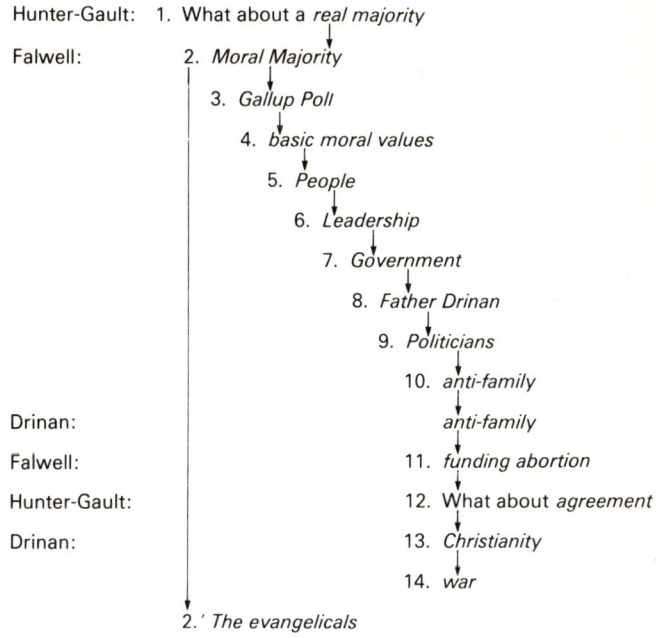

Figure 3.3

3.5.2 Examples of UMTs

(33) *Audience*: What is the average cost of this therapy?
Ms. Dreyer: Um, I'd—
Mr. Donahue: Give us a ball park, can you? I mean—
Ms. Dreyer:
I would say that it is about a hundred dollars a week. It's very, very expensive. And one of the reasons that I'm on this program is that I feel that there are many things available to people in this country who can afford it. Okay. But this is not a program that is available at our major universities. They have sexual dysfunction clinics, but they don't have the availability of working with surrogates yet. Okay.
Mr. Donahue: Do you think they ought to?
Ms. Dreyer:
I feel they should. But, then, you're the audience here, how would you feel if your tax dollars were going to support a, you know, a thing like this? I mean, see it, it's a complicated issue, isn't it?
Audience: The way that it remains is upper-middle class therapy.
Ms. Dreyer: That's right.
Audience: I think that's immoral.
Audience: So do I.
Mr. Donahue: So much of psychiatric care remains that.
Ms. Dreyer:
That's true, Phil, but to a certain extent, there is very good psychiatric care available through major medical universities.
Mr. Donahue: True.
Ms. Dreyer: THAT SORT OF THING, THIS IS NOT. [Donahue transcript No. 09249] [author's emphasis]

Schematically the topical progression here is illustrated in Figure 3.4, which shows that the UMT, *that sort of thing*, does not re-establish an earlier discourse topic, as PRMTs do; rather, it maintains a discourse topic. In this example, the UMT is co-referential with the immediately preceding topic, *psychiatric care*.

Another example of an UMT is:

(34) *Mr. Donahue*: Why can't I be aiming at reducing misery?
Dr. Shockley:
Well, you were aiming at reducing misery by making things perfect across the board. Now—
Mr. Donahue:
Well, no. I'm merely saying, 'Let's have more equitable distribution of wealth.' Let's have wealth go to people on the basis of merit, not on whether or not they own multi-national corporations and exploit third world governments and people, that's all.
Audience: (applause)
Dr. Shockley:
Well, I'd rather stick to the U.S. in this point. And now I was bringing

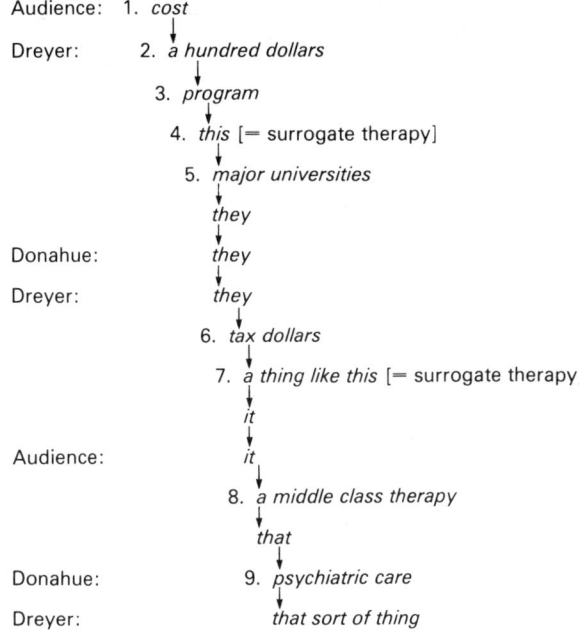

Figure 3.4

something up about this thing, which I say is the biggest threat for any minority group in our nation. And this is the high birth rate at the bottom of the black population. And we got as far as saying that taxpayers are gonna suffer from this, and that brought a response from the audience. And I was gonna say there was a more fundamental moral issue, to my way of thinking. AND THAT I DIDN'T FINISH. And that moral issue is that these babies that come into the world at the bottom of this scale, at this lowest socio-economic status, are, in effect, getting an unfair shake from a badly loaded parental genetic dice cup. [Donahue transcript No. 03250] [author's emphasis]

Schematically the topical progression is as shown in Figure 3.5. Again, the UMT, *that*, maintains a current discourse topic, rather than re-establishes an earlier discourse topic.

Consider also:

(35) *Jim Lehrer*:
Senator, what kind of limit would you put on coal severance taxes?
Sen. Dale Bumpers: Twelve and a half percent.
Lehrer: Why?
Bumpers:
Well, number one, that is an arbitrary figure, Jim, and I recognize that. But I think it's a reasonable figure. It certainly would do more than

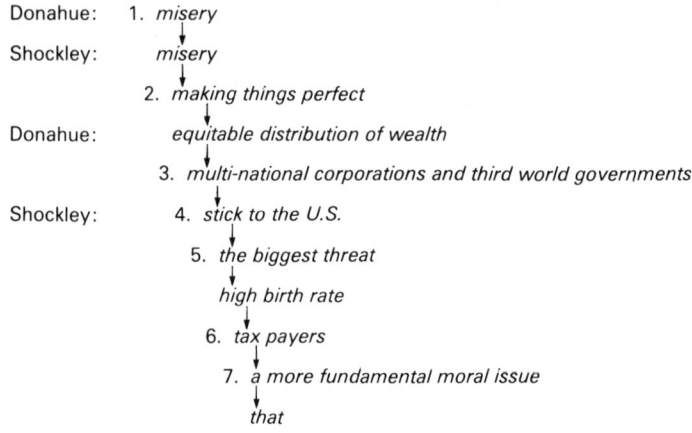

Figure 3.5

enough to accommodate the impact of the increased energy production, particularly in states like Montana and Wyoming. But I think there's one point that has not been made in yours and Robin's opening, and THAT I WANT TO STRESS RIGHT NOW. My bill only goes to federal coal, and I'm not talking about coal that is owned by the United States. [MacNeil/Lehrer transcript No. 1285] [author's emphasis]

Schematically the topical progression is illustrated in Figure 3.6. Again, the UMT maintains a current discourse topic. The UMT, *that*, is co-referential with the immediately preceding topic, *one point that has not been made*. The function of the UMT is to maintain the topic.

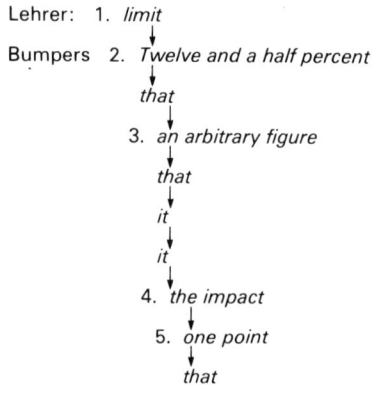

Figure 3.6

To characterize more precisely the distribution of structures with UMTs and PRMTs, one could make the following generalizations:

- UMTs are co-referential with the topic in the immediately preceding sentence.
- PRMTs are co-referential with a topic in an earlier sentence, x-sentences away from the PRMT, where x = 2.

Or to describe the distribution relationally, one would say that the UMT is co-referential with the immediately preceding discourse topic, but the PRMT is co-referential with an earlier discourse topic, where there is at least one intervening topic between the PRMT and its antecedent topic. One could schematically illustrate the relational description of distribution by Figure 3.7.

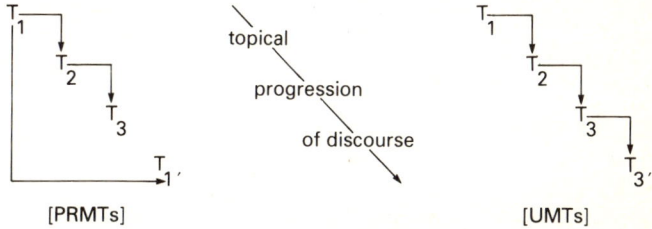

Figure 3.7

3.6 WORD ORDER STUDIES

Having examined the syntactic, semantic and distributional differences between structures with UMTs and PRMTs, one now can make a claim about the relationship between function and form. It may be the case that the differences in the syntactic forms of sentences with UMTs and PRMTs derive from their functions in discourse. Intuitively, one might guess that any construction that functions to re-establish an earlier discourse topic must be 'richer' in semantic content than any construction that functions to maintain a topic.[11] A structure maintaining a topic, which can be assumed to be in the immediate consciousness of the audience, requires a 'leaner' semantic content compared to the structure that must re-establish an earlier topic, which cannot be assumed to be in the immediate consciousness of the audience.

Three syntactic facts support these intuitions about the relation of form to function. First, nearly one-half of all the UMTs in the corpus are pronouns. Pronouns themselves are 'leaner' in semantic content than their co-referential, full noun phrases. Secondly, all of the PRMTs in the corpus are definite, full noun phrases. So on the basis of their sentence initial constituents, structures with PRMTs are 'richer' in semantic content than structures with UMTs, and this is exactly what one would predict given the discourse function of PRMTs to re-establish topics not in the immediate consciousness of the audience.

Thirdly, the structural differences between sentences with UMTs and

PRMTs also provide PRMTs with a 'richer' semantic content. That is, PRMTs have co-referential pronouns within their clauses that serve to reinforce the semantic content of the PRMT in much the same way as reflexive pronouns can reinforce their antecedents in sentences like *John himself ate the pizza*. UMTs do not have this kind of pronominal reinforcement of their sentence initial constituents, so they are comparatively 'leaner' in semantic content.

These three syntactic facts bear out one's intuitions about the kinds of structures needed to maintain, as opposed to re-establish, a discourse topic. One could hypothesize, therefore, that the form of structures with UMTs and PRMTs is (partly) determined by their distribution and function in discourse.

3.7 CONCLUSIONS

By determining the syntactic properties of structures with UMTs and PRMTs, one is able to explain the semantic properties and discourse functions of those structures. Further, by studying the discourse distribution of structures with UMTs and PRMTs, one can discover how differences in discourse functions create differences in syntactic forms. Those studies, discoveries, allow a number of conclusions:

— the semantic properties of UMTs and PRMTs provide a definition of topichood through the notion of presupposition;
— the (discourse) functions of presentation, connection and contrast follow directly from the semantic properties of structures with UMTs and PRMTs;
— structures with UMTs and PRMTs are in complementary distribution; i.e. they do not occur in the same discourse environment;
— one can hypothesize (based on the discourse functions of UMTs and PRMTs, their semantic properties and their discourse distribution) that the form of the structure is at least partly determined by its function.

As a final note, one should recognize that these generalizations can only be made after a careful corpus study of the structures involved.

NOTES

1. A note about terminology: these constructions are labelled differently in different grammatical theories. Transformational-generative theory prefers the labels 'topicalization' and 'left dislocation'. The formal, scholarly grammars, such as Quirk *et al.* (1985), often use 'thematic fronting'. Those labels imply, unquestioningly, a movement analysis of the non-canonical word orders, suggesting that they are somehow derived from more basic types of sentences or from their canonically ordered corresponding sentences. Following the Prague school, Halliday (1967, 1985) uses the general label 'marked theme' to characterize non-canonically ordered structures. Marked themes in an independent declarative clause include the structures studied here in addition to sentence initial adverbials (i.e. adjuncts).

Further, Halliday (1985: 45, 81) clearly labels marked themes without pronominal reinforcement as 'thematic complements' or 'marked-thematic complements'. It is not certain if he would include marked themes with pronominal reinforcement in the category of (marked-) thematic complements. And given the evidence to follow in this study, one has reason to distinguish the two different structures, for as Halliday (1985: 384) notes, 'All of them differ in meaning in some respect, and given a functional grammar we can say what that respect is'.

So, in this study, I prefer the labels 'pronominally reinforced marked themes' (PRMTs) and 'unreinforced marked themes' (UMTs) over the more specific label '(marked-) thematic complement'. First, as Halliday mentions himself, not all of those marked themes are complements in Halliday's system, as in *the other one, that needs to be taken apart*, where the marked theme functions as subject, or in *Some things I do think you have to spank 'em on the butt a little [for]*, where the marked theme functions as object of a (subvocalized) prepositional phrase. Secondly, as we shall see, those constructions are grammatically, semantically and functionally distinctive, justifying separate labelling.

2. Markedness here is determined by (1) frequency of occurrence, (2) structural complexity in sentences beginning with PRMTs, and (3) restricted distribution: i.e. not all unmarked structures have corresponding sentences with UMTs or PRMTs appearing in the same contexts.
3. All of the impromptu speech data for this chapter comes from the unedited transcripts of two television interview programmes, the *Donahue Show* and the *MacNeil/Lehrer Report*.
4. Compare Prince (1981) for her interesting and useful explication of the concepts 'given' and 'new'.
5. This review of the literature was meant to outline some of the problems that arise in word order studies. A major source of problems when one studies word order might be called the poverty of surface syntactic information, i.e. the number of distinctions serial order can make as an information-carrying device. Serial order can provide only two possible pieces of information: (1) two constituents can be sequential or not (i.e. serial order can describe adjacency relations), and (2) if the constituents are sequential, their order may be either X–Y or Y–X (i.e. serial order can describe precedence relations).

Through the relationships of adjacency and precedence, serial order, supplemented in the surface representation by morphology and intonation, provides information about grammatical relationships of subject, object, etc; about thematic structure of theme/rheme or topic/comment (the 'psychological' subject of Sandmann 1954); about the participant roles of agent, patient, etc. (the 'logical' subject of Sandmann 1954); and about information structure of given and new. As Chafe (1976: 27) puts it, 'A noun in its sentence plays many roles, or has the potential of doing so'.

So part of the difficulty in determining the contribution of linear order to one's understanding of language results from the interplay of various language processes. These linguistic processes 'conspire' to determine the serial order of clausal constituents. Out of context, or in a controlled context, it is possible to isolate the functions of end-focus, thematic prominence, and euphony in determining linear order, but *in vivo*, as it were, it becomes more difficult to characterize precisely the contribution of individual language processes.

Neutralization processes provide an analogous situation to the 'conspiracy' described here. Neutralization rules, at any level of linguistic analysis, eliminate a potential contrast, thereby creating the potential for ambiguity. At some level of analysis, one would want to explain the ambiguity by positing different forms, which are no longer overtly distinguished at the surface level because of a neutralization process. Likewise, different sentence types seem to neutralize some distinctions between grammatical, thematic, psychological and logical subject, for example, in order to express some distinction that otherwise may be missed. That is, in appropriate contexts, language users may need to be explicitly clear about information structure, or thematic structure, etc., for efficient language processing. For example, when speakers need to be explicit about the 'packaging' of information within a clause, the cleft and pseudo-cleft constructions allow a distinction between GIVEN versus KNOWN information. See Prince (1978) for a discussion of the discourse contexts that require such explicitness.

For more details about the confusion that arises through the poverty of surface syntactic information, see Chafe (1976).

6. Sentence (17b) is acceptable only if one assumes a contrast with other kinds of tea that could be asserted as possible answers to the question. Without this contrastive sense, (17b) is unacceptable.
7. Sentence (23) is intonationally marked because focal stress falls on a non-focal constituent. But it is not marked if it answers the question *Who ate the pizza?*, which requires an answer like (23).
8. Quirk *et al.* (1985) provide a more detailed account of the relationship between marked theme and intonation.
9. Firbas (1966), Reinhart (1982), and Simon-Vandenbergen (1987) present evidence that indefinite NPs with specific reference may also serve as marked themes. For example, Simon-Vandenbergen discusses *Now, a friend of mine, he had the same problem*. Simon-Vandenbergen explains this apparent discrepancy by citing Langendonck's study of indefinites. Langendonck argues that for some classes of indefinites, like the one above, 'the individuals are presupposed in the speaker's world, though not in the hearer's for whom an introduction is needed' (1980: 216). So it seems that SPECIFICITY OF REFERENCE (in addition to definiteness, plurality and generic reference) can provide the necessary conditions for topichood by creating existential presuppositions (at least in the speaker's world). Thus, 'This presuppositional status of [this class of] indefinite entails that these NPs tend to figure in the front of the sentence, just like definites' (Langendonck ibid.).
10. Note also that the marked themes in examples (13) and (33) have a concessive force.
11. Givón believes that there is an iconicity principle at work here: '... the more disruptive, surprising, discontinuous or hard to process a topic is, the more coding material must be assigned to it' (1983: 18).

BIBLIOGRAPHY

Bever, T. (1975), 'Functional explanations require independently motivated functional theories', in Grossman, *et al.* (eds), *Papers from the Parasession on Functionalism*, Chicago, Chicago Linguistic Society.
Bolinger, D. (1977), *Meaning and Form*, London, Longman.
Chafe, W. (1974), 'Language and consciousness', *Language*, 50, 111–33.
—— (1976), 'Givenness, contrastiveness, definiteness, subjects, topics, and points of view', in Li (ed.), *Subject and Topic*, New York, Academic Press.
Chomsky, N. (1965), *Aspects of the Theory of Syntax*, Cambridge, Mass., MIT Press.
Duranti, A. and Ochs, E. (1979), 'Left dislocation in spoken Italian', in Givón (ed.), *Syntax and Semantics, Vol. 12, Discourse and Syntax*, New York, Academic Press.

Firbas, J. (1964), 'On defining the theme in functional sentence analysis', *Travaux linguistiques de Prague*, 1, 267–80.
—— (1966), 'Non-thematic subjects in contemporary English', *Travaux linguistiques de Prague*, 2, 239–56.
Friedman, L. (1976), 'The manifestation of subject, object, and topic in American Sign Language', in Li (ed.), *Subject and Topic*, New York, Academic Press.
Gary, N. (1976), 'A discourse analysis of certain root transformations', Bloomington, Ind., Indiana University Linguistics Club.
Givón, T. (1979), *On Understanding Grammar*, New York, Academic Press.
—— (1983), 'Topic continuity in discourse' in Givón (ed.), *Typological Studies in Discourse*, Vol. 3, Amsterdam, John Benjamins.
Green, G. (1980), 'Some wherefores of English inversions', *Language*, 56, 582–602.
—— (1982), 'Colloquial and literary uses of inversions', in Tannen (ed.), *Spoken and Written Language, Vol. 9, Advances in Discourse Processes*, New York, Academic Press.
Gundel, J. (1977), 'Role of topic and comment in linguistic theory', Bloomington, Ind., Indiana University Linguistics Club.
Halliday, M. A. K. (1967), 'Notes on transitivity and theme in English: Part 2', *Journal of Linguistics*, 3, 199–244.
—— (1985), *An Introduction to Functional Grammar*, London, Edward Arnold.
Hetzron, R. (1975), 'The presentative movement, or why the ideal word order is VSOP', in Li (ed.), *Word Order and Word Order Change*, Austin, Texas, University of Texas Press.
Jackendoff, R. (1972), *Semantic Interpretation in Generative Grammar*, Cambridge, Mass., MIT Press.
Katz, J. (1972), *Semantic Theory*, New York, Harper and Row.
Langendonck, W. V. (1980), 'Indefinites, exemplars, and kinds', in Van der Auwera (ed.), *The Semantics of Determiners*, London, Croom Helm.
Lyons, J. (1977), *Semantics, Vol. 2*, Cambridge, Cambridge University Press.
Prince, E. (1978), 'A comparison of *Wh*-clefts and *It*-clefts in discourse', *Language*, 54, 883–906.
—— (1981), 'Toward a taxonomy of given-new information', in Cole (ed.), *Radical Pragmatics*, New York, Academic Press.
Quirk, R., Greenbaum, S., Leech, G. and Svartvik, J. (1972), *A Grammar of Contemporary English*, London, Longman.
—— (1985), *A Comprehensive Grammar of the English Language*, London, Longman.
Reinhart, T. (1982), 'Pragmatics and linguistics: an analysis of sentence topics', Bloomington, Ind., Indiana University Linguistics Club.
Rodman, R. (1974), 'On left dislocation', *Papers in Linguistics*, 7, 437–66.
Ross, J. (1967), 'Constraints on variables in syntax', Bloomington, Ind., Indiana University Linguistics Club.
Sandmann, M. (1954), *Subject and Predicate*, Edinburgh, Edinburgh University Press.
Simon-Vandenbergen, A. M. (1987), 'Left dislocation revisited', to appear in *Studies in Honour of René Derolez*, Ghent

4 Functional sentence perspective in the context of systemic functional grammar

M. P. Williams
Department of Languages, Heviot-Watt University, Edinburgh, UK

4.0 INTRODUCTION

The purpose of this chapter is to show how a functional sentence perspective (FSP) understanding of THEME and RHEME can both fit into, and indeed enrich, the understanding which systemic grammarians have of the textual component by making these notions at once more delicate and more responsive to varying textual environments. Much of the work on which this chapter is based was done on Arabic and my initial concern with FSP arose as I sought to deal with thematization in a VSO language. However, the points made can all be adequately illustrated from English, which in the context of the present collection of works would seem to be more suitable and is therefore adopted. The passage analysed in section 4.3 and the system networks and realization rules given in section 4.4 originally appeared in Williams (1987).

The chapter is organized as follows. In section 4.1, I shall contrast the orthodox systemic and the FSP approaches to theme and rheme and seek to point up some shortcomings within the orthodox system approach to this subject. Then, in section 4.2, I shall show how the concept of communicative dynamism (CD) relates to terms more familiar to British and American linguists. In section 4.3, I shall elaborate a method for the FSP analysis of a text and show how it applies to a text. Finally, in section 4.4, I will show how the FSP definitions of theme and rheme can be profitably used within a still totally systemic understanding of the textual component to yield a dynamic analysis of a text.

4.1 THE SYSTEMIC AND FSP DEFINITIONS OF THEME AND RHEME CONTRASTED

4.1.1 The systemic approach

In his book *An Introduction to Functional Grammar* (1985: 38), Halliday defines the theme in functional terms, as 'the element which serves as the point of departure of the message; it is that with which the clause is concerned'. It does not have to be 'given' information for, '... while "given" means "what you were talking about" (or "what I was talking about before"), "theme" means "what I am talking about" (or "what I am talking about now")' (Halliday 1967). With this functional definition as a basis, Halliday goes on to discuss the realization of the theme in English:

As a general guide, the Theme can be identified as that element which comes in first position in the clause. [Halliday 1985: 39]

There is always an ideational element in the Theme. There may be, but are not necessarily, interpersonal, and/or textual elements as well. [ibid.: 53]

The Theme of any clause, therefore, extends up to (and includes) the topical Theme. The topical Theme is the first element in the clause that has some function in the ideational structure. [ibid.: 56]

Working with these definitions, the theme can be a group as in the following example:

(1) His father's raincoat | was too small.
        Th | Rh

or a clause as in Example (2):

(2) When the bank had closed, | the thieves began to drill.
        Th | Rh

or a number of groups bounded on the right by a group having a function within the ideational component, as in example (3):

(3) Well then, David, perhaps Susan | will arrive tomorrow.
        Th | Rh

4.1.2 The FSP approach

By contrast, the FSP definition of theme is as follows:

The thematic elements are those elements which form the foundation of the utterance, from which the speaker proceeds. They are the elements that contribute least to the communicative dynamism (CD) of the utterance, where CD means 'the extent to which the sentence element contributes to the development of the communication'. [Firbas 1964: 270]

The rest of the sentence composes the rheme, which is in turn divided into transition (usually a relation or a process), and the rheme, where the rheme is defined as those elements which contribute most to the CD of the utterance. In Firbas (1975), and again but perhaps not so clearly in Firbas (1979), four factors are said to determine the distribution of CD within the unit:

  (i) the principle of linearity;
 (ii) semantics;
(iii) context;
(iv) the communicative intention of the speaker.

The principle of linearity corresponds in large part to the principles of end-weight and end-focus discussed in Quirk *et al.* (1972) and states that other things being equal words towards the end of a sentence have more CD than those coming towards the beginning of the sentence. The factor of semantics attributes CD according to the semantic function attributed to an element within a sentence according to the following two scales:

Scene–Appearance/Existence–Phenomenon Appearing/Existing
Quality Bearer–Quality–Specification

which can be combined as follows:

Scene–Appearance/Existence–Phenomenon Appearing/Existing//
Quality Bearer–Quality–Specification–(Further Specification)

These two scales can perhaps be best described as Terms in a functional semantics in which: 'Scene' describes the possible world to which the proposition pertains; 'Phenomenon Appearing/Existing', the entity that is introduced into this world; 'Appearance/Existence', the process by which the object is introduced into this world; 'Quality Bearer', the entity appearing or existing in this world viewed as the bearer of an attributed quality, that about which something is said; 'Quality' the process attributed to the quality bearer; and 'Specification' specifying the range of operation of the process specified.

Three examples of how this can be applied to sentences may help:

(4) There | was | a little girl. Scene–Appearance/Existence–Phenomenon Appearing/Existing.
(5) She | had | a little curl. Quality Bearer–Quality–Specification.
(6) A man | came | into the room | and sat down. Phenomenon Appearing/Quality Bearer–Appearance–Scene–Quality.

The factor of context states that where an element is retrievable from the previous text, it is thematic, whatever the outcome of consideration of the previous two factors. But taking precedence over all is the factor entitled 'the communicative intention of the speaker'. This allows for the illocutionary intention of the speaker/writer to overrule any previous consideration. Thus in a text in which there are a number of participants, where a sentence like *The lion entered the cave* would be quite acceptable in reply to the notional question *What happened then?*, the fact that *the cave* is retrievable from the previous text is immaterial in the light of the fact that it is the heart of the communicative intention of the speaker (see Williams 1987: 64–83 for a fuller description of FSP).

4.1.3 The contrast illustrated

The practical difference between the results obtained by the two methods of determining the theme can be illustrated by the following examples:

(7)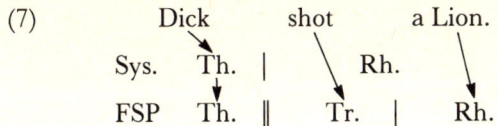

(8)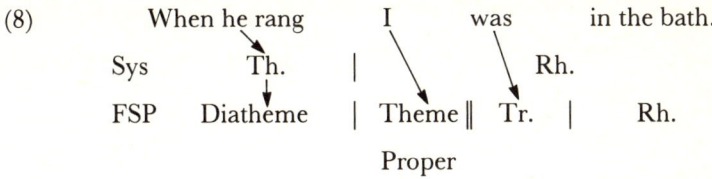

(9)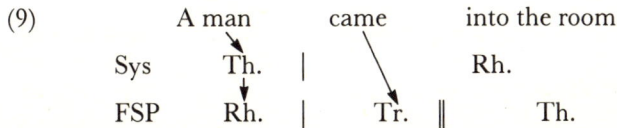

This comparison shows two problems with the orthodox approach to theme. Although the two methods of analysis agree in example (7), notwithstanding the secondary division of the rheme made in FSP, example (9) shows total divergence. The problem with the orthodox analysis is that although the first ideational element is formally the theme, in no significant sense is it the 'point of departure of the message' (although it may turn out to be the topic of the whole text from which this sentence is notionally extracted). It is rather the whole point of the message.

Moreover, even accepting Halliday's definition of theme as it stands, it is unfortunately not sufficiently delicate to handle helpfully cases where there is, so to speak, more than one point of departure. Example (8) is a typical example. In most texts, the first element functions contrastively, whereas the second element is continuative. These two functions of the theme are of major importance in text, and appear to be totally ignored in systemic literature in this area. As I will show later on in this chapter, both these shortcomings can be coped with by adopting the FSP definitions. However, before this can be done convincingly, one problem needs to be overcome.

4.2 COMMUNICATIVE DYNAMISM AND RELEVANCE

The major problem in FSP is a tight definition of the term COMMUNICATIVE DYNAMISM, in terms of which—as we have seen above—the terms *theme* and *rheme* are defined. This admittedly serious problem can, I believe, be solved by relating CD to 'relevance', as Sperber and Wilson (1986) define the term. In their book they define relevance in terms of the contextual effects that the utterance under consideration has on the cognitive environment of the hearer counterbalanced by the effort which the hearer has to exert in order to process it. It is my contention that this is a formalization—and a needed formalization—of the term FSP as used by the Prague school. In this framework, the degree of communicative dynamism (the degree to which a certain element contributes to the message conveyed by the whole) can be defined in terms of the number of analytic implications which the element in question gives rise to, this number being assessed cumulatively following a modified dependency scale. In other words, with the slight change made in the previous sentence, the degree of CD should coincide with Sperber and Wilson's 'focal scale' (1986: 208–9), defined by them as 'a strictly ordered subset of analytic implications', this ordering being achieved in my slight modification by means of a dependency scale, the exact nature of which will be described below. Moreover, one can follow Sperber and Wilson in saying that:

> when an implication in the focal scale of an utterance has contextual effects of its own, and hence is relevant in its own right, it is a FOREGROUND IMPLICATION, and that otherwise it is a BACKGROUND IMPLICATION. Then the focus of an utterance will be the smallest syntactic constituent whose replacement by a variable yields a background rather than a foreground implication. [1986: 209]

One could quite happily identify the term 'foreground implication' with 'rheme' and 'background implication' with 'theme'. The tendency would be that the later an element occurred in a sentence, the more implications it would give rise to, and therefore the greater the CD. Moreover, where an element is given, and therefore included in the thematic part of the sentence, it will have no contextual effects and will therefore be backgrounded. Conversely, elements giving rise to contextual effects in their own right, and therefore foregrounded, will form the rhematic section of the sentence. The rheme is in other words the focus of the sentence.

Let us see how this would work in a couple of examples:

(10) John was hunting lions.

Following Hudson's *Word Grammar* (Hudson 1984), the dependencies are as follows:

John was hunting lions.

This represents the ideational plane of relationships. Hudson also suggests that there is a dependency the other way between *John* as subject and *was*. In support of this he cites a number of arguments which we need not enter into here. However, if we substitute for the term 'subject' the FSP terms 'Quality Bearer' in the case of the Quality Bearer–Quality–Specification chain and 'Scene' in the case of the Scene–Appearance/Existence–Phenomenon Appearing/Existing chain, and see this as the decoders point of entry, then we have a framework for a dynamic approach to the textual component. The ammended dependency chain is now as follows:

John was hunting lions.

Starting from the Quality Bearer (*John*), the item at the top of the chain, one can then substitute logical labels as do Sperber and Wilson to achieve an ordered list of analytic implications.

(11) John is relevant in some way.
(12) John had a certain attribute.
(13) John was doing something.
(14) John was hunting something.

John by itself implies (11); *John was* implies (11) and (12); *John was hunting* implies (11), (12) and (13); and *John was hunting lions* implies (11), (12), (13) and (14).

Another example, taking the other type of chain, is as follows:

(15) A man came into the room.

This gives us the following chain:

A man came into the room.

Starting from the Scene, the item at the bottom of the chain, this gives us the following ordered list of analytic implications:

(16) Something happened in the room.
(17) Something or someone came into the room.
(18) A man came into the room.

Into the room implies (16); *came into the room* implies (16) and (17), and *A man came into the room* implies (16), (17) and (18).

In both these cases, it should be clear that the basic degree of CD can be determined in terms of the number of implications set up by the addition of each element on the scale. Where an additional implication does not change the cognitive environment of the hearer (in other words is not relevant), then that implication is backgrounded and the element giving rise to it is thematic.

More work needs to be done on this, but it does go a considerable way towards tightening up the definition of the term CD. For the purposes of this chapter it is sufficient to establish the connection and to move on to the next section, the purpose of which is to set theme and rheme (defined in terms of FSP) in the context of systemic grammar.

4.3 THE FSP DEFINITIONS OF THEME AND RHEME SET WITHIN A SYSTEMIC FRAMEWORK

In this section, I shall elaborate a method for the FSP analysis of a text. To do this, I shall define various types of theme, various types of rheme, show how they can be distinguished and used, and then apply them in the analysis of a text. Following this analysis, in section 4.4, I shall give two systems networks for thematic and rhematic choices, and show two examples of how speakers select from these systems.

First of all, though, let us define the various types of theme and rheme. In the literature, the following types of theme are discussed (they contribute in ascending order to the CD of the sentence):

theme proper
theme proper oriented theme
diatheme oriented theme
diatheme

The theme proper and the theme proper oriented theme are the elements that contribute least to the information of the thematic sphere, being purely continuative in function. It is these elements that give continuity to a text. The diatheme and the diatheme oriented theme are those elements that contribute most to the information of the thematic sphere. These elements help to develop a text by introducing into the thematic sphere new entities or entities already introduced into the rhematic sphere or by reiterating or making a contrast with entities already in the thematic sphere. When both theme proper and diatheme are present, it is usually easy to tell which is which. However, when only one is present, it is sometimes difficult to tell which category to put it in. This can be clarified and somewhat formalized by specifying the characteristic functions of the diatheme. These are as follows:

1. refocusing thematic information;
2. bringing information from the rhematic to the thematic spheres;
3. introducing rhematic information directly into the thematic sphere.

The four types of theme described above are usually expressed by numerical subscripts. In addition to these four, I have found it useful to introduce a fifth category, that of 'dummy theme', which contributes absolutely nothing to the CD of the sentence. With this addition, the five types are listed below, along with the numerical subscripts that express them:

dummy theme   (10)
theme proper   (11)
theme proper oriented theme   (12)
diatheme oriented theme   (13)
diatheme   (14)

The rhematic sphere is characteristically divided in the literature between 'rheme proper' and 'rest of rheme'. Not much research has been done in this area. However, there would seem to be a primary difference between those rhematic elements that give a satisfactory completion to an utterance without reference to the context, and those that do not. The latter can be divided between those that I will call 'dummy rhemes' (either *wh* words or ellipted rhemes as in the clause *The question is O: . . .* (coded (30)) and those constituents of the rheme that still carry with them the need for further specification or addition (coded (31)). This need is expressed in speech by intonation, and in writing by punctuation. These incomplete rhemes are of two types. Some are simply used as build-up to a more important element elsewhere—usually later—in the sentence. The second type comprises superordinates whose referent is still to be specified in the succeeding text, and Winter's Vocabulary 3 items (see Winter 1977 for a fuller discussion of these). As for the 'rheme proper', it can usually be coded (32), but where there are a number of rhematic elements, the second digit may increase accordingly, reflecting incidentally the increased rhetorical weight of such elements. Thus the coding of the rhematic sphere is as follows:

dummy rheme   (30)
incomplete rheme (31 — 3n)
rheme proper   (32 or 3n + 1)

In addition, though not really relevant to this study, the transition is traditionally divided between the 'transition proper' (consisting of the temporal and modal elements, coded (21)), and the 'rest of the transition', consisting of the notional element of the verb (coded 22).

The following shows this method of analysis applied to an actual text:

Whenever the enlightened reformers expect the crowd to choose Christ (14), it (11) cheers for (21/2) Barabbas (32). Whenever some Weimar republic gets rid of some old monarchy (14), the liberated crowd (13) turns (21/2—) its republic (31) over (—22) to some Hitler (32). Then (11) what consolation (31) remains for (21/2) the brute fact that sustained progress is impossible (14)? Sheer self-deception (32) is (21) the hope of overcoming man's doom by founding a more exact social science (14). How (30—) can (21—) there (10) ever (30—) be (—21) an exact science dealing with man (14)? Science is exact (11) when dealing with predictable chemicals (32); only art (32) can (21/2—) deal with flesh (14). There (10) are indeed (32) consolations for man's precariousness (11), but they (11) consist (21/2) not of trying to end it (31) but of learning to find in it not only the lowest but also the highest reaches of the spirit, not only cruel social wrongs but the holy welding flame of the lyric imagination (32) transfiguring (21/2—) frailty (31) into (-21/2) beauty (32). This (14) is (21) the Baudelairian truth (31) that the best roses grow from manure (32).

4.4 SYSTEM NETWORKS FOR THEME AND RHEME

Figures 4.1 and 4.2 show two systems networks for the selection of different combinations of theme and rheme. It is perhaps necessary to explain some of the terminology used. 'XTheme' is a term invented to cover any type of theme, whether diatheme-oriented or theme proper-oriented. The term 'commitment' is used to cover cases where a sentence in some way signals what follows. This can be done in any of the four ways listed in the following system. The term 'Vocabulary 3' is taken from Winter 1977 and covers those nominal or verbal items which act as signals to the succeeding text, indicating clause relations in a similar way to conjunctions and discourse adjuncts. Examples are: 'cause', 'effect', 'contrast', 'similar', 'different', 'problem', 'solution', etc.

Tables 4.1 and 4.2 show the realization rules respectively for Figures 4.1 and 4.2. A few of these are somewhat speculative. This is indicated by placing these rules in brackets. Where one term in a system is mentioned and the

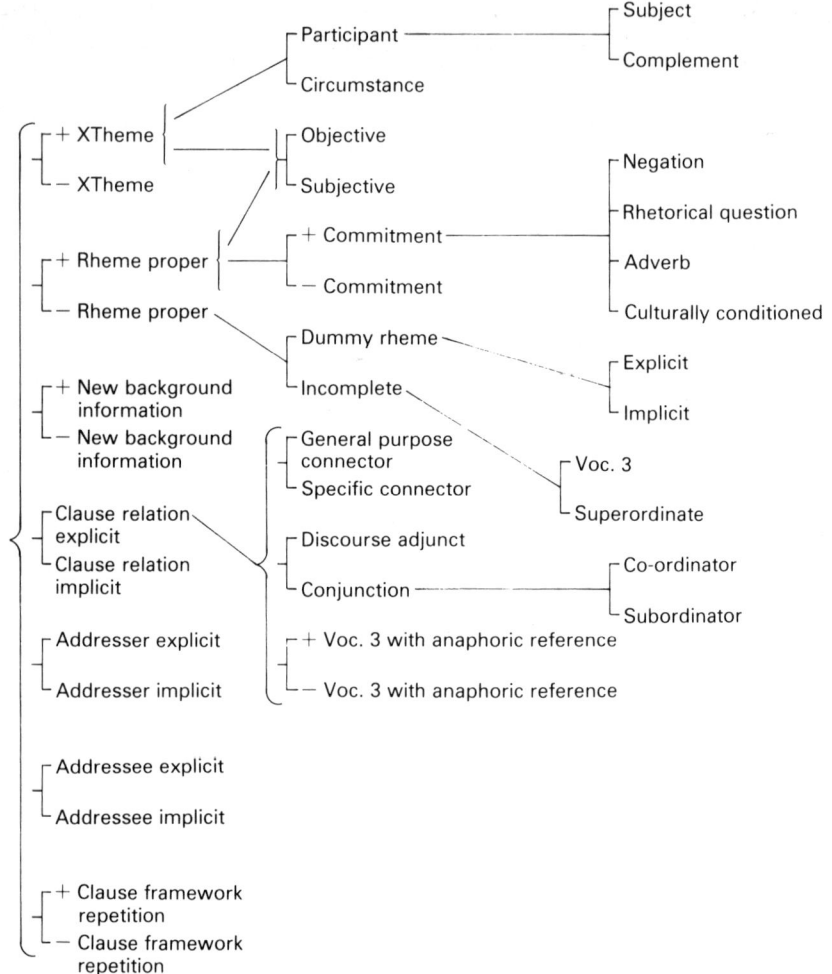

Figure 4.1 Systems at the clause level

other not, the one(s) that are not are best regarded either as negative choices which do not add to or modify the structure, or as gates whose only function is to lead into more delicate systems. Where a whole system is not found, this is because the exact way in which it is realized requires further study.

The realization operands adopted are those of Mann and Matthiessen (1985) with the addition of Berry's 'Include' operand, and are listed in the appendix.

Example 19, taken from the text used above, shows how these networks could work in practice:

(19) Whenever the enlightened reformers expect the crowd to choose Christ, it cheers for Barabbas.

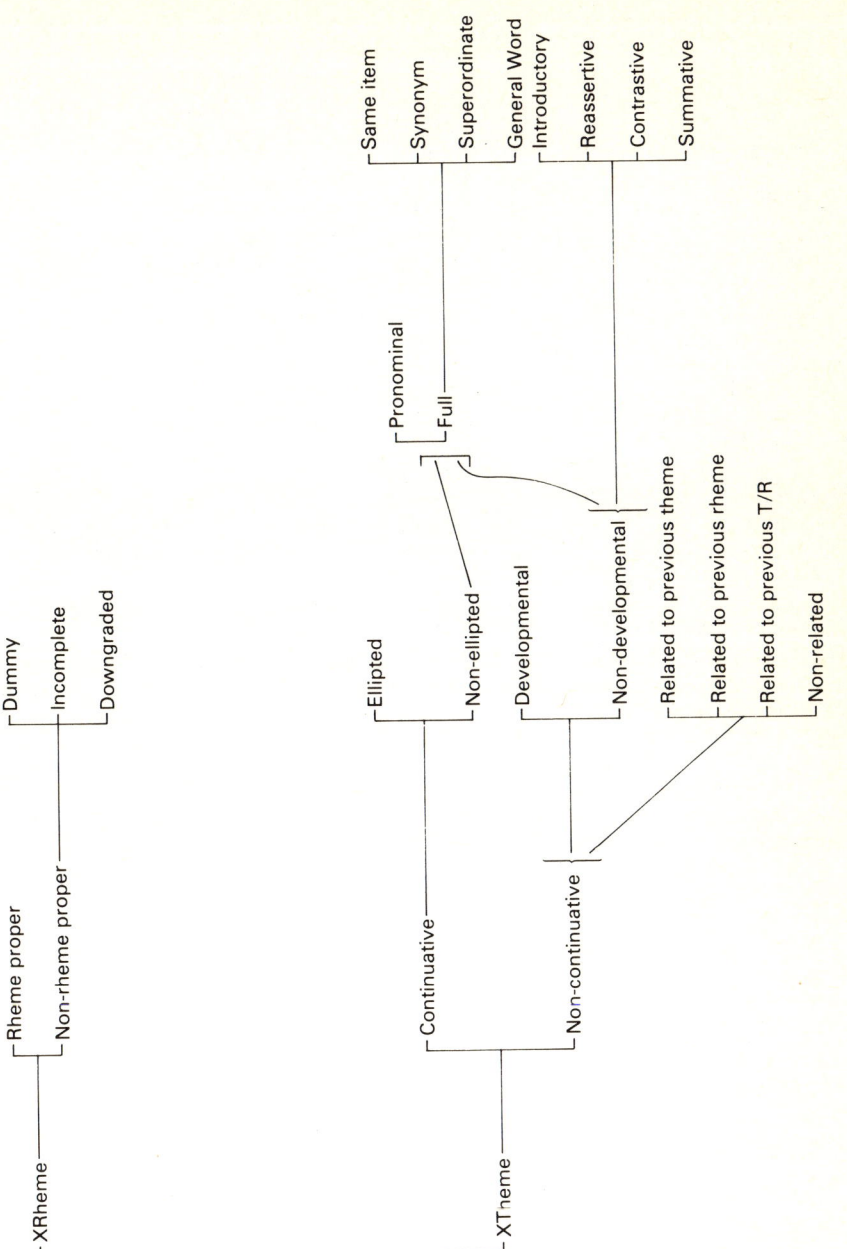

Figure 4.2 Systems at group level

Table 4.1 Realization rules for systems at clause level

Feature	Realization
+ XTheme	Include XTheme
	Enter group level system
Circumstance	Conflate XTheme Adverbial
	Reenter XTheme system
Subject	Conflate XTheme Subject
	Reenter XTheme system
Complement	Conflate XTheme Complement
	Reenter XTheme system
+ Rheme proper	Insert Rheme proper
Dummy rheme	Include Dummy rheme
Explicit	Insert Dummy rheme
Incomplete	Insert Incomplete rheme
Voc. 3	Classify Incomplete rheme Voc. 3
Superordinate	Classify Incomplete rheme Superordinate.
Subjective	OrderAtFront Rheme Proper
Negation	Expand Predicate Negative Polarity.
Rhetorical question	Preselect Rhematic clause Interrogative.
Adverb	(Insert Text ordering adverb)
Culturally conditioned	(Classify Pragmatic Structure Incomplete)
Clause relation explicit	Insert Clause relator
General Purpose connector	Preselect Clause relator General Purpose.
+ New background information	(Insert preposed B clause)
Specific connector	Preselect Clause relator Specific.
Discourse adjunct	Preselect Clause relator Discourse adjunct.
Conjunction	Preselect Clause relator Conjunction.
Coordinator	Preselect Conjunction Coordinator.
Subordinator	Preselect Conjunction Subordinator.
+ Voc. 3 with anaphoric ref.	(Classify one argument in clause Voc. 3.)
Addresser explicit	Insert addresser
Addressee explicit	Insert addressee
+ Clause Framework repetition	(Preselect Structure of RC Structures of previous Clause.)

This clause has chosen the following features from the clause level network:

+XTheme, participant, subject, +rheme proper, −commitment, objective, +new background information, clause relation implicit, addresser implicit, addressee implicit, −clause framework repetition.

The nominal group *it* has chosen:

XTheme, non-continuative, non-developmental, pronominal.

The nominal group *Barabbas* has chosen:

XRheme, rheme proper.

Table 4.2 Realization rules for systems at group level

Feature	Realization
Rheme proper	Preselect XRheme rheme proper
Dummy	Preselect XRheme dummy rheme
Incomplete	Preselect XRheme incomplete
Downgraded	Preselect XRheme downgraded
Continuative	Preselect XTheme theme proper
Non-ellipted	Insert theme proper
Pronominal	Preselect XTheme pronoun
Same item	(Preselect XTheme same as connecting element X)
Synonym	(Classify XTheme synonym of connecting element X)
Superordinate	(CXlassify XTheme superordinate of connecting element X)
General word	(Classify XTheme general word with same referent as connecting element X)
Non-continuative	Preselect XTheme diatheme
Developmental	(Outclassify head of XTheme same referent as connecting element X)
Introductory	(Classify diatheme same referent as previous rheme proper)
Reassertive	(Classify diatheme same referent as previous XTheme)
Contrastive	(Classify diatheme antonym of connecting element X)
Summative	(Classify referent of diatheme previous theme–rheme nexus)
Related to previous theme	Classify connecting element previous XTheme
Related to previous XRheme	Classify connecting element previous XRheme
Related to previous T/R nexus	Classify connecting element previous T/R nexus
Related to ellipted item	Classify connecting element previous ellipted item

4.5 CONCLUSION

Having carried out one's analysis in the way described, the search for identity chains and patterns of development can be pursued in the manner suggested, for instance, by Hasan (1983) and Lemke (1983). The main advantages of the procedure I have outlined above are that it is more delicate, showing clearly the differences between continuative and contrastive elements; and at the same time it maintains a tighter and more functional distinction between the thematic and the rhematic spheres of the text.

This brief chapter, then, should give the reader some idea of the way in which the insights of functional sentence perspective can be used to enrich the systemic approach to the textual component. It is my belief that these insights can add a dynamism to the systemic analysis of text that is otherwise lacking.

APPENDIX

Realization operands

Structure-building realization operands

Include incudes a new grammatical function in the structure while allowing it to be ellipted (operand taken from Berry 1977).
Insert places a new grammatical function into the overt realization of the unit being formed.
Conflate constrains two grammatical functions in the overt realization to be realized by the same unit at lower rank.
Expand creates structure within the overt realization, relating one grammatical function to another in a relation of constituent to subconstituent.

Feature-associating realization operands

Preselect associates a grammatical feature with a function.
Classify associates a lexical feature with a function.
Outclassify indicates that a lexical feature must be absent in a particular feature set.
Lexify specifies a particular lexical item uniquely.

Order-constraining realization operands

Order introduces left–right relations into the overt realization, constraining one group of functions to be realized immediately to the left of another.
Partition is equivalent to 'Order' in requiring left-to-right precedence, but it does not require adjacency.
OrderAtFront and **OrderAtEnd** are used to order functional constituents in initial and final positions respectively.

System negotiation operands

Enter instructs the chooser to enter another system.
Reenter instructs the chooser to enter a system previously entered, thus allowing for recursion.

BIBLIOGRAPHY

Allwood, J., Andersson, L.-G. and Dahl, O. (1977), *Logic in Linguistics*, Cambridge, Cambridge University Press.

de Beaugrande, R. and Dressler, W. (1981), *Introduction to Text Linguistics*, London, Longman.
Berry, M. (1977), *Introduction to Systemic Linguistics, Vol. 2*, London, Batsford.
Firbas, J. (1964), 'From comparative word-order studies', *Brno Studies in English*, 4, Univerzita J.E. Purkyne.
—— (1975), 'On "Existence/appearance on the scene" in FSP', *Prague Studies in English*, 16, University of Prague.
—— (1979), 'A Functional View of "Ordo Naturalis"' *Brno Studies in English*, 13, Univerzita J.E. Purkyne.
—— (1981), 'Scene and perspective', *Brno Studies in English*, 14, Univerzita J.E. Purkyne.
Halliday, M. A. K. (1967), 'Notes on transitivity and theme in English', Part II, *Journal of Linguistics*, No. 3.
—— (1985), *An Introduction to Functional Grammar*, London, Edward Arnold.
Hasan, R. (1983), 'Coherence and cohesive harmony', in Flood, J. (ed.), *Understanding Reading Comprehension*, International Reading Association Inc.
Hudson, R. (1984), *Word Grammar*, Oxford, Blackwell.
Leech, G. (1981), *Semantics*, 2nd edn, Harmondsworth, Penguin.
Lemke, J. (1983), 'Thematic analysis: systems, structures, and strategies', *Recherches semiotiques/Semiotic Enquiry*, 3, No. 2.
Mann, W. G. and Matthiessen, C. M. I. M. (1985), 'The realization operators of the Nigel Grammar', *Network*, No. 7.
Quirk, R., Greenbaum, S. *et al*. (1972), *A Grammar of Contemporary English*, London, Longman.
Sperber, D. and Wilson, D. (1986), *Relevance: Communication and Cognition*, Oxford, Blackwell.
Svoboda, A. (1983), 'Thematic elements', *Brno Studies in English*, 15, Univerzita J.E. Purkyne.
Williams, M. P. (1987), 'A comparison of the text structures of Arabic and English written texts', unpublished Ph.D. thesis, Department of Linguistics and Phonetics, University of Leeds.
Winter, E. O. (1977), 'A clause-relational approach to English texts: a study of predictive items in written discourse', *Instructional Science*, 6, Elsevier Scientific Publishing Company, Amsterdam.

5 Thematization in legislative language: the observations of Bentham and Coode in relation to the FG definition of Theme

Frederick Bowers
University of British Columbia, Vancouver, Canada

5.0 INTRODUCTION

This examination of two draftsmen's explicit reasons for thematizing particular elements of a legislative sentence is intended to underline the fact that ordinary users of language have quite definite intuitions about sentence structure in general and about thematization in particular. Motivation of thematic selection is not at one level alone, but embraces factors of semantic role, vocative address, ease of processing by the reader, and representation of real time in the order of elements in a sentence.

The intuitions of these draftsmen point to quite definite communicative functions governing choice of Theme and very much complement the observations made by Kies about thematic fronting and its motivation in speech, and the chapter as a whole is in agreement with Kies's observation that an adequate description of thematization must give a great deal of weight to function.

The chapter also implicitly agrees with the claim made by Williams that standard FG treatments of Theme are more formal than functional, but one of the theoretic conclusions of the paper queries the identification of Theme in both FG and FSP models.

In standard Functional Grammar (FG) the identification of Theme in English as 'that element that comes in first position in the clause' (Halliday 1985: 39) is distinguished from the definition of Theme, which is expressed in functional and presumably universal terms as the element serving as 'the point of departure of the message; it is that with which the clause is concerned ...' (38), the starting point of the message that the speaker wants to send—what the speaker wants to tell the hearer about. The constitution of Theme is such that it must include some ideational element realized in one of the SPCA constituents of clause, but it may also include textual and interpersonal elements. The natural, ordinary, unexceptional Theme in English is also the structural Subject of a clause, a non-Subject Theme being selected only if there is 'good reason' for doing so, and such a marked Theme is said to be foregrounded.

The problem with these functional definitions is that they are obviously true in general but vague in particular such as what specific functions might motivate a speaker's choice of Theme, both in relation to a scale of markedness and to particular features of Theme that the speaker takes for granted. In order to determine particular functions of Theme, it is necessary either to examine real non-literary discourse and to infer qualities of Theme and possible reasons for Thematic choice, or to look for explicit reasons that a speaker might consciously have in mind for his choice of Theme in a particular situation. I have chosen the second alternative, because I think that the observations of a writer about the language he uses in the transaction of his particular business has greater relevance for grammatical theory than do any number of inferences from a given text, especially a literary text, where no real uptake in action is demanded and which makes a virtue of ambiguity. For the language-theorist, the clear pane of practical language is more revealing than the stained glass of literary language.

The observations that I shall examine here concern statutory instructions made by a legislature to be followed by the ordinary citizen and monitored by the courts. The kind of language used in statutes is practically revealing about the functions of language generally, and it is concerned with real action. Indeed, law and language are ultimately inseparable, in that language is the indispensable instrument of law. The social outcome of legal language is serious, and its users take it seriously, relating the gravity of Field to that of Mode. Most important of all, both courts and draftsmen make explicit comments on matters of intention, expression and interpretation within the confines of particular social and legal situations.

The observations to be examined here are those of two of the most influential reformers of British statutory drafting in the nineteenth century—Jeremy Bentham, academically concerned with jurisprudence and professionally involved with the drafting of codes, and George Coode, a conveyancer who drafted many bills for the governments of his day and who was responsible for the consolidation of the Poor Laws and the revision of many other social statutes. The objects of my examination are the comments on sentence structure and thematization made by these two draftsmen, and especially their reasons for preferring the thematization of one element over another. The aim of the examination is to relate their explicit comments to the standard Halliday definition of Theme, and to suggest extensions of the definition where their comments indicate that extension may be necessary. The implications of their observations will be seen to have theoretic relevance for the current FG identification of Theme.

Bentham's commentary appears in his monograph 'Nomography' which was published posthumously in 1839. His concern is with the practical purposes of legislative language, and it leads him to two interconnected principles: first, that law is 'addressed always to a person or set of persons at whose hands compliance is constantly looked for' in respect to their intellectual, volitional and behavioural capacities (Bentham 1839: 233); second, that the form of law as the subservient but essential instrument of the matter of law should be principally concerned with facilitating the reader's understanding of legal provisions as the necessary preliminary to attaining the practical purpose of those provisions. The achievement of intended effect, Bentham notes, 'will depend in the instance of each individual on whom the law calls for his obedience, on the hold which it has happened to take upon his mind' (237). Thus, the address of a law and its intelligibility to the reader constitute the fundamentals from which all Bentham's specific compositional recommendations derive, and both principles underlie his frequent references to sentence structure and thematization.

The principle of addressing a person leads Bentham to prefer the categorial, Subject–Predicate form of sentence—'Every person who fails to pay his rate by the due date shall be liable to a fine', over the hypothetical form that thematizes a conditional clause—'If a person fails to pay his rate by the due date, he shall be liable to a fine', which he derides as difficult to understand, prone to indefinite extension and addressed to no one in particular. He might also have observed that this older, Anglo-Saxon form assumes the primary audience to be the Court rather than the citizen, as it looks at the law in terms of penalties under the presumption that the law has already been broken. Such address and presumption, of course, runs entirely counter to Bentham's view of the written law as a means of leading the reasonable man to legal compliance. Bentham is at pains to suggest that if law-makers want to achieve the practical end of compliance, they must clearly identify the Agent of the intended action by thematizing it wherever possible; moreover, the sections of an Act should be arranged in terms of the set of Agents, whereby the Agent-Theme of the sentence becomes also the Topic of the section in which the sentence occurs. In this recommendation, Bentham is relating theme structure with information structure to serve the aim of Agent identification from the points of view of both the draftsman and the reader. The directness of expression in the Agent-Action structure is complemented by accessibility of reference in terms of a constant given Theme and a series of enumerated Rhemes. However, the primary purpose of thematizing the Agent remains that of getting the reader's attention so that he takes note of the action expressed in the Rheme, which will thereby 'have presented and fixed itself in that person's mind' (235).

The thematization of the Agent is a special case of Bentham's broader dictum regarding sentence structure: 'Rule: Whatever be the principal object which your sentence is designed to bring into view, bring forward as early as you conveniently can the word employed in the expression of it—if you can make the sentence begin with the same word, so much the better' (268). This broader rule turns out to be concerned with ease of processing by the reader, in that Bentham justifies the rule thus: 'If a word expressive of another idea come before it [i.e. the 'principal object'] the mind is in the first instance put upon a wrong scent; and a sort of correction and partial change of conception must have place, before the idea meant to be conveyed is apprehended' (268). Further, Bentham suggests that thematizing the principal object brings about expressive liveliness by allowing the reader to grasp the meaning of the sentence quickly: 'the idea of spiritedness in the discourse is suggested . . . the idea meant to be conveyed being apprehended on the instant, and without further trouble' (268). In the rule as a whole, Bentham assumes that Theme has a function of prominence that closely relates to a reader's mental processing of the sentence in real time.

Bentham's concern with ease of processing is particularly apparent in his discussion of exceptions and limitations in statutory provisions. Where a provision is not intended to operate universally, the exception should be thematized, because

> Being placed at the very commencement of the sentence, it gives a sort of WARNING which has the effect of anticipating and keeping the door of the mind shut against all those false conceptions which in the first instance ... would be among the effect of a proposition if presented in the first instance, a degree of extent which was not intended and which as the sentence advanced would receive contradiction. [269] [author's emphasis]

Similarly, he suggests that limitative clauses should be prefixed to each of the principal clauses of provisions with more than one clause, on the grounds that thematization of limitative clauses gives notice

> that the proposition which is about to follow is not meant to be given as expressive of its author's meaning, till after the portion of extent, indicated by the antecedent, the limitative clause which is thus employed to introduce it, has been taken out of it. Thus it is, that to the reader the unpleasant sensation, the sort of false step in question, is saved. [254]

Although Bentham, like some modern rhetoricians, seems incapable of writing clearly about clear writing, one may infer that one of the major advantages he sees in appropriate thematization, whether of 'principal object', reader-Agent or limitative clause, is ease of processing by the reader and a consequent effect of pleasure that will make the reader more willing to obey the law. He frequently criticizes contemporary statutory expression for the unpleasantness, unease and uncertainty that it engenders in the mind of the reader; presumably, his promotion of ease of reading is an instance of his more general pleasure-principle. The quality of expression whereby meaning is made quickly accessible he calls 'notoriety', and he presents as a major principle of nomography that: 'It is only in the proportion that it is thus notorious that a law can be productive of any of the smallest particle of good effect' (243). A sentence has notoriety when it gains by its form the immediate attention of the reader and permits the reader to grasp its meaning without rescanning. The appropriate choice of Theme is, for Bentham, a significant if not crucial factor in achieving notoriety and thus constitutes a fundamental principle of statutory composition. Moreover, Bentham sees his prescribed sentence formula of (Exception) + Addressed Agent + Action as an aid to the draftsman as well, in that the formula sharpens the definition for the writer and helps avoid the situation where 'the legislator is himself prevented from understanding what he himself is doing when he writes' (242).

In terms of the characteristics of Theme and Given, Bentham's motivations for Theme selection seem to introduce a fresh element that cuts across the primarily writer-oriented nature of Theme and reader-oriented nature of

Given, in that what Bentham presupposes about Theme is its iconic and real-time effect as a means of address and attention-getting, and as a kind of limitative 'frame' within which a provision operates. The iconic nature of Theme seems to be consciously recognized by Bentham in that he uses expressions such as 'to bring into view', 'to bring forward', and 'to present' in reference to thematization. Because the intention and effect of thematization are to make interpretation easier for the reader by having the sentence structure mimic the order of attention, it appears that Bentham's assumption about the major metafunction served by Theme is interpersonal rather than textual.

I shall return to the question of iconic thematization later, but now I turn to George Coode's observations (Coode 1848) which appeared first as an appendix to his revision of the Poor Laws, but which have been reissued many times as a monograph and have had a very marked effect on Commonwealth and American drafting practice. Like Bentham, Coode stresses that his rules of legislative composition are entirely natural, both in their relation to law and to 'the common popular structure of English' (376), and whose application may be observed in the bills prepared by the best draftsmen, which are 'remarkable for their simplicity and directness, and . . . for the popularity of their style and construction' (377). Throughout his treatise, Coode draws attention to the way in which his rules maintain a harmony between concept and expression, relating the fundamental legal notions of rights and duties to the structure of the legislative sentence.

Coode opts for thematization of the affected person ('legal subject') whether Agent or Patient in a provision, because the purpose of law is to secure or limit some benefit for some person or persons:

It is obviously impossible to confer in effect a right, privilege or power on a thing, or to impose an obligation on a thing, or in other words to affect a thing with a command, or prohibition, or permission . . . It is only possible to confer a Right, or Privilege, or Power on one set of persons . . . The Person is the LEGAL SUBJECT of legal action . . . None but persons are the legal subjects of a law, however they may be verbally disguised or kept out of view. [324–5] [author's emphasis]

From this jurisprudential principle Coode develops a formula similar to Bentham's, whereby every universal legal provision consists of a Legal Subject as Theme and a Legal Action as Rheme. The essential feature of the Theme is that it must be Agent or Patient of the Legal Action. Coode does not make a rule that only the Agent and active voice should be used, but says: 'When the subject is to be active the whole of the enacting verb will be active, SHALL FORFEIT etc., and where the subject is to submit . . . the whole enacting verb will be passive, as in SHALL BE IMPRISONED etc.' (329) (author's emphasis). What is important for Coode in terms of voice is that where it is intended that the legal subject should take action, the verb should be active, so that expressions like 'notice shall be given by the surveyor' are avoided. Semantically agentive propositions expressed in the passive voice Coode finds 'weak and inexpressive . . . and frequently wholly unintelligible' (329).

Impersonal expressions such as 'It shall be lawful for any person to . . .' Coode thinks to be 'needlessly indefinite where the person on whom the right, power or privilege is to be conferred are easily denoted' (328). His rejection of this kind of predicated Theme is interesting in that it underlies his concern for achieving some kind of personal address in the Theme, even though the predicated Theme is in fact more consonant with the basic illocutionary force of a statute, which is declarative rather than directive. His jurisprudential stance is clearly in support of what is really a rhetorical charade in which the draftsman appears to be immediately, or as immediately as the third person permits, addressing the reader with directive speech-act force, rather than enumerating the rights and duties declared by Parliament in its Act. His rejection of the impersonal form suggests that, like Bentham, Coode is concerned with thematic address as well as with agency. To this implied function of address, Coode adds the motivation of specifying the extent of a provision's application in the Theme: 'The description of the LEGAL SUBJECT determines the EXTENT of the law . . . Hence the importance of rules for securing the highest possible degree of clearness in the description and enumeration of the LEGAL SUBJECTS' (324). Coode further supports his preference for a thematized legal subject on iconic grounds, pointing out that 'The LEGAL SUBJECT of an enactment is always conceived as existing before the LEGAL ACTION can operate' (328) (author's emphasis).

Coode's secondary motivation for thematization is also similar to Bentham's desire for 'notoriety' in that he sees the consistent choice of address agent as Theme to permit greater clarity and easier accessibility of meaning. The legal subject and legal action can be kept 'distinct in form and in place from other parts of the legal sentence' (328) and thus may be quickly identified by the reader. Legal subjects and actions should, he advises: 'not only be distinguished by the construction of the sentence, but they should be instantly discovered by the eye, and each distinguished by the other' (338). The aim for clarity is mixed with the wish to address the legal subject directly: 'it is . . . all important that the attention of the public and of the legislators should be certainly and easily directed' (325).

Like Bentham, Coode advocates thematization of limiting case and conditions; however, unlike Bentham, he justifies his rule on both jurisprudential and iconic grounds as well as on grounds of non-redundant processing by the reader. His legal principle is that 'legislation is not a science, but a practical art' (333) because it has to apply itself to particular cases. Perhaps with Bentham in mind, he says: 'Generalising the expression of the law is more the work of the scholastic professor; specializing the law the proper task of the practical legislator' (333). However, he finds that without some compositional

> rule for expressing the limitation of the law to its specific occasions, the draftsman first draws an enactment in terms too general for his purpose; he then attempts to detract from its generality by interpolated limitations, qualifications, exceptions, and by that bane of all correct composition, the Proviso. [333–4]

Coode, therefore, makes the rule that the circumstances in which the law is intended to operate 'should be invariably described BEFORE any other part of the enactment is expressed' (334).

Coode motivates his choice of Theme position for the phrase or clause expressing the *casus legis* primarily on grounds of easy processing by the reader. The proper place of the legal Case, he says, 'is at the beginning of the sentence, as it is misleading the reader to commence an enactment as if it were universal, and to wind it up by a parenthetical qualification or proviso which limits it to certain occasions only' (334). He is extremely critical of 'wretched provisos' that often introduce mere exceptions rather than limiting cases; in his criticism, he shows not only a concern for ease of processing, but also a revulsion against placing the least general case in the information Focus position of the legislative sentence. It is clear from his many remarks on the syntactic position of the words expressing the legal action that he wants the Rheme and New positions of his legislative sentence to be devoted to legal action only, uncluttered by other content. However, his motivation is more to prevent unnecessary reading on the part of the statute-user rather than one of logical proportioning of whole and part, as is shown by his observation that: 'The case being placed first, the first few words of the sentence answer immediately to the enquirer whether his case is included in the provision or not; whether he need read on or should proceed to seek the law applicable to his circumstances in another clause' (344).

Coode's concern for interpretative accessibility and economy of action makes him also put the legal conditions (the steps that must be taken before the legal action can operate) after the statement of limiting case but before the legal subject, as a kind of appositive Theme: 'Having ascertained that there is law applicable to his case, [the reader] next learns what is to be done to make it operative' (344). It seems from this remark that Coode is maintaining an iconic–tactical dimension of motivation, both in terms of the law itself and its operative steps in real time, and in terms of action to be taken by the statute-user. He observes that the legal conditions are invariably precedent to the legal provision itself, and he is quite literal in his emblemism of reader-action, saying that because the steps to be taken by the statute-user are always serial,

> The order of performance in time ought to be carefully observed in expressing them; so that the person . . . on whom they are imposed may see the order in which to proceed to realise all the conditions of the legal action, and may be in no doubt when those conditions are all complied with. For the reason that the legal action is postponed and cannot act upon the legal subject until all these conditions are complied with, the expression of the conditions ought immediately to precede that of the legal subject. [342]

What conclusions may one draw from the commentaries of Bentham and Coode about the nature of sentence Theme? Both commentators see Theme as most naturally realized by an Agent or Patient, as doer or sufferer of the action expressed in the Rheme. Such a realization provides a semantically unmarked Theme in the sense that, for English, agents and perceivers constitute the highest elements in the hierarchy of case-marked propositional arguments for promotion to syntactic Subject. However, each commentator adds reasons besides that of case superiority for his choice of animate Theme. Bentham sees the animate Theme in terms of the addressed person, as a necessary first step in the sentence to gain the reader's attention for the injunction that follows in the Rheme; Coode's reasons are both semantic and iconic—only persons can do things, and the legal person pre-exists the command in the Rheme; what constitutes the cause of the action in the Rheme and what is first in time should come first in the sentence. Both commentators are quite certain that the choice of an animate Theme will normally lead to easier sentence-processing by the reader.

Bentham's emphasis on address may be related theoretically to Halliday's interpersonal vocative element, not as a separate item in a multiple Theme, but rather as a combined interpersonal and ideational Theme in the third person. Although it may seem paradoxical to talk about a third person vocative, the general modal expression of a statute in terms of *shall* and *may* makes statutory provisions similar to utterances like *Class will stand*, where a representative sentence with an ambiguous modal is passed off as a directive sentence. If such quasi-directives are admitted, then the thematic function of address assumed by Bentham confirms the interpersonal vocative function in Halliday's definition.

Coode's iconic functions of Theme, of course, can operate only where Theme is positionally fronted, as it is in English but not, apparently, in all languages, so his observation need not be universally valid, a constraint that might account for the Thematic characteristics of logical cause and temporal priority not being counted as definitional features of Theme in Halliday. However, for English and other SVO languages, these features are significant features of Theme.

The comments made by Bentham and Coode about the thematization of case, condition and exception as a means of preventing the reader from having to read the whole of a provision that ultimately does not apply to his situation, or to rescan a sentence in order to understand it at all, fall within Halliday's observation that the Subject will normally constitute clause Theme unless there is good reason for choosing something else, and, more specifically, that a Thematic non-Subject element may be chosen because 'it is being explicitly foregrounded as the Theme of the clause' (45). However, the reasons of economy of scanning and of mental processing that Bentham and Coode offer to justify the selection of a marked Theme do not, I think, appear as a function of Theme in standard FG, though they constitute for SVO languages a rather important quality.

Of course, agency, address, cause–effect and temporal order are all different aspects of sentence iconicity; they are also hearer-oriented, whereas Theme is usually thought of as primarily speaker-oriented. The hearer-orientation of the Bentham–Coode observations about Theme might, therefore, be thought to disqualify them as Theme features. However, as Halliday points out (278), Theme is always selected by the speaker, so features which might in fact be chosen with the hearer in mind are none the less Thematic features; moreover, they are features which add a great deal of particular detail to the general characteristics of Theme as they are at present described in FG. The observations of Bentham and Coode clearly confirm the general definition of Theme, but they extend and particularize the definition considerably.

Furthermore, the iconic nature of Thematic function inferred from the Bentham–Coode commentaries raises interesting questions about Thematic function in non-SVO languages, and these questions lead in turn to questions about the theory itself. One must ask whether Theme may ever occur elsewhere in a clause than at the beginning, in view of the fact that all the particular characteristics of Theme enumerated here depend on the Theme's appearing as the first element. Of course, what I have been calling Theme might, in fact, be Given, but if so, it cannot be in the Halliday sense of 'This is not news', because in all its uses as address, agent-identification and temporal presentation, the Theme certainly is 'news' of the greatest significance to the reader. We are left, consequently, with the conclusion that in any but the most general sense, not only the identification but also the definition of Theme essentially depends upon its syntactic position at the front of a clause. This conclusion entails that any other kind of apparent Theme, for example, one marked morphologically but not ordered as first element in a clause, cannot satisfy any of the functional definitions of Theme at all. It follows then that either the FG characterization of Theme is unworkable in any detailed way for non-SVO languages, or that non-SVO languages are unable to thematize at all in any but the narrow FSP sense of suppressing communicative dynamism.

BIBLIOGRAPHY

Bentham, Jeremy (1839), 'Nomography, or the art of indicting laws', in Bowring, John (ed.), *Works of Jeremy Bentham, Vol. III*, London, Barton, 231–83.
Coode, George (1848), 'On legislative expression', in Driedger, E. (1976), *The Composition of Legislation*, Ottawa, Department of Justice, 317–78.
Halliday, M. A. K. (1985), *An Introduction to Functional Grammar*, London, Edward Arnold.

Part III
Insights from discourse analysis

6 The structure of family conversation in Yoruba English*

Femi Akindele
University of Ife, Ile-Ife, Nigeria

6.0 INTRODUCTION

Most researchers on institutional discourse have concentrated on native English settings for their analysis and description of data (see, for instance, Sinclair and Coulthard 1975; Coulthard and Ashby 1976; Stubbs 1974; Harris 1980; Tucker, this volume). It seems that no attempt has been made to examine the structure of any type of institutional discourse in non-native, English-using communities where English is used as a second language. This chapter examines the structure of family conversation in Yoruba English context where English is used as a second language. More specifically, it investigates speakers' rights to initiate conversation by finding out whether speakers' rights differ with different types of initiation in the Yoruba English family conversations. In investigating this, the chapter explores the relationship between socio-semantic concepts like 'control' and 'dominance' and their manifestations in the discourse.

This work and the others on institutional discourse are not only different in terms of data and settings; they also differ in methodology. For example, while this chapter investigates the pattern of social dominance as independent variables, takes discourse patterns as dependent variables, and then considers the linguistic realization of socio-semantic patterns on the linguistic level of discourse, Tucker in the following chapter takes discourse structures as given and studies their realization in syntax and intonation by making use of a service encounter corpus of data collected in a bookshop. In order to be able to appreciate fully the preoccupation of this chapter, I shall explain briefly the notion of Yoruba English.

---

* This is a revised version of the paper given at the International Systemic Workshop held at the University of Kent at Canterbury in July 1986. I am grateful to the members of the workshop for their various suggestions on the chapter. I am particularly grateful to Margaret Berry, Chris Butler, Jean Ure, Robin Fawcett, Hilary Hillier and Ruth Riley for their useful comments on the chapter.

6.1 THE CONCEPT OF YORUBA ENGLISH

Among the various non-native users of English in Nigeria are the Yorubas. They constitute one of the largest ethnic groups with a population of about nineteen million. Yoruba English is developed and widely used among them.

Yoruba is the language of the Yoruba people found in Western Nigeria. The co-existence within the Yoruba-speaking community of English and Yoruba over a long period of time results in the blend of the two languages into a special variety of English referred to as Yoruba-English. The influence of the Yoruba language on English seems noticeable at the various levels of linguistic description, namely phonology, lexis, grammar and discourse (see Afolayan 1968; Atoye 1980; Bamgbose 1971, 1983 for a full discussion of such influences).

Yoruba-English is influenced by the culture of the community in which it is used. As English undergoes thorough acculturation in the Yoruba context, it shows various degrees of Yoruba culture.

Since culture cannot be divorced from language, and since the Yoruba community would exhibit its norms of social interaction, it could be argued that although the Yoruba-English bilinguals may share the English language with the native speakers in an interactional discourse, the structural organization of such discourse may not be the same. The older adults initiate and control conversations particularly when issues of importance are being discussed and decisions have to be taken. The occupant of the lower role usually behaves according to the dictates of the occupant of the higher role. If he behaves contrary to the expectations of his social position in the interactional event, he may be reprimanded by the sanctioning power of the occupant of the higher role. However, the occupant of the lower role may violate the norm. He may do this by seeking permission from the occupant of the higher role before making any important contributions to the ongoing talk. The occupant of the higher role may decide to honour or refuse his request.

Rigidity in the social hierarchy may account for why certain participants, for example, have restricted speaking rights while others are free to use their participation rights. As Gumperz (1972: 220) stresses:

Before we can judge a speaker's social intent, we must know something about the norms defining the appropriateness of linguistically acceptable alternates for particular types of speakers; these norms vary among subgroups and among social settings.

It seems clear from the foregoing claim that an understanding of the cultural life of the Yoruba-English bilinguals will be necessary for the interpretation of the use of speakers' rights and the structural organization of discourse of Yoruba-English.

6.2 DATA FOR THE STUDY

Ten families were recorded for this study, made up of parents aged 50–56, and children aged 18–25. There are five participants in each of the recordings, made up of two males and three females. The parents' group comprises one male and one female, while the children's group comprises one male and two females.

In an attempt to record the data, I did not contact any of the members of the families; neither did I inform them about my intention. The reason is that socio-culturally in Yoruba tradition, one does not need to inform friends, relations or acquaintances formally about one's intention to visit unless such a visit is special. Therefore, I visited the families I recorded on many occasions before the data were actually collected. The recordings were carried out surreptitiously.

The participants were told about the recordings after the exercise was over, and the intention of the researcher was made known. The participants were surprised at the recordings, but, however, allowed the transcripts to be used, provided that their identities were made confidential, and the tapes were returned to them.

In an attempt to transcribe the data, all the tapes were listened to repeatedly in order to gain more detail about the conversations. Then from each of the recordings, ten long passages were selected for transcription. The selection of the passages was based on the audibility of the recordings.

6.3 ON ANALYSING THE FAMILY DATA

In order to analyse my data in terms of the preoccupation of this chapter, I reviewed research in discourse analysis. Sinclair and Coulthard's (1975) (henceforth SC) work on classroom interaction and the subsequent development of the theory turned out to be very useful; see also Coulthard and Brazil (1979, 1981) (henceforth CB). They are useful in the sense that they show who initiates and controls discourse, what strategies are used, and how the roles of speaker and listener pass from one participant to another. These frameworks are further adapted and expanded to accommodate the data for this study.

It should be stressed that the framework discussed in this chapter is a brief one, showing how the basic categories used in the analysis of the data were arrived at. The reader is, therefore, referred to Akindele (1986) for details of the framework.

6.4 FRAMEWORK FOR ANALYSIS

Sinclair and Coulthard (1975: 21) say that a typical exchange in classroom interaction 'consists of an INITIATION by the teacher, followed by a RESPONSE from the pupil, followed by FEEDBACK' (author's emphasis).

Three types of exchange are identified. They are Inform, Elicit and Direct. The moves which initiate the exchanges have, respectively, Informative, Elicitation and Directive as their head acts.

Sinclair and Coulthard (1975: 28) define an ELICITATION as an act which functions to request a linguistic response; a DIRECTIVE is described as an act which functions to request a non-linguistic response; and an INFORMATIVE is an act which functions to pass on information and to which the appropriate response is simply an acknowledgement that one is listening. These three acts determine the exchange types which Sinclair and Coulthard label Inform, Elicit and Direct.

It seems clear from the definition of the acts which determine exchange types that Sinclair and Coulthard do not offer a definition of initiation in general. What can be inferred from their proposals are the definitions of initiating moves of exchange types—Inform, Elicit and Direct.

I tried to apply SC's categories to my data. I found that the problem that arises from their definition is not that of identifying each of the exchange types in my data. The problem came when I wanted to find a working definition of exchange which would apply to all exchanges in my data. This matters because if exchanges have nothing in common, then there is no motivation for regarding the exchange as a unit. Similarly, if there is nothing that all initiating moves have in common, there is no motivation for regarding the initiating moves as a distinct category.

As can be seen from the discussion of SC's exchange types above, although SC have criteria for identifying each type of exchange—Inform, Elicit and Direct—they do not have any motivation for regarding them as members of the same unit. What they say about the exchange being the minimal unit of interactional discourse needs to be translated into precise recognition criteria before it can be considered a working definition usable in the analysis of data other than their own. In the light of this, I examined Coulthard and Brazil's (1979) work on exchange structure.

Coulthard and Brazil (1979) define an Initiating move as a move which predicts a succeeding move. A Response move is predicted but it does not predict a Following move, though feedback may occur following it.

From these definitions one could infer that an Initiating move is defined as a move which predicts a Following move, and consequently a marker of exchange boundary.

CB's definition of initiation provides me with a clear way of identifying the initiating moves in my data, and consequently a clear way of recognizing the boundaries of exchanges. It provides a definition of initiation in general which SC do not provide.

6.5 TOWARDS A WORKING DEFINITION OF THE EXCHANGE

The examination of various attempts to define and identify Initiating moves and Exchange types shows that Coulthard and Brazil's definition of Initiating moves seems to be the most useful in the sense that it suggests precisely a reliable criterion for identifying all initiations and, consequently, exchange boundaries. In other words, all Initiating moves are alike in that they are predictive.

In view of this criterion, I adopt Coulthard and Brazil's predictiveness of the Initiating moves. More specifically, Coulthard and Brazil (1979: 39) suggest that all types of Initiating move are predictive in the sense that they begin a new and set-up expectation of responses. I shall, however, try to show that in my data responses to Initiating moves of Inform exchanges are just as obligatory as are the responses to the Initiating moves of other types of exchange, so that the Initiating moves of all exchanges can truly be seen as predictive.

In this way, all Initiating moves Inform, Elicit and Direct will be considered to be alike in the sense that they predict a following move.

The predictiveness of Initiating moves can be illustrated with the following extract from the family data:

```
Ye.  Bring some sugar—D. please       1 I ⎫ A  predicting
D.   ((non-linguistic activity))       2 R ⎭    predicted
            (15)                       3
Su.  Have you seen K recently?         4 I ⎫ B  predicting
Ye.  No                                5 R ⎭    predicted
F.   Is he around?                     6 I ⎫ C  predicting
Ye.  No                                7 R ⎭    predicted
F.   K sells insurance policy
     and nobody wants to buy
     before christmas                  8 I ⎫ D  predicting
Ye.  That's right                      9 R ⎭    predicted
            (Ib. YESLFD)
```

I shall attempt to show the predictive power of the Initiating move, particularly that of the Inform exchange by demonstrating that participants in the family conversations orient to the predictiveness by protesting when the predicted response does not occur.

6.6 PARTICIPANTS' ORIENTATION TO INFORMING MOVES

In this section, I shall try to show that co-participants themselves orient to the fact that an Informing move expects a Succeeding move to follow; that is, a Response move is obligatory in discourse. I shall show how a 'violation' of this organization, and the reaction to such a 'violation', may show that co-participants actually orient to the contributions of one another in discourse. Let us examine the following extract to support the argument.

```
Ad.  I'll be attending my friend's     1 ⎫ A
     wedding next week—dad               ⎬
Su.  Yes                               2 ⎭
Ad.  He is getting married to R        3 ⎫ B
Su.            (6)                     4 ⎭ Su searches for
                                           something on the floor
```

Ad.	Are you listening—?	5	C
Su.	Yes	6	
Su.	He is getting married to his former girlfriend	7	D
Im.	That's right	8	

Participant Ad. initiates the talk with an Informing move 1 and participant Su. responds to the initiation (move 2). After exchange A has been successfully negotiated, speaker Ad. initiates exchange B with an Informing move 3. However, there seems to be a 'breakdown' in exchange B. Indeed, such an exchange could be regarded as incomplete in some sense because the expected Succeeding move fails to occur.

I will argue that this type of breakdown is a pointer to participant Ad.'s orientation to Su. and his contribution, and the fact that Su.'s contribution must necessarily follow. The six-second pause indicates the lapse which occurs. Ad. then shows his reaction to the absence of Su.'s contribution by checking whether he is attending to what he is saying to him. The check (move 5) can be considered as a kind of initiation of another type of exchange labelled C, which is followed by Ad.'s response (move 6) that he is listening to the ongoing talk. Ad. then carries on with his series of contributions which continue to receive Su.'s response. Su. does this perhaps to avoid being censored again.

The type of breakdown which occurs in the talk and the subsequent censor that follows is evidence that the type of move which initiates exchange A is predictive. It can further be claimed that such a breakdown and the attempt to rectify it show how participants orient to a stretch of discourse.

In the foregoing section, I have attempted to solve the problem by defining and identifying initiations in the family data. I have shown that even an Inform predicts a response, and that when such a response fails to occur after an Inform the absence is perceived, in ethnomethodological terms, as a NOTICEABLE absence. This means that Inform, like the other types of initiation—Eliciting and Directing—can be regarded as +predicting. There is, then, a feature that all Initiating moves have in common, predictiveness. Therefore, it means that there is now a criterion for analysing a move as an Initiating move. It also follows that there is now a criterion for analysing exchange boundaries.

On the basis of my recognition criteria for Initiating moves, I define an exchange as the minimal unit of interactional discourse marked by a move which predicts a Following move. The predicted move which occurs as a result of the prediction does not predict any succeeding move, but a voluntary move(s) may occur following it.

However, the definitions of the unit exchange and the identification of Initiating moves do not provide all the answers to the issues I want to investigate. As well as identifying exchanges as exchanges, I need to be able to classify the different types of exchange that may be found in my data. For this reason, I examine how Sinclair and Coulthard's and Coulthard and Brazil's proposals could help in the classification of exchanges in my text.

6.7 ON CLASSIFYING EXCHANGES

Sinclair and Coulthard (1975) propose two types of exchange labelled Boundary and Teaching exchanges. Boundary exchanges are realized by Framing and Focusing moves. Teaching exchanges are subdivided into Free and Bound exchanges. Those that are regarded as free are Teacher Inform, Pupil Inform, Teacher Elicit, Pupil Elicit, Teacher Direct and Teacher Check.

The function of the exchanges are said to be informing, eliciting, directing and checking, respectively. The structure of the exchanges is as follows: Teacher Inform—I(R), Pupil Inform—IF, Teacher Elicit—IRF, Pupil Elicit—IR, Teacher Direct—IR(F), and Teacher Check—IR(F). The enclosed elements are optional.

The exchanges that are regarded as Bound are (i) Reinitiation and (ii) Repeat, Listing and Reinforce. All Bound exchanges are claimed to be produced by the Teacher.

It should be stressed that in analysing the extracts, I was aware that there were no teachers and pupils in my data. However, like the classroom which is hierarchically structured into higher and lower social roles occupied by the teacher and pupil respectively, the family seems to be hierarchically ordered into pairs of higher and lower roles. Parents occupy the higher roles while children occupy the lower roles. Participant roles in classroom and family can therefore be compared on the basis of hierarchical ordering. The teacher is comparable with parents, and the pupil can be compared with children. In view of this, I try to find out whether what Sinclair and Coulthard say about teachers is relevant to parents and whether what they say about pupils is relevant to children in my data.

In addition, I try to find out whether the exchange types summarized above fit my data in respect of the four defining criteria—participant roles, the structure, function and position of the exchange types.

The analyses show that Sinclair and Coulthard's classification of exchanges can be used in analysing my data. All that needs to be done is a modification/redefinition of, and probably a change in the terminology used for, some of the categories. I changed the terminology Free Teaching Exchanges which include Inform, Elicit and Direct initiated by both the Teacher and Pupil. This is because I cannot use the terms Teacher Elicit or Pupil Elicit in my analysis. I regard Inform, Elicit and Direct as types of Informatory exchange. Further, where Sinclair and Coulthard's categories were inadequate, I proposed new categories.

The framework also enabled me to classify my data into Bound exchange types—Repeat and Reinitiation which I labelled Regulatory Positive exchange.

I then considered CB's classification of exchanges. I found that their classification does not consider all possible exchange types in discourse, and indeed it does not help in classifying the remaining exchange types in the family data.

I therefore proposed two categories which I labelled Prefatory and Regulatory Negative exchanges, since none of the categories examined above fit the examples in my data.

The analyses carried out therefore show that there were broadly three exchange types in the Yoruba-English family conversations labelled Prefatory, Informatory and Bound exchanges. These categories are briefly described in the following sections.

6.8 THE PREFATORY EXCHANGE

It seems that Prefatory exchanges occur frequently in naturally occurring interactional discourse, and there could be several criteria for recognizing them. The criteria that are proposed for recognizing the Prefatory exchanges in the family data for this study will be discussed under the following headings: (a) the predictive power of the exchange, (b) its non-terminality in discourse, and (c) its linguistic markers.

6.8.1 Predictive nature of the Prefatory exchange

I have suggested that one important aspect of the definition of an exchange is that its initiating move predicts a following move. The Prefatory exchange, like other exchange types, has an initiating move which predicts a succeeding move.

There is, however, a second type of prediction which the Prefatory exchange makes. This type of prediction is made by the Prefatory exchange itself, rather than the Initiating move making such a prediction. In this way, the Prefatory exchange predicts something to follow immediately. That 'something' is not precise, as any type of move which expresses information content can occur. In other words, unlike the first type which makes precise predictions, the second type predicts a wide range of 'responses' as the reasons for the occurrence of the exchange itself, as in:

Ye.	Mama B?	1	A
Su.	Yes	2	
Ye.	Do you want more beer?	3	
Su.	Yes	4	B
	thanks (12)	5	
	(Ib. YESLFD)		

In this example, exchange A is the Prefatory exchange. The Initiating move in the exchange, that is 1, predicts the occurrence of 2. The 'response' to the Initiating move shows that the recipient has accepted the invitation or call predicted, by giving his attention in readiness for the 'message' that is going to be passed on by the initiator. The prediction is not just a prediction that anything can follow; it is a prediction that a particular response must follow a limited range of possible responses.

The second type of prediction can be explained in terms of exchange A predicting the occurrence of exchange B. There must be some reason why A has occurred; the reason is expected to be made clear in B. However, although some indication of the reason can be predicted, there is no clear prediction as to what the reason will be or what form it will take. What occurs as the 'reason' for the occurrence of exchange A is a further questioning (move 3).

The predictive power of the Prefatory exchange itself can be explained in the light of the fact that it seems to be the case that whenever an exchange such as A in the above example occurs, an exchange such as B must also follow. That is, exchange A depends on exchange B for its interactional completeness. This non-completeness or non-terminality of the Prefatory exchange is another defining criterion of this type of exchange.

One other defining characteristic of the Prefatory exchange as suggested is that it cannot stand properly as a final exchange in discourse. In other words, it is non-terminal. The interactional completeness of the exchange can be noticed if the exchange terminates there without any further talk following it. One can predict that the participants would hear it as incomplete.

6.8.2 Types of Prefatory exchange

Three types of Prefatory exchange can be distinguished in the family data for this study. The three are differentiated here with the notional/functional labels. They are: Prefatory I—Summons, Prefatory II—Permission-seeking, and Prefatory III—Greetings. The three types can be exemplified with the following examples:

B.	Daddy	1	Prefatory I
S.	Yes	2	Summons
B.	Can I make my point now?	3	Prefatory II
S.	Yes	4	Permission-seeking
Jm.	Morning—dad	5	Prefatory III
Al.	Morning my dear	6	Greetings

These exchange types, although differing from each other, are alike in their predictiveness and non-terminality. Indeed, one or more of these types could precede a free exchange.

The linguistic markers for recognizing the Prefatory exchange in the family discourse are derived from the family data. Although the list of linguistic markers for the Prefatory exchange to be summarized here is not exhaustive, and therefore cannot be claimed to account for all types of moves that can be described as a Prefatory exchange, nevertheless, the list of the items to be presented would be sufficient for the need of this chapter in that it accounts for all the types of Prefatory exchange found in the corpus on which this chapter is based.

The Initiating move of a Prefatory exchange may take the form of:

1. an address term, namely, names, e.g. *Alison* or titles of participants, e.g. *Dad, Mum, Uncle, Darling, Mother*;

2. courtesy phrases, such as *pardon me* or *excuse me* or their equivalents;
3. an opening greeting, e.g. *hello, good morning*.
4. forms of mitigation like *Can I*, *Could I*, plus self-referential meta-statement such as *come in at this point, speak on this issue, make my point*.

In fact, the Initiating move can combine items (1) and (4), (1) and (2) or (1) and (3).

The Response move in a Prefatory exchange can be realized by any of the following surface markers:

1. *Yes, Yeah, uh huh*, with rising intonation, *what is it?*, or *what?*;
2. *Yes, Yeah, uh huh*, with falling intonation;
3. Reply greeting, e.g. *hello, good morning*.

Functionally, I consider the Prefatory exchange as a minimal interactional exchange which has no content information as far as the 'business' of talk is concerned, but which, however, provides an opportunity to make the participants available for more talk in discourse. It is therefore a type of preliminary or preparatory talk which helps to establish social contacts before the actual 'subject matter' of the discourse is introduced. The Prefatory exchange thus serves as what Stubbs (1983: 182–3) describes as 'a superficial linking device employed by a participant in an attempt to turn the conversation to his own topic'.

6.9 THE INFORMATORY EXCHANGE

In discussing the Prefatory exchange, I suggested that the exchange type cannot be regarded as an interactionally complete unit of discourse. Rather, it is meant for establishing social contact between the participants in talk, and therefore 'further talk' must necessarily follow. It is this further talk that I have labelled the Informatory exchange.

The notion of Informatory is derived from the definition of an exchange as a unit concerned with negotiating the transmission of information (Coulthard and Brazil 1981: 101). An Informatory exchange is considered as an exchange which has information content. However, it is suggested in Berry (1981) that not all exchanges transmit information. Some may be concerned with the negotiation of actions. It is true that these distinctions exist in the making of discourse. Nevertheless, for the purpose of this chapter, I shall, following Leech (1981: 124), consider an action as another kind of information.

An Informatory exchange is therefore defined in this chapter as any exchange that is concerned with negotiating the transmission of information or non-verbal action. The information content of such an exchange is NEW. More specifically, an Informatory exchange is defined as a unit of discourse which has a propositional content and new information. In addition, its initiating move predicts a following move.

The notion of proposition in this chapter refers to the meaning or sense expressed by a declarative, interrogative or imperative sentence. Here sentence is used in the sense of a 'text sentence'; that is, as the product of a bit of language behaviour (Lyons 1977: 29–30). This definition of proposition is derived from Searle (1969: 23) and Leech (1981: 124), who suggest that utterances with declarative, interrogative and imperative do express propositional content.

Another defining characteristic of an Initiating move in an Informatory exchange is that it has something new in terms of information content. Young (1983: 63) employs the term 'new' in her definition of Initiating moves but she does not define it. However, Burton, in an earlier study (1978: 143), employs the term 'new' while defining a category she calls 'Opening moves'. She defines Opening moves as 'essentially topic-carrying items which are recognizably new in terms of the immediately preceding talk'. That is, the moves make no anaphoric or backward reference to the preceding moves.

The category defined by Burton in terms of newness of topic is similar to what I have considered as Informatory Initiating moves. They are similar in the sense that both serve as Opening moves of the exchange, and they also both have new content. They are, however, different in the sense that not all the moves I regard as Initiating will Burton consider as Opening moves. Prefatory moves, for instance, will not be classified by Burton as Opening moves.

However, because of the similarities between what I consider as Initiating moves and Burton's Opening moves, I employ her definition of newness, modify it, and relate it to the propositional content of the Initiating moves of Informatory exchanges.

The criteria that are used in identifying newness of Informatory initiations are the range of reference, substitution, ellipsis, conjunction and lexical ties in the data. These criteria are borrowed from Halliday and Hasan (1976), who describe them as cohesive devices in texts. For a full discussion of these devices, see Halliday and Hasan (1976). In the meantime, I shall demonstrate how the cohesive devices help in differentiating between Informatory and Bound exchanges.

Let us consider the following stretch of discourse from the family data in the light of the above criteria.

(11) Ad. Dad   1 | A Pref I
     Su. Yes—my dear   2 |
     Ad. Is our conversation being recorded?   3 | B Free
     Su. I don't know   4 | Inf.
     Ad. Can you stop it now?   5 | C Bound
     Su. Okay   6 |
                         (5)   7
     Ad. Do you know when the recording began?   8 | D Bound
     Su. No—   9 |
     Ad. Are you serious—dad?   10 | E Bound
     Su. Yes—(3)   11 |
     Su. I never knew any recording was going on   12 | F Bound
     Ad. I see   13 |
                    (Ib. YESLFD)

In this extract, exchange A is an example of Prefatory type discussed above. However, the Initiating move 3 has new information in the sense that it does not tie with the preceding moves by means of any of the cohesive categories outlined above. Exchange B is therefore analysed as Free Informatory type.

The rest of the initiating moves and the exchanges in which they occur, that is C–F, cannot be regarded as having new information because each of them ties with the preceding move(s) by means of the cohesive categories already stated. Having considered Informatory exchange, I shall discuss briefly the category Bound exchanges.

6.10 BOUND EXCHANGES

In the discussion of the Prefatory exchanges I observed that such exchanges were interactionally incomplete and they were therefore considered as a type of Bound exchange.

Also, in the description of the Informatory exchange, I observed that a certain pattern of organization emerged, which cannot be regarded as a 'real' Informatory type of exchange. This pattern of organization is what I labelled Bound Representational exchanges.

There are three other types of Bound exchange which I observed while analysing my data in terms of Sinclair and Coulthard's categories. These are Repeat and Regulatory Positive and Negative exchanges. The Bound Prefatory type mentioned earlier becomes the fifth of the Bound categories.

Although Prefatory exchanges are a type of Bound exchange, I shall not discuss them further, since I have already dealt with them. I shall here concentrate on the other four types of Bound exchange.

6.10.1 The Bound Representational exchanges

The notion of 'Representational' is derived from Halliday (1973: 16), who uses it to describe a function of language. Halliday uses the term Representational to refer to the use of language as a means of 'communicating about something, of expressing presuppositions'. I use the term in this chapter to describe any Informatory exchange that ties with the content of the preceding exchange(s) in the discourse.

A Bound Representational exchange is therefore by definition a category which always makes backward reference to the content of the preceding exchange(s). It exemplifies, expands or justifies the content of the preceding exchanges. This category, like all types of exchange, can be recognized by the fact that its initiating move predicts a following move.

The range of features determining backward reference or when a move can be regarded as bound have been discussed. It is sufficient to state here that they are signalled by reference, ellipsis, substitution, conjunction and lexical cohesion.

Like the Informatory types, Bound Representational exchanges can be seen to be of three types corresponding to the three Informatory exchange types—Inform, Elicit and Direct.

6.10.2 Bound Regulatory exchanges

The use of the notion Regulatory in this study is borrowed from Halliday (1973: 12) who uses it to describe a 'model of language'. Halliday defines the term Regulatory as 'the use of language to regulate the behaviour of others'. It is used in this chapter to refer to the type of exchanges labelled Bound Regulatory. These exchanges cannot stand on their own as interactionally complete exchanges in discourse. They rely on the preceding exchange for their completeness. In addition, such exchanges, as we shall see shortly, function for regulating the interactional behaviour of others in conversations.

For the purpose of clarification of this type of category, I shall present here extracts from the data for this study.

(14) B. Daddy   1 ⎱ A Pref. I
    S. Yes   2 ⎰
    B. Can I make my point now?   3 ⎱ B Pref. II
    S. Yes   4 ⎰
    B. Don't you realize that men
        of today are trying to
        prevent women from liberating
        themselves?   5 ⎱ C Informatory
    S. Yes   6 ⎰
    Fr. Despite these attempts there
        are many of er of them—still
        believe strongly that yes (2)
        they have the goal which they
        er they must achieve—   7 ⎱ D Bound Rep.
    D. yes—   8 ⎰
    D. we have—er   9   Violation of
                                          speaker's
                                          rights

    Fr. Would you wait until I
        finish?   10 ⎱ E Regulatory
                                      ⎰ Negative
    D. Sorry   11
              (6)
    Fr. What I'm saying is that
        er that women are ranking
        themselves with men   13 ⎱ F Bound Rep.
    S. Yes   14 ⎰
    Fr. They are trying to raise
        themselves to the er the
        same pedestal as er erm with
        their husbands—   15 ⎱ G Bound Rep.
    S. that's correct—(5)   16 ⎰

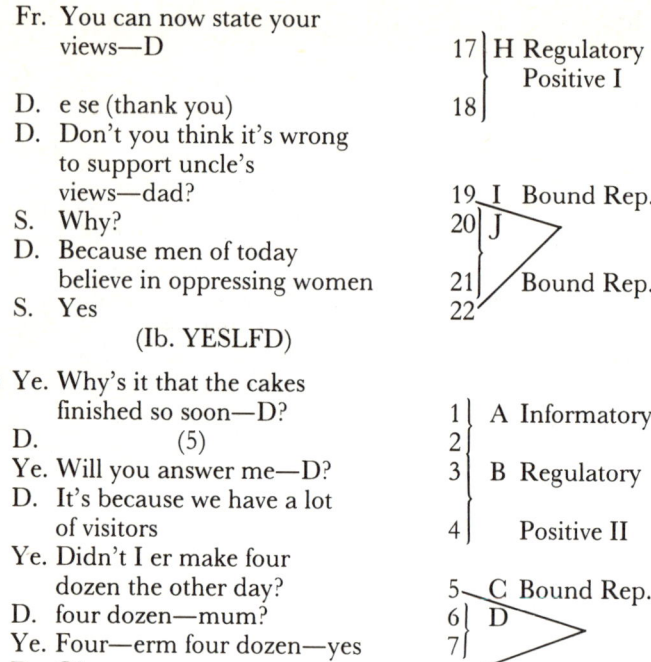

```
    Fr. You can now state your
        views—D                          17 ⎫ H Regulatory
                                            ⎬     Positive I
    D.  e se (thank you)                 18 ⎭
    D.  Don't you think it's wrong
        to support uncle's
        views—dad?                       19   I  Bound Rep.
    S.  Why?                             20   J
    D.  Because men of today
        believe in oppressing women      21      Bound Rep.
    S.  Yes                              22
            (Ib. YESLFD)

(15) Ye. Why's it that the cakes
         finished so soon—D?             1 ⎫  A Informatory
     D.              (5)                 2 ⎪
     Ye. Will you answer me—D?           3 ⎬  B Regulatory
     D.  It's because we have a lot
         of visitors                     4 ⎭     Positive II
     Ye. Didn't I er make four
         dozen the other day?            5    C Bound Rep.
     D.  four dozen—mum?                 6    D
     Ye. Four—erm four dozen—yes         7
     D.  Oh: yes                         8
            (Ib. YESLFD)
```

In extract (14), exchanges A and B are examples of the Bound Prefatory type, exchange C makes a new contribution to the talk, and exchange D, a Bound Representational type, develops the content of exchange C further.

Exchange E, however, seems different from the preceding ones. As can be seen from the extract, participant Fr. (move 10) who initiates exchange E feels that participant D. (moves 8 and 9) has misused his speaking rights by interrupting the talk and has therefore disrupted the smooth flow of the discourse. Having noticed such a violation, he attempts to repair the breakdown in the talk by reprimanding the interruptor. His sanction produces exchange E. I consider this as a type of Bound Regulatory negative exchange. I label it 'negative' because the exchange seems to function as a reprimand of a negative interactional behaviour. It is a reprimand in the sense that participant D. (moves 8 and 9), by virtue of his lower social position in the interaction, is not expected to make the contribution he has made at that instance. The contribution is therefore considered by speaker Fr. (who is an occupant of a higher role in the talk) as a violation of the norm of speaking in the interaction event, hence the reprimand (move 10).

However, exchange H differs from any of the preceding exchanges. It can be regarded as an attempt to ask the participant who interrupted in moves 8 and 9 to make his contribution at the time participant Fr. (who reprimanded D.'s behaviour in move 17) feels is appropriate. Participant D. (move 18) appreciates Fr.'s gesture, and begins to make his contributions in exchange I which immediately follows. I consider this organization as another type of Bound Regulatory exchange, and I label it Bound Regulatory positive exchange I (Encourage). I consider it 'positive' because its function seems to be to encourage participants with limited speaking rights to make contributions to the ongoing talk at some stages thought to be appropriate by privileged participants in the discourse.

When we examine extract (15) we find that there is a breakdown in the talk (exchange A) because participant A. (move 2) fails to respond to Ye.'s initiation (move 1). Consequently, participant Ye. presumably regards such a failure as a violation of an interactional norm, which results in a breakdown in the talk. She then makes an attempt to regulate the ongoing discourse by checking whether the supposed responder, participant A., is still on the same wavelength with her or not. This repair mechanism constitutes exchange B. I label this type of exchange employed by the participant with a view to repairing the breakdown in the discourse as a type of Bound Regulatory positive exchange II (Repair). This exchange type, is like Sinclair and Coulthard's Reinitiation in respect of function and position in discourse. They are, however, different in respect of participant roles and structure.

This exchange differs from the type described above in the sense that the breakdown which it repairs results from an implicit rule of conversation which expects an initiation to be followed by a response of some kind. On the other hand, Positive I occurs as a result of the violation of the social norm of speaking.

In the light of the preceding examination of the extracts from the family data for this study, four sub-types of Bound Regulatory exchanges clearly emerge. The four types can be represented as follows:

	positive	positive I (encourage)
Bound regulatory exchanges		
	negative	positive II (repair)

6.10.3 Repeat exchange

This exchange type is like Sinclair and Coulthard's Repeat. The Initiating move of Repeat in the family talk either repeats what has been presented by the immediately preceding initiation or predicts a repetition of the content of the preceding initiation. This type of exchange usually occurs as the second (inserted) exchange in talk which I have, using the ethnomethodologists' term, analysed as an 'insertion exchange'. It occurs as a result of participants' lack of attention to the preceding initiation. Instead of producing the expected response to the preceding initiation, such participants usually ask the initiator to repeat the initiation or confirm it before they (the supposed responders) provide the expected response.

Repeat exchanges can be exemplified with the following examples:

Su. I brought home—some Christmas cards
Ye. What?
Su. I've got some Christmas cards
Ye. I see

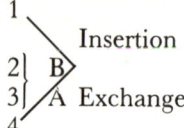

6.11 HYPOTHESES TESTING

Having proposed a framework for the analysis of the family conversations in terms of initiations, I tried to find out who initiates and controls the discourse. In the light of this, I postulated two hypotheses which I shall consider in the following sections.

6.11.1 Method of analysis

First, I calculated the total number of Informatory initiations produced by the parents and children in the family conversations. Second, I calculated the number of Inform, Elicit and Direct Initiating moves produced by the participants. For instance, the proportion produced by parents when they interacted with the children was investigated along with the children's contributions. The proportion of the Informatory initiations produced by the pairs was expressed in terms of the percentage of the total number of each type of Informatory initiations. Then the percentage of the total number of Informatory initiations produced by the older people, and that produced by the younger people, were also calculated.

6.11.2 Hypothesis 1

In the Yoruba-English family conversations, the proportion of initiations that the older adults will produce will be greater than that of the younger adults.

A summary of the results is presented in Table 6.1. The contributions of the parents in the Yoruba-English family conversations comprise those of ten fathers and ten mothers, while those of the children comprise the total

Table 6.1 Distribution of initiation types

Participants	Baseline	Ini	%	Bnd	%	Pre	%
Parents	4,125	600	14.5	1,620	39.3	25	0.6
Children	1,875	150	8.0	440	23.3	105	5.6
Total	6,000	750	12.5	2,060	34.3	130	2.3

Key: Ini—Initiation; Bnd—Bound Initiation; Pre—Prefatory.

contributions made by ten sons and twenty daughters from the five-family talk.

The baseline used for the calculation of the figures in Table 6.1 is the total number of moves produced by each group of participants in the family conversation. For example, the parents' group in the Yoruba-English family talk initiated 4,125 moves. Out of this figure, they initiated 600 initiations. The percentage of initiations produced by the parents is 14.5 per cent, that is, 600 initiations per 4,125 moves.

6.11.3 Discussion

The results in Table 6.1 show that the proportion of Informatory initiations produced by the parents in the Yoruba-English family talk is greater than that of the children. It is greater by 6.5 per cent, which is about the total proportion of initiations produced by the children. The hypothesis can be said to be clearly supported in that the difference between the proportion of initiations produced by the parents and children is significant.

The figures on Bound initiations also show that the proportion produced by the parents is greater than that of the children. The difference between the proportion of the category produced by the parents and children is 16 per cent. This figure is more than the proportion of Bound initiations produced by the younger adults. Since the difference is very significant, one can conclude that the hypothesis is clearly supported by the data.

The results of Prefatory initiations show that the proportion of the category produced by the children is greater than that of the parents. In fact, it can be said that the parents rarely produced the category since they produced only 0.6 per cent, while the younger adults produced 5.6 per cent. Since the difference between the proportion of Prefatory initiations produced by the children and parents in the Yoruba-English family talk is small, it can be concluded that the findings clearly go against Hypothesis 1.

The reason why the figures go against the hypothesis is probably because Prefatory initiations, as defined in this chapter is a category often used by participants with restricted rights in conversations. It is likely that the younger adults realized that they were participants with such rights in the Yoruba-English family conversations; hence the proportion of Prefatory initiations that they produced was higher than that of the older adults.

From the figures it can be claimed that Hypothesis 1 is clearly supported to a great extent by the data obtained from the Yoruba-English family conversations.

6.11.4 Hypothesis 2

In the Yoruba-English family conversations, not all types of initiation will be produced by both parents and children. Parents will produce all types of initiation except the type that was classified as the 'Permission-seeking' moves, and the children will produce all types of initiation except those that were categorized as 'Directives', and 'Regulatory Positive I (encourage)' and 'Regulatory Negative' moves. The findings are summarized in Table 6.2.

Table 6.2 Distribution of initiation types

Participants	Basel	Inf	Elc	Dir	Ibf	Ibl	Ibr	PI	PII	Ng	PRI	PRII	PRIII	Rpt
Parents	4,125	270	172	48	800	500	60	20	70	20	16	—	9	150
Percentage		6.5	4.2	1.2	19.4	12.1	1.5	0.5	1.5	0.3	3.6	—	0.4	3.6
Children	1,875	50	60	—	230	150	—	—	20	—	38	33	9	40
Percentage		2.7	3.2	—	12.3	8.0	—	—	1.1	—	2.0	1.8	0.5	2.1

Key: Basel—Baseline; Inf—Inform Initiation; Elc—Elicit Initiation; Dir—Direct Initiation; Ibf—Bound-Inform; Ibl—Bound-Elicit; Ibr—Bound-Direct; PI—Bound Regulatory Positive I; PII—Bound Regulatory Positive II; Ng—Bound Negative; PrI—Prefatory I—Summons; PRII—Prefatory II—Permission-seeking; PRIII—Prefatory III—Greetings; Rpt—Repeat Initiation.

A consideration of the figures in Table 6.2 reveals that the parents in the Yoruba-English family conversations produced all types of initiations—Inform, Elicit, Direct, Bound Inform, Bound Elicit, Prefatory I (Summons), Regulatory Positive I (Encourage), Regulatory Positive II (Repair), Regulatory Negative and Repeat initiations, except the type labelled Prefatory II or Permission (Permission-seeking) moves. In addition, the figures show that the children produced all types of initiation—Inform, Elicit, Bound Inform, Bound Direct, Prefatory I and II, Regulatory Positive II and Repeat initiations, but they did not produce Directives, Bound Direct, Regulatory Positive I and Regulatory Negative initiations.

Prefatory II, as said earlier, is used by the participants with restricted speaking rights in an 'unequal' interaction. This seems to be the reason why the parents did not use the category at all. Regulatory Positive I and Regulatory Negative initiations, as defined earlier, are used by the participants of higher social positions for reprimanding deliberate violations of the speaking norms by persons of restricted speaking rights in conversations. This may account for the reason why only the older adults produced all the twenty instances of Regulatory Negative initiations that occurred in the Yoruba-English data.

In view of the figures presented in Table 6.2, it will be concluded that Hypothesis 2 is clearly supported.

It will be recalled that the participants that took part in each of the conversations comprised two males and three females. I attempted to find out whether the asymmetry in the distribution of sex had affected the results. I therefore examined the Yoruba-English family data for cross-sex conversations, that is, male/female contributions. The results of the findings are shown in Table 6.3. The figures in the table show that the proportion of initiations produced by the males is greater than that of the females.

Table 6.3 Male/female contributions

Participants	Baseline	Initiations	%
20 Males	3,980	2,100	52.8
30 Females	2,020	840	41.6

The reasons why males dominated females is perhaps because of the role associated with males and females in the Yoruba society. Socioculturally, males are regarded as head, breadwinner and protector who should be honoured and respected by women. On the other hand, females are considered weak and therefore occupants of lower or subservient role. This status of women in the Yoruba society seems to have been reflected in the proportion of initiations produced by females in the conversations.

From the findings, it can be argued that asymmetry in the sex of the participants did not affect the results. This is because the children's group which comprised twenty females and ten males produced less initiations than the parents' group which consisted of ten males and ten females.

One other factor which did not seem to have influenced the findings is the asymmetry in the distribution of the subjects. As pointed out earlier in this chapter and reflected in Table 6.2, thirty children interacted with twenty parents in the ten-family conversations recorded. But the children produced less initiations than the parents. On the basis of these findings, it can be concluded that the postulated hypothesis in this chapter are supported.

6.12 CONCLUSION

The results of the investigation showed that the proportion of initiations produced by the parents was greater than that of the children. The findings also showed that in the Yoruba-English family conversations not all types of initiations were produced by both the parents and children. The parents produced all types of initiation except the type that have been categorized as Prefatory I; while the children produced all types of initiation except those described as Directives, Regulatory Positive I and Regulatory Negative initiations.

It seems possible to distinguish between the point where children join the ongoing talk and the point of entry of the parents in the Yoruba-English family conversations. That is, structurally, the parents rarely prefaced much of their contributions before making them, but the children did so most often in the conversations.

As regards the influence of speakers' rights on the structure of the family conversations, it can be claimed that the points of entry of the children in the Yoruba-English family conversations were marked by Prefatory I and II, and sometimes by Regulatory Negative and Positive I exchanges. On the other hand, such markers were not found with the parents' contributions.

Finally, the findings of the investigation of the structure of family conversations in Yoruba-English point to the fact that parents dominate and control social interactions just as they control other aspects of the family life. Children are considered as subservient to their parents and could only interact with them as equals only when they are given such permission.

BIBLIOGRAPHY

Afolayan, A. (1968), 'Linguistic problems of Yoruba learners/users of English', unpublished Ph.D. thesis, University College London.

Akindele, D. O. (1986), 'Speakers' rights in English-English and Yoruba-English family discourse', unpublished Ph.D. thesis, University of Nottingham.

Atoye, R. O. (1980), 'A sociolinguistic study of phonological interference in Yoruba-English', unpublished Ph.D. thesis, University of Sheffield.

Bamgbose, A. (1971), 'The English language in Nigeria', in Spencer. J. W. (ed.), *The English Language in West Africa*, London, Longman, 35–48.

—— (1983), 'Standard Nigerian English: issues of identification', in Kachru, B. B. (ed.), *The Other Tongue*, Oxford, Pergamon Press, 99–111.
Berry, M. (1981), 'Systemic linguistics and discourse analysis: a multi-layered approach to exchange structure', in Coulthard, M. and Montgomery, M. (eds), *Studies in Discourse Analysis*, London, Routledge and Kegan Paul, 120–145.
Burton, D. (1978), 'Towards an analysis of casual conversation', *Nottingham Linguistic Circular*, 7, No. 2, 131–64.
Coulthard, M. and Ashby, M. (1976), 'A linguistic study of doctor–patient interviews', in Wadsworth, M. and Robinson, D. (eds), *Studies in Everyday Medical Life*, London, Martin Robertson.
Coulthard, M. and Brazil, D. (1979), 'Exchange structure', *Discourse Analysis Monograph 5*, English Language Research, University of Birmingham.
Gumperz, J. J. (1972), 'The speech community', in Giglioli, P. P. (ed.), *Language and Social Context*, Harmondsworth, Penguin.
Halliday, M. A. K. and Hasan, R. (1976), *Cohesion in English*, London, Longman.
Harris, S. J. (1980), 'Language interaction in magistrates' courts', unpublished Ph.D. thesis, University of Nottingham.
Kachru, B. B. (1981), 'The pragmatics of non-native Englishes', in Smith, L. E. (ed.), *English for Cross-Cultural Communication*, London, Macmillan.
Leech, G. N. (1981), *Semantics*, Harmondsworth, Penguin.
Lyons, J. (1977), *Semantics: Volume I and II*, Cambridge, Cambridge University Press.
Searle, J. R. (1969), *Speech Acts*, Cambridge, Cambridge University Press.
Sinclair, J. McH. and Coulthard, M. (1975), *Towards an Analysis of Discourse*, Oxford, Oxford University Press.
Stubbs, M. (1974), 'The discourse structure of informal committee talk', mimeo, University of Birmingham.
—— (1983), *Discourse Analysis*, Oxford, Blackwell.
Tucker, G. (1988), 'From illocution to syntactic and prosodic realization in making requests', in Steiner E. H. and Veltman, R. (eds), *Discourse and Text: Exploration in Systemic Semantics*, London, Pinter Publishers.
Young, J. (1983), 'An essay in child language', mimeo, Department of English Studies, University of Nottingham.

7 From illocution to syntactic and prosodic realization in making requests*

G. Tucker
Computational Linguistics Unit, University of Wales, College of Cardiff

7.0 INTRODUCTION

The relationship between speech acts and the language which realizes them has rarely been explicated. Speech-act theorists have not always been concerned with the 'language component' of acts, and linguists, for their part, have not always sought to explain how utterances are meaningful outside of the semantics contained in their models. The lack of mutual explicit recognition which Butler refers to in Part I has not helped in showing how the two systems interact.

Utterances must always relate to a context. If there were no such link, speakers would be deprived of 'guidelines' in selecting from the whole range of meanings options made available to them by the semantics of the language. It is argued here that speakers exploit such a range of linguistic meaning to address features of the immediate context, such as the presuppositions and contextual knowledge which they hold. Where the speech function or illocutionary function of the utterance may be made clear extra-linguistically, the role of language is to provide the means of relating a generalized speech act—such as requests—to their particular context. This, as the chapter shows, is necessary if speech acts are to be acceptable and interactants are to avoid loss of face and unsuccessful performance as conversationalists. How else are we to explain how the same speech act can, potentially, be realized by a wide range of lexicogrammatical and prosodic realization signalling considerably different linguistic meaning?

The choice of bookshop requests made here allows us to examine not only which linguistic forms are used to realize the act, but how they relate to a set of genre-specific contextual features. From a vast number of ways of making a request, a small number only are massively found in the corpus of encounters. Detailed analysis of their linguistic structure and the meanings they realize shows clearly how they, and not others, match the contextual configuration

---

* The research on which this chapter is based is funded by a (40 per cent) grant from the Italian Ministero della Pubblica Instruzione.

and allow successful interaction, even if in transactional terms there is no positive outcome.

This chapter examines the lexicogrammatical and prosodic form of requests in one specific type of service encounter in an attempt to throw some light on the relationship between the illocutionary force or speech function of an utterance and its linguistic realization.

All the utterances examined are taken from a corpus of over 150 encounters audio-recorded in a Central London bookshop. Given the importance of context to an understanding of speaker choice in realization, a more detailed account of the bookshop setting is given in section 7.1.

Considerable importance is attributed to the use of naturally occurring data. Although there should be no need to restate the case for such an approach, so much work is still carried out, especially in the field of pedagogically oriented applied linguistics, on the basis of material elicited, for example, through role play (the Bochum project, see Edmondson *et al.* 1984) and completion techniques (CCSARP, see Blum-Kulka and Olshtain 1985). Indeed, one of Hyme's four components in a speaker's communicative competence concerns a knowledge of 'Whether (and to what degree) something is in fact done, actually *performed*, and what its doing entails' (Hymes 1971). In such a well-circumscribed activity as requesting books in a bookshop it is possible, in purely statistical terms, to ascertain what 'is in fact done' and the results of the work discussed here confirm this. What is important to this particular study is that certain forms occur massively and other request realizations which might have been predicted do not. As was suggested above, it is precisely the relationship between linguistic choice and contextual features which is under examination.

What I wish to suggest is that lexicogrammatical and prosodic realizations do not directly or indirectly determine speech function but, rather, relate speech acts to their contexts by attending to some more or less relevant aspect of the performance of the act itself. In performing the numerous speech functions a speaker must necessarily exploit the limited set of options in the mood system of the clause. Apart from stating, commanding and asking (three of what Halliday (1985) refers to as PRIMARY SPEECH FUNCTIONS), which correspond to declarative, imperative and interrogative mood, there is no direct link between function and mood. It is in fact the lack of a one-to-one relationship which allows speakers greater delicacy in performing acts. I shall maintain here that a speech act is realized by any utterance susceptible of being interpreted as such in a given context by reference to the various types of knowledge which speakers share. The semantic options and their lexicogrammatical representations are concerned more with factors such as appropriacy, acceptability and perhaps success of the speech act in its immediate context.

7.1 CONTEXT AND SHARED KNOWLEDGE

Service encounters and the acts which are performed during them allow us to work from a circumscribed set of contextual features. The acts are inherent to the overall activity itself, here buying and selling. There is a clear role structure (customer and shop assistant) which suggests transactionally oriented speech rather than speech of an interactional nature. In the case of the Central London bookshop, a good number of features are likely to constitute shared knowledge between customer and assistant. People who enter bookshops, apart from known publishers' representatives, etc., will be assumed by the sales assistants to be customers looking for books or categories of books with the probable intention of purchasing. Customers, for their part, will assume that the individuals located behind desks at service points are there to provide assistance. The departmental, self-service layout and organization of the shop (e.g. labelling and signposting) indicate that the only obligatory interaction will be the final sales transaction. Contact with the departmental assistants is necessary only when self-help strategies fail, whenever, for example, the customer is unable to locate what he is looking for. We can predict in many cases, therefore, that if the customer has made an unsuccessful search before addressing an assistant, the likelihood of the book's availability is greatly reduced.

The features described here differ considerably from other service encounter genres. In the particularly popular (among linguists!) small greengrocer's, for example, the whole, comparatively narrow range of vegetables is usually clearly on display. Sprouts and aubergines are bought by weight or number and often according to quality. The assistant is both server and cashier, and not always can the customer serve himself. It should not be surprising to discover that, given the differences in generic features between bookshops and greengrocers, the respective request forms also show differences.

The kind of knowledge described above for the bookshop can be partially expressed as a set of presuppositions which might be held by the customer, as follows:

(1) (i) The book is available from the assistant.
 (ii) The book exists and is stockable (i.e. in print, not hopelessly obscure, etc.).
 (iii) The book is a category dealt with by this department.
 (iv) The book is not READILY available by other means (e.g. not immediately visible).
 (v) The customer is interested in buying the book.
 (vi) The reference is contextually adequate to ensure:
  a. recognition as a request.
  b. recognition of the book.

As well as contextual knowledge, Faerch and Kasper (1985) suggest other types of pragmatically relevant knowledge that speakers possess. They include knowledge of a set of speech-act constitutive rules for requests of the type proposed by Searle (1969) or a similar set proposed by Labov and Fanshel (1977) which are given below:

(2) 1a. (an action)   X should be done.
    1b. (a hearer)   B would not do X in the absence of the request.
    2.   B has the ability to do X.
    3.   B has the OBLIGATION to do X or is willing to do it.
    4. (a speaker)   A has a RIGHT to tell B to do it. [Labov and Fanshel 1977]

Other types of knowledge will include conversational principles and maxims of the kind discussed by Grice, Leech and Levinson *inter alia*, discourse knowledge, contextual knowledge, knowledge of the world, and, of course, linguistic knowledge. No strict validity or exhaustiveness is claimed for any of the listed conditions or presuppositions. What is important, however, is the way such contextual features relate to linguistic realization.

7.2 THE NATURE AND FORM OF REQUESTS

In this section, the forms found with statistical significance in the data are analysed in lexicogrammatical terms. The underlying systemic options selected are then related to features in the context. Given the warning made earlier with regard to the role of lexicogrammatical realization in determining (and consequently indicating) speech function, we are already faced with the problem of defining and identifying a request. It might be glossed as a speech act by which person A attempts to get something done by person B—something that A cannot or does not wish to do himself and which he cannot, through status, oblige B to do in the normal course of events. What B is requested to do may fall within a range of activities, such as giving things (objects, information), even permission for doing things (opening windows, moving cars, etc.). A's request is for something to his own advantage, although mutual advantage is an inherent characteristic of buying and selling.

Content and context analysis on the data reveals the subject matter for requests in the bookshop; customers almost exclusively make requests about specific works or categories of books. Whatever the lexicogrammatical dressing of this content, wherever specific or categorial reference is made encounter-initially by a customer, we may expect a request to have been made. This is confirmed by the assistant's response behaviour. Most significantly, the linguistic uniformity of response seems related more to the act of requesting itself than to the form the request takes; the lexicogrammatical realization (especially in terms of mood) does not seem to constrain the form of response.

In order that an utterance may function as a request, clearly, it must be recognized and acknowledged as such by the assistant. Once its validity as a request and its acceptability have been recognized, the assistant must then make a reasonable attempt to satisfy it or clarify why he cannot. The issue of acceptability relates not to whether the utterance functions as a request or not but whether it conforms to social and conversational norms such as reasonableness and accessibility. Customers often have difficulty in getting their requests right, especially in terms of acceptability. It is not so much the danger of failing to have an utterance recognized as a request but the risk of loss of face through producing an unacceptable request. As Anderson *et al.* (1986) have shown, a considerable amount of linguistic work is done by customer and assistant alike in order to prevent failure in terms of an inability to do things and to make talk together as a 'joint product'.

The choice of linguistic realization is closely related to request acceptability. This applies both to basic 'canonical forms' which the data reveal and to modification of these forms, whether internally (modifying the lexico-grammar and prosody of the canonical form) or externally, by prefacing and/or extending the basic form. Figure 7.1 shows the discourse structure of requests, in these terms, along the lines of accounts posited by Faerch and Kasper (1985) and Anderson *et al.* (1986). Although much of the research on these data has tended towards the analysis of request extension and consequent overlap and latching, as reported in Anderson *et al.* (1986), it is the core request form and internal modification which comes under attention here. We shall be concerned with three aspects of realization: the clause structure of the core request, the nominal group structure of the central referent indicator, and the prosodic structure. The term 'referent indicator' relates to the book or category enquired about by the customer and, as will be seen, is the only obligatory element in request structure. It is interesting to note that what appear to be significant modifications of canonical forms are realized almost exclusively through options at the level of clause and group.

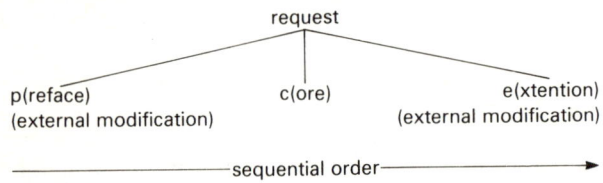

Figure 7.1 The discourse structure of requests

By far the majority of utterances which referred to specific books or categories of books took one of the following forms:

— Polar interrogative with *have*
— *wh*-interrogative with *where*
— Declarative with *looking for*
— Incomplete clause syntax (isolated nominal group)

No other commonly accepted forms of request such as *Can I have X* or *I'd like X* occur. It is the above forms alone which relate the customer to the act in context and allow him to produce acceptable behaviour.

Immediately noticeable is the absence of an imperative mood (often associated with requests) and the presence of declarative mood and of forms where mood is not realized. If we accept the MOOD system as one of the major grammatical devices for realizing interpersonal and especially interactional meaning, in that it establishes basic speech roles, then clearly such roles do not all correspond directly with the roles in operation, in this case requester–requestee. What I wish to argue here is that those basic speech roles established through mood remain constant, irrespective of the nature of the overall speech act. By sharing the same linguistic knowledge as the speaker, the hearer understands that he is formally being asked to provide polarity when a polar interrogative utterance is addressed to him. Through the very nature of the utterance a hearer cannot be denied a polarity-providing response, and if in certain circumstances he responds or reacts as if this interrogative were not a question but a suggestion or order, etc., it is because contextual knowledge leads to a different interpretation and the formal option has not been taken up. Similarly, declaratives always declare and incomplete clause syntax in the form of a nominal group can only formally refer. What needs to be analysed specifically is the association between the mood options selected, together with other variables such as lexical items, and the overall act of requesting. Each of these major options are now discussed in turn.

7.2.1 Incomplete clause syntax

This form will be considered both as a request and as the referential device central to the overall bookshop request activity. Although the nominal group does appear in isolation, it usually fills the complement in all clauses realizing requests. A nominal group, in the absence of an operator and predicator, does not carry mood and cannot therefore be related directly to any basic speech role. It does little more than refer and realize within ideational meaning aspects such as deixis, modification, quantification of the class of things referred to. The speaker may, however, hint at the inherent role the nominal group has or at its syntactic function as in:

(3) any books on XC

suggesting that it is to be treated as a complement. On other occasions it constitutes a thematized element followed by a clause with anaphoric pronominal reference:

(4) workbooks on chemistry, where can I find them (1b07c)

By appearing formally only to refer or indicate theme, the customer can create illocutionary or functional ambiguity. He is appealing to no condition or presupposition other than that of ensuring recognition of the book or category. As we discussed above, it is the speaker's right to have the formal 'face value' of his utterance taken into consideration. There is no way in which an assistant can claim that customer's utterance is unacceptable (other than being considered incomplete), since through the very absence of mood it avoids making implicit, contextually unjustified presuppositions. Nominal group requests for individual items in the data are not found with *please*, the presence of which would indicate request and might consequently involve false presuppositions. It is, however, used in requests for categories such as:

(5) Latin texts, please, classical Latin (1a08)

Such a request presupposes the existence of the category, the availability of books in it, etc. As a request for single items it is more typical of a newsagent's where:

(6) *The Guardian*, please.

presupposes very strongly that the newspaper is available and will be handed over by the newsagent.

The frequency of occurrence of the isolated nominal group suggests that customers know it works as a successful request format and are aware of avoiding face loss which fuller clause structure implying unwarranted presuppositions might cause. Its effectiveness is again substantiated by the assistant's response. Anderson *et al.* (1986) have found that completion of the referent indicator constitutes pragmatic completion of the act to which it contributes. Once an acceptable referent indicator has been uttered—and usually never before—the assistant may begin his response. In the few cases of interruption before completion of the referent indicator the assistant completed or joined in completion of the utterance. A customer selecting thematization of the referent indicator before selecting mood in the clause risks, therefore, being interrupted by the assistant for whom this part is enough to signal the request.

The major threat to acceptability with nominal group format is the inaccessibility of the reference. Transactionally, if not interactionally, success of the encounter can be registered in terms of how accessible the details of the book are made by the customer. The nominal group allows combinations of T(itle), A(uthor), P(ublisher) and hardback/paperback edition. TA, AT and T are the most common forms of referent indicator, AT being the most frequently used. Where the customer is aware of his own referential inadequacy there is often considerable remedial work done, especially in terms of request extension. Lack of awareness naturally leads to dispreferred responses on the part of the assistant.

7.2.2 Polar interrogatives

The corpus includes mainly *have you got/do you have* + lexical variants *keep/stock*. In other service encounters (see Merritt 1976; Levinson 1979) such forms have been treated as a pre-request establishing necessary conditions such as availability before a true request of the type *could I have three, please* can be made. This is not confirmed by the bookshop data; polar interrogatives appear to be as much fully formed requests as any other form and by far the most frequently used.

They do relate to relevant conditions or presuppositions, however. Of the list in (1), (i) is not held, while the others are. The syntax expects a polar response but does not seek positive or negative polarity in particular, as a negative interrogative or a tagged declarative would. A negative answer to the request may therefore be disappointing, in real world terms, to a customer who is thus informed that he will not be able to obtain the book, but in formal linguistic terms, given that *yes* and *no* are both permitted, neither can be considered linguistically dispreferred. Other presuppositional differences are made through the lexical choice of *have/keep/stock*. A hypothetical utterance such as:

(7) do you stock X

is presuppositionally weaker than a request with *have*; an item may be stocked as a rule but out of stock at any particular moment.

It is mainly with this form of polar interrogative that ambiguity regarding the request sub-type may be created. It appears to be an information-seeking question of the type found in Merritt's data, but even if a positive answer is obtained there is no third turn such as:

(8) could I have a copy, then?

Equally it would be odd for an assistant to provide nothing more than a positive response. The data in fact show that positive response is followed by location or direction instructions; thus the customer may resume his autonomous search. If the customer's intention is therefore to request guidance or even the handing over of a copy, a negative response could constitute loss of face and be interpreted as a refusal to comply. The guise of 'request for information', however, means that the customer can take *no* as providing acceptable and non-dispreferred information and can of course terminate the purchase attempt immediately on receiving such a response without loss of face.

7.2.3 Looking for

The declarative with lexical *looking for* has only one occasional variant, *I was looking for*, as well as the present tense form. It would be difficult to associate declaratives directly with requests, yet again the assistant's response behaviour confirms this form as a request. The form is non-modal and speaker-oriented. In presuppositional terms, in this case (i) and (ii) are not made. (iii) is, however, since the customer is asking in a department which he believes to correspond to the book in question. Declaratives do not directly require physical or verbal response from the hearer; one may assume at most that the hearer has undergone a change of state in his knowledge of the world; here, he has become aware of the speaker's quest for and apparent difficulty in finding a book. His intervention is not triggered off by the syntax of the request but by his knowledge of context and role. Awareness of an interlocutor's particular state is often a necessary condition for speech-act constitution. Person B cannot merely make suggestions or give advice to person A unless A's need for such is either orally communicated or understood from B's behaviour. In the bookshop the customer's declaration is sufficient enough a signal for the assistant to offer expert guidance.

The past tense variant *was looking* might perhaps be interpreted in terms of temporal distancing with the effect of lessening the directness of implied request. By our principle of 'face value consideration', the assistant could understand that the customer was no longer looking for a book and consequently cannot be held to be requesting it.

7.2.4 *Where*-interrogatives

This form is the one most directly concerned with syntactically realized modality. The following variants are found:
— where might/would I find
— where is
— where would X be
— where do you keep

By selecting a *where*-interrogative, the customer is no longer doubting the existence and availability of the book he wishes to find nor the fact that his interlocutor is able to provide the answer. The presuppositional load implicit in the utterance is therefore considerable, with a consequently higher risk of face loss. The employment of modal devices such as *might/would* introduces a degree of probability/uncertainty and thus tones down the presuppositions held. The same strategy is also employed by the assistant especially when the customer's request does not include modality and where the item requested is outside the assistant's departmental competence as in:

(9) Um, well: probably yes, that would be in the next department, on the left (1b50)

7.3 PROSODY

By examining one part of how speakers realize a request we are inevitably limiting our approach to prosody. The domain of the enquiry has been limited, in fact, to syntactically determined stretches of discourse. Requests have been discussed in terms of mood selection especially. Now that we wish to investigate the role and contribution of prosodic features, we are consequently forced into assuming a close relationship between syntax and prosodic unit. Whereas on the basis of the analysis of all the data there is general agreement with Brown *et al.* (1980) on the difficulty of establishing tone units and units which correspond with syntactic units, perhaps the brevity and straightforwardness of request realization allow us to avoid the problem. On the whole, with these brief utterances, there is little difficulty in recognizing such units. Furthermore, the identification of tonic syllables seems to be unproblematic, even though again, in general, there is confirmation of Brown *et al.*'s view on the difficulty of establishing one tonic syllable per tone group. A tone group and tonic syllable structure can confidently, therefore, be imposed on the data.

As with the lexicogrammar, prosodic realization evolves from a set of options on the basis of which differences can be made and exploited. This is not essentially different from what happens with segmental phonology, which again is the exploitation of a set of distinctive elements, although we shall want to claim in the case of prosody a more direct link to the semantics, i.e. one not always mediated by syntax. Briefly we are concerned with major features such as tonicity, pitch movement, range and height, unit boundaries and key. The functions exploiting these features discussed by Brown *et al.* (1980) are: affective meaning, interactional structure, topic structure, information structure, speech function or illocutionary force. Information structure and interactional structure in a discourse-oriented approach are dealt with in depth by David Brazil and collaborators (Brazil 1985; Brazil *et al.* 1980).

Here we shall limit ourselves to observing prosodic tendencies over the range of request realizations and attempt to associate such tendencies with the various functions mentioned above. We shall wish to show that prosodic mapping, like lexicogrammatical mapping, does not constitute the illocutionary force of utterances, but that such features relate directly to interpersonal and textual functions in particular within the specific context.

It is perhaps tone which has been most associated with speech acts. Halliday (1970) suggests that the unmarked tone for polar questions is a rising tone (his tone 2), whereas for all other basic mood options including *wh*-questions the unmarked tone is falling (tone 1). This derives from his generalization that a fall indicates certainty with regard to polarity and a rise indicates uncertainty. What is significant in the bookshop data is that even with polar interrogatives rising tone is extremely rare and used in the fifteen occurrences of it mostly by non-native speakers. Only two tones are present with any statistical significance: (a) falling tone, in most cases and exclusively with declaratives and *wh*-interrogatives, and (b) falling–rising tone (Halliday's tone 4 and Brazil's referring tone) as a significant alternative to falling tone with polar interrogatives.

Any attempt to associate tone with lexicogrammatical realization or illocutionary type is to reduce the value of prosodic potential. Of course, certain tone patterns may correspond with certain grammatical forms or illocutions but if prosody were so contextually conditioned it would be practically redundant. Here it is suggested that the basic meanings which we can attribute to various tones hold always, and interact with the meanings realized by the lexicogrammar and with the contextually determined speech function or illocutionary force. Thus we can use a falling tone with a polar interrogative indicating that, syntactically, polarity is sought, yet according to the prosodic signal polarity is not a central concern. Brown *et al.* (1980) claim that low termination—in the bookshop data usually a fall from mid to low— indicates the conduciveness of the question, again reinforcing the idea that polarity is not as central a concern as the syntax suggests. This correlates well with a request realized through such a mood option—but the combination of syntactic and prosodic options does not, all the same, constitute the act.

If we remember that low termination might also indicate end of topic and end of turn (the 'I have nothing more to say' function) it might be expected to be predominant in the case of short, straightforward requests for books. We can, however, also introduce the element of uncertainty. The introduction of a rise (in combination with a fall), thus falling–rising tone, allows the customer to express modality. Here the uncertainty suggested by the rise is not simply prosodic redundancy alongside the polar interrogative which, as we have suggested, provides the same meaning. Indeed, in Halliday's terms, it is the high rising tone (tone 2) which is unmarked in this respect. It is allowing generalized uncertainty to be expressed, which could be with regard to the assistant's answer or to the acceptability of the request.

The use of tone 2 (rising) seems to be restricted to indicating the 'more to come' function. It is found often when the central request element is extended as in:

(10) //2 have you got Robert Burchfield's the English LANguage//1 or have you sold OUT// (1a04a)

or

(11) //2 got Popper's Conjectures and RefuTAtions or//1 (1b25c)

Tonic prominence appears to be reserved for the referent indicator, which in most cases comes at the end of the request or constitutes the request alone. When the referent indicator is thematized, it forms its own tone unit. Tonicity almost always follows the principle of the last lexical item (in our case within the referent indicator):

(12) // 1 Bill Duran's story of PhiLOsophy // (1b18c)

There is some small degree of evidence in the data that falling tone and falling–rising tone may contrast to indicate whether, as Brazil *et al*. (1980) claim, the information in the tone unit is being R(EFERRED) or P(ROCLAIMED), that is, taken as shared by the speakers or assumed by present speaker as new. There are few examples of a series of tone units where /p/ and /r/ tones can be observed, but it is suggested here that, especially with incomplete syntax, tone contributes to indicating the functional value of the utterance. Thus in:

(13) //r4 Cambridge LAtin texts// (2a17d)

the referring function is indicated by the tone. The assistant's response *yes* clearly confirms this and invites the first speaker to proceed to third turn and proclaim something about his referent, whereas:

(14) //1p recent European HIstory// (2a17c)

seems to suggest that the referent indicator is new information and being proclaimed and is, in fact, taken by the assistant as a signal to act as if this were a request. If we also map in features such as low termination (no more to come) or not-low termination (more to come) we begin to build up a picture of what the complete contour is indicating.

Even in this informal examination of the role of prosody we find some evidence for the various semantic and discourse functions claimed. But this takes us back to our initial point. Syntactic, lexical and prosodic realizations can be mapped into structure with a considerable degree of independence.

What is uttered is a complex set of meanings, and meanings which may even appear to contradict one another, as in the example of an interrogative with intonation suggesting that the answer is already known. The temptation is to view such a resultant structure as having been programmed to realize a certain illocutionary force. Clearly some realizations will be identified with certain acts. This, however, must be attributed to the fact that the meanings options selected relate, as we have seen, to a number of unmarked features, conditions and presuppositions which accompany the act. When informants are asked how to make a request they will produce one of the commonly employed formulae, a decision which might give rise to the suspicion that there is a direct link between formula and act. The data presented here, together with other researchers' data show that speakers are both highly selective with regard to encounter genre and fully exploit the linguistic system in order to tailor basic requests to their contexts and thus produce more acceptable and successful social behaviour. In exploiting a language's meaning potential for social ends people are not simply concerned with 'how to do things with words', but rather 'how to do things better'!

BIBLIOGRAPHY

Anderson, L., Aston, G. and Tucker, G. (1986), 'The joint production of openings in service encounters', paper presented at the 20th Annual TESOL Convention, March 1986, Anaheim, Calif.
Blum-Kulka, S. and Olshtain, E. (1985), 'Requests and apologies: a cross-cultural study of speech act realisation patterns (CCSARP)', in *Applied Linguistics*, 5, No. 3.
Brazil, D. (1985), *The Communicative Value of Intonation in English*, Birmingham, ELR.
Brazil, D., Coulthard, M. and Johns, C. (1980), *Discourse Intonation and Language Teaching*, London, Longman.
Brown, G., Currie, K. L. and Kenworthy, J. (1980), *Questions of Intonation*, London, Croom Helm.
Edmondson, W., House, J., Kasper, G. and Stemmer, B. (1984), 'Learning the pragmatics of discourse: a project report', *Applied Linguistics*, 5, No. 2.
Faerch, C. and Kasper, G. (1985), 'Pragmatic knowledge: rules and procedures', *Applied Linguistics*, 5, No. 3.
Halliday, M. A. K. (1970), *A Course in Spoken English: Intonation*, London, Oxford University Press.
—— (1985), *An Introduction to Functional Grammar*, London, Edward Arnold.
Hymes, D. (1971), 'On communicative competence', in Pride and Holmes (eds) (1972), *Sociolinguistics*, Harmondsworth, Penguin (excerpts from the paper published 1971, Philadelphia, University of Pennsylvania Press).
Labov, W. and Fanshel, D. (1977), *Therapeutic Discourse: Psychotherapy as Conversation*, New York, Academic Press.
Levinson, S. C. (1979), 'Activity type and language', *Linguistics*, 17.
—— (1983), *Pragmatics*, Cambridge, Cambridge University Press.
Merritt, M. (1976), 'On questions following questions in service encounters', *Language in Society*, 5.
Searle, J. R. (1969), *Speech Acts: An Essay in the Philosophy of Language*, Cambridge, Cambridge University Press.

Part IV
The text as a product of interaction and cognition

8 Grammatical metaphor: an initial analysis

L. J. Ravelli
English Language Research, University of Birmingham, UK

8.0 INTRODUCING

Since Halliday's *Introduction to Functional Grammar* (1985a), there has been an increasing interest in the resource of GRAMMATICAL METAPHOR. While his work provides a descriptive framework or background to this phenomenon, there is a need for a more detailed explanation and model of grammatical metaphor. This chapter highlights some of the reasons why it is important and, most significantly, proposes a method of analysis so that it can be studied in detail. Like all attempts at categorization or classification, the proposals are hardly definitive, but hopefully suggestive and useful for further text analysis.

When analysing a text, one of the primary aims is to understand how the text does what it does: how it means. Currently the systemic functional model, although far from being fully developed, does provide a way of studying text which helps us to understand how meanings are expressed. It gives us insight into generalities of meaning: language that signifies a particular relationship between the speaker and the receiver: language that signifies a particular event or feeling in the speaker's world of experience; and language that signifies a particular textual organization of these meanings. It also gives us insight into the specifics of realization: how choices in meaning are reflected in, and conveyed by, the lexicogrammar, and organized over a whole text. Further, it allows us to understand and represent the complexity of language: multi-layered, recursive, interwoven.

The notion of meaning potential is central to a systemic description of language: there are many things we CAN mean, and in order to communicate we CHOOSE from this range of potential meanings. Therefore a theory of language must be able to describe both the potential, and the instantiation of a choice from that potential. If the relationship between the meaning potential and the realization of a choice was totally random, then language would be impossible to describe and study, and probably useless as a communication tool. Evidently, the relationship is not random. Halliday (1985a: 321) has said that '... for any selection in meaning there will be a natural sequence of steps leading towards its realisation'. In a tri-stratal model of language (consisting of semantics, lexicogrammar and phonology), this 'sequence of steps' constitutes a flow-on of choices between the strata, described as PRE-SELECTION, a concept closely bound with that of REALIZATION. For example, if a speaker wants to represent an event or happening, the corresponding choice in the semantics will be that of 'process' (and not, say, 'participant'). This pre-selects a particular process type in the lexicogrammatical stratum represented by a verbal group, which may consist of, for instance, an auxiliary verb and a verb. Simultaneously, participants and, optionally, circumstances will also be chosen.

Such movement between the strata gives rise to the notion of a TYPICAL selection in language following through from the semantics to the phonology. Typical here refers to the expected flow-on of choices between the various linguistic levels and ranks. Martin (1985) elaborates this notion of typicality when he discusses expected lexicogrammatical realizations for generalized semantic concepts. For example, semantic representations of people, places and things are usually realized by nouns; actions by verbs; logical relations by conjunctions and so on.

Yet an examination of almost any adult text soon reveals that these generalized meanings are not always realized in the expected way. I can choose, for example, to represent a particular event as *She sailed out of the room*. That is, I mean that this is a process, carried out by a participant in a particular location. A certain impact is created through metaphor by transferring a meaning from its typical referent to a new and different one. (When someone says *she sailed out of the room*, we do not (usually!) imagine a flooded house and a woman saving herself by an innovative use of the bathtub. Rather we understand that the movement of a water vessel has been transferred to the movement of a person, to suggest something about her: perhaps she is puffed up with pride or anger as a spinnaker is puffed up by the wind.)

However, a different representation may encompass a closely related meaning, as in *Her sailing out of the room caught us by surprise*. Here, although a similar event is represented as in the first example, I now mean that it is a participant integral to another process. This situation is similar to that found in metaphor: there is some kind of transference going on. But it is no longer transfer of referent from the literal to the figurative, between the same grammatical categories, but transfer of representation between different grammatical categories. It cannot be said that *She sailed out of the room*, and *Her sailing out of the room* . . . mean the same thing, because they both do something different in the communication process. Yet they are close in meaning, primarily because of shared experiential content. The difference in the message is the kind of meaning variation which Halliday (1985a: Ch. 10) has called GRAMMATICAL METAPHOR.

Although many others have recognized this process in their work, usually under the term 'nominalization', Halliday recognizes its far-ranging importance in language and suggests that the motivation for grammatical metaphor lies in the register variables in a text. His introduction provides a descriptive framework for examining the phenomenon. The transferred METAPHORICAL forms are essentially variations in grammatical form, 'systematically related in meaning' and 'co-representational' with CONGRUENT forms. Thus *sailed* in the above examples would be the congruent realization of a process, whereas *her sailing* would be the metaphorical realization: the idea of a process is still encoded, and yet it is a Thing which has been realized.

As Halliday emphasizes, neither form is inherently 'better', 'more frequent' nor more of a 'norm' than the other; nor can they be said to be totally synonymous. Further, it should be emphasized that metaphorical forms are not permutations of congruent forms: one does not 'become' the other; there is no 'base form'. Each is a lexicogrammatical form arrived at by a pass through the system network: they are independent realizations, but share a certain core of meaning.

However, it is the case that when presented with two such similar forms, native speakers both recognize the similarities and 'feel' that one is in some way an extension of the other. 'Part of knowing a language is to know what is the most typical "unmarked" way of saying a thing' (Halliday 1985a: 322). This, of course, begs the question of just how we, as native speakers, 'know' this, and of what it is that characterizes a form as congruent or otherwise. From a linguistic point of view, the congruent is that which is the 'most straightforward coding of the meanings selected' (Halliday 1985a: 345). The metaphorical is interpreted by reference to the congruent, and thus the congruent appears to have the status of something like a base form. This, however, is merely a descriptive convenience to facilitate the interpretation of metaphors. Corroboration of adults' intuitive understanding, and linguists' explanation, of the differences between congruent and metaphorical forms is found in an examination of children's speech. They do not use some forms which adults do: they do not use metaphorical forms.

Halliday's discussion of metaphors, both ideational and interpersonal, gives us the basic understanding that '... some aspect of the structural configuration of the clause ... is in some way different from that which would be arrived at by the shortest route ...' (1985a: 345). Yet in order to apply this to discourse analysis much more work is needed. Among other things, one could explore the possibility of different types of metaphor (within the major subsets of interpersonal and ideational), ways to recognize it, and ways to quantify it for textual comparisons.

These areas are examined below. Although an extension of Halliday's work, the following is but a springboard for—hopefully—further study. It does provide a starting point for text analysis, even though more questions may be raised than answered. The research which led to the following conclusions was undertaken in the context of testing Halliday's hypothesis regarding the relationship of metaphor to complexity in language (see Ravelli 1985). This aspect of the study is presented at the end of the chapter.

8.1 MODELLING

It is first necessary to extend the explanation of metaphor, and provide some model of this explanation. Grammatical metaphor may be most simply explained as an alternative lexicogrammatical realization of a choice in the semantics. Thus in the example:

the MOBILITY of the system ...

the speaker is representing some participant (the system) and some quality of that participant (its mobility). However, he has not chosen to realize the quality as some attribute of identification (the system is mobile) but as a participant in its own right, with *the system* as Qualifier. The semantic choice is very much the same, but the lexicogrammatical realization is different. Similarly, with:

VERIFICATION will be a major hang-up

the process of verifying something has been realized as a participant, and the Goal of the process is no longer retrievable. A comment on the likelihood of new agreements has been realized as a participant in the following:

the POSSIBILITY of new agreements ...

thus presenting this comment as a fact, rather than an interpretation of a situation. In:

the art of GENERALSHIP ...

a process (of being a good general) is realized as a participant.

This view of grammatical metaphor, as an alternative lexicogrammatical realization, may be represented diagrammatically as shown in Figure 8.1. Here, one meaning may be realized in two (or more) ways: congruently and metaphorically. This is a simple model, allowing an easy description of the typical and atypical as different lexicogrammatical forms related in meaning. It is possible to network metaphor given this description. A choice in the semantics, such as 'process', would be regarded firstly as congruent, that is as a process, and secondly as metaphorical, that is as a participant. The usual realizations for the choices of process and participant would then carry through to the lexicogrammar, as illustrated in Figure 8.2.

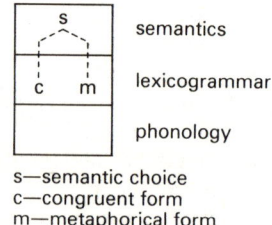

s—semantic choice
c—congruent form
m—metaphorical form

Figure 8.1 Grammatical metaphor interpreted as realization choice

Recursion (which, as explained below, is a feature of metaphor) would be included in the lexicogrammatical networks, as is already the case for descriptions of congruent realizations. Unfortunately there is a great deal of redun-

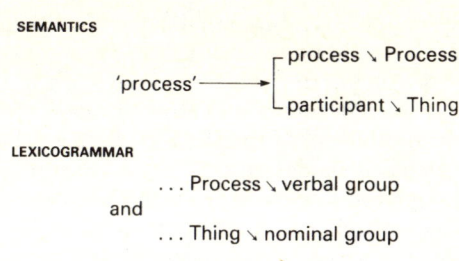

Figure 8.2 Networking metaphor

dancy in such a model, as it would be necessary to make a similar double statement for every different type of metaphor. Further, like many simple models, this interpretation does not account for all the facts, and indeed even misrepresents them. For it is not true that the meaning is the same in both cases: the grammatical category itself has a feedback effect into the semantics, and alternative lexicogrammatical realizations may omit or include different parts of the message (as in the VERIFICATION example, where it is not possible to identify specifically what is being verified, although of course one can make an educated guess at the context). Each representation thus shares some semantic content, but differs in detail.

A preferable model would be one which could encapsulate both the similarities and differences of the comparable realizations. Such a model has been proposed by Halliday (personal communication 1985) and is illustrated in Figure 8.3. In this interpretation, metaphor is seen as a combination of semantic features. That is, two (or more) meaning choices come together in the semantics, forming a compound entry condition for a (combined) meaning, which gives rise to a metaphorical realization in the lexicogrammar.

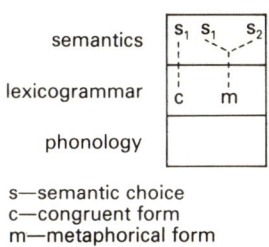

s—semantic choice
c—congruent form
m—metaphorical form

Figure 8.3 Grammatical metaphor interpreted as semantic compound

On the other hand, a congruent lexicogrammatical realization derives from a simple semantic choice. For example, a process meaning combined with a circumstantial meaning (of temporal location, say) may give rise to a metaphorical process, such as *follows* in *night follows day* (*follows* being a combination of, say, *be* and *after*).

This explanation of metaphor has several advantages. Firstly, it does not imply the distinction between meaning and form which is implicit in the first model. Secondly, it is possible to pinpoint the meaning difference between the two forms. Although it would be necessary to represent the level of semantics with system networks as for the lexicogrammar—which has not yet been done—our understanding of metaphorical processes in the language would develop as our understanding of the semantics developed. In contrast, the first interpretation has reached its descriptive limits: metaphor is an alternative realization—it only remains to describe the alternatives.

Other models of metaphor may be proposed—what they say about language, and how they interact with the descriptive framework within which it is suggested, will provide the basis for choosing among them. The first model, despite its inadequacies, was the basis for the following analyses. Its simplicity was its attraction, given that the whole area of grammatical metaphor is underdeveloped.

8.2 ANALYSING

An exploration for possible different types of metaphor was undertaken within a set of eight texts, produced by adults, on the general field of nuclear disarmament. Primarily the focus was on ideational metaphors, although some note was taken of the interpersonal, and both have consequences for the textual metafunction. Table 8.1 lists the types of grammatical metaphor which were found in the texts. Ideational metaphors are revealed through a transitivity analysis (see Halliday 1985a: Ch. 5) by identifying the participants, processes and circumstances of each clause, and determining if the meaning behind the clause is realized congruently or not. This analysis assumes that a speaker knows, for example, that a process meaning is congruently realized as a verbal group, and not by a nominal group. The table presents the alternative realizations which were found for a given semantic choice. Note that grammatical terms have been used to label the semantic choices. Although a taxonomy of generalized concepts for the semantics has not yet been developed, it is counter-intuitive to suggest that such generalized concepts do not exist. They are therefore described with recourse to terms with which we are familiar—namely grammatical terms—which are here to be interpreted as names of semantic choices. The table is followed by an example of each category, and some discussion of the categories.

Examples of each category (in small capitals) are as follows:

1a — the APPOINTMENT of an ambassador
1b — it changed our PERCEPTION of the situation
1c — the sheer COST of it
1d — we had no TALKS last year
1e — its CONTINUATION
2 — INCOMING Soviet missiles
3a — peace through STRENGTH
3b — its INTRINSIC worth
3c — a sense of SECURITY
4a — the POSSIBLE outcome

Table 8.1 Categories of grammatical metaphor

No.	Semantic choice	Metaphorical Realization Function / Class	Congruent Realization Class
1a	material process	Thing / nominal group	verbal group
1b	mental process	Thing / nominal group	verbal group
1c	relational process	Thing / nominal group	verbal group
1d	verbal process	Thing / nominal group	verbal group
1e	behavioural process	Thing / nominal group	verbal group
2	process	Epithet, Classifier / adjective	adjective
3a	quality of a Thing	Thing / nominal group	adverb
3b	quality of a process	Epithet, Classifier / adjective	adverb
3c	quality of a process	Thing / nominal group	(modal) adverb
4a	modality	Epithet / adjective	adjective, passive verb
4b	modality, modulation	Thing / nominal group	conjunction
5a	logical connection	Thing / nominal group	conjunction
5b	logical connection	Process / verbal group	prepositional phrase
6	circumstance	Process / verbal group	nominal group
7a	participant	Classifier / adjective	nominal group
7b	participant	Thing / nominal group	
8a	expansion	Relative Act, Clause / embedded clause	ranking clause
8b	projection	Fact / embedded clause	ranking clause
9	circumstance	Epithet, Classifier / adjective	prepositional clause

4b — first strike CAPABILITY
5a — for that REASON
5b — the arms race CONTAINS the threat
6   — night FOLLOWS day
7a — ECONOMIC development
7b — the art of GENERALSHIP
8a — WWIII is more likely than [[PEACE BREAKING OUT]]
8b — [[ALL IT CAN DO]] is [[to retaliate]]
9   — HISTORICAL experience

The first category, with its various subtypes, was by far the most frequent example of metaphor, averaging about 35 per cent of all instances in each text. This perhaps explains why 'nominalization' is the type of metaphor of which there is the greatest awareness. One other type of process—the existential—has the potential to fall into this category. No examples were found in the texts and so it was omitted from the sub-categorization. Sub-categorization for different process types in the second category was not warranted, because of a lack of sufficient examples.

A type of metaphorical dependence is established between categories 1 and 3b. That which congruently qualifies a process must metaphorically qualify a Thing. For example, if one talks of someone who *behaves irrationally*, one may also realize the process metaphorically, as *behaviour*. In this case the Quality associated with the process is realized as part of the Thing, as in *irrational behaviour*.

Although the study was essentially limited to an examination of ideational metaphors, the fourth category takes some account of interpersonal metaphor. The congruent realization of category 4a (modality) is as a model adverb (commenting on the likelihood of an event). An example might be *it will POSSIBLY turn out like that*. Congruently, category 4b (modality or modulation) is realized by an adjective or a passive verb, as in *they are CAPABLE of striking first*. In both cases, the speaker is projecting his opinion about the validity—or otherwise—of the statement. Metaphorically, these categories are realized respectively by an Epithet or Thing, the corresponding examples being *the POSSIBLE outcome* and *their first strike CAPACITY*, where the speaker's opinion now appears either as an intrinsic part of a Thing, or as a Thing itself. This has the effect of objectifying (and backgrounding) the speaker's opinion.

A distinction was made between categories 5b and 6; however, the differences between them are minimal. In 5b, the participants themselves are metaphorical, thus congruently the logical connection is between PROCESSES. In 6, the participants are congruent; thus the logical connection is between PARTICIPANTS.

An extremely important aspect of grammatical metaphor is illustrated by categories 3c, 4b and 7b. Each illustrates the phenomenon of PARADIGMATIC PLURALITY—or RECURSION—in grammatical metaphor. In such cases, a metaphorical realization has the potential to pass through the network a second time, again being realized metaphorically. Table 8.2 exemplifies this for category 3c.

Table 8.2 Stages of metaphor in category 3c

Semantic choice	quality of a process
Congruent realization	they feel SECURE
1st metaphorical realization	their SECURE feeling
2nd metaphorical realization	their feeling of SECURITY

The three categories exhibiting recursion in these texts each have as their input to the system a metaphorical Epithet or Classifier (in categories 3b, 4a, 7a). This suggests that paradigmatic plurality is limited to such cases. Yet there is no obvious reason why recursion should be a feature of these categories only: it is possible that recursion is general to all categories of metaphor. Note that the recursive option as described here is not an option in the network, but a rewiring mechanism at a point of realization, to bring a realization of the network back into the system at a less delicate point. Apart from paradigmatic plurality, grammatical metaphor also exhibits the feature of SYNTAGMATIC PLURALITY, where the recursive option IS the network feature. This allows more than one metaphor to be realized in the same clause.

In order to reinterpret these categories in light of the second model proposed above, the semantic choice of each category would have to be defined as a combination of meanings. Also those categories exhibiting recursion would be examples of a combined choice linking with another, to form a further combined entry condition.

The detection of grammatical metaphor is not always obvious, and there are at least two devices which may be useful in determining whether a realization is congruent or not. The first of these is derivation. Derivational suffixes are often a sign that the form in question may be metaphorical and should be investigated. Examples include *-ment* in appointment, argument, *-ism* in idealism, and so on. It should of course be remembered that many metaphorical examples are found without any derivational suffixes, and that further, not every suffix indicates a metaphorical form.

The second useful device is agnation. Any form which is metaphorical will have an agnate form corresponding to its congruent realization. For example, a metaphorical realization of a process meaning will have an agnate verbal form, as illustrated below:

 process meaning: *explode*
— metaphorical realization: THE EXPLOSION
— verbal agnate (congruent realization): EXPLODE

Agnation can be more difficult if lexical metaphor has been involved as well, but nevertheless, it remains a valuable and essential criterion in recognizing grammatical metaphor.

Having established the categories of metaphor to be considered, the next step is to quantify the amount of metaphor in a text. For my purposes this was necessary so that the extent of metaphor between texts could be compared with other variables. Quantification was simply a matter of counting the number of instances of metaphor per clause and giving a value of one to each instance. The measure thus represented the proportion of total instances of grammatical metaphor over the total number of clauses in the text.

Two levels of measurement can be considered when quantifying grammatical metaphor: the macro level and the micro level. The micro level accounts for those categories of metaphor as outlined above. Here, the instances of metaphor are treated as syntagmatically INDEPENDENT of other processes of metaphor. The macro level accounts for those instances which are syntagmatically INTERDEPENDENT on other metaphorical processes. At this level, grammatical metaphor can be seen to exhibit syntagmatic plurality, as well as the paradigmatic plurality already discussed. These two levels are illustrated by the example, *it will have a real impact on political thinking*. Here, there are four instances of metaphor at the micro level: *real* (category 3b); *impact* (1a); *political* (7a); and *thinking* (1b). These four instances cluster into two groups at the macro level: *real impact* and *political thinking*.

For comparative purposes, only the measure of metaphor at the micro level was used. The measure at the macro level reveals little about the variation in the extent of metaphor used in a text, as one macro count can include any number of micro processes. However, it is a useful way of highlighting those metaphorical processes which are syntagmatically interdependent. Perhaps a more sophisticated method of quantification will be able to account for this aspect of metaphor, as well as for the potentially different contributions made to the text by the different categories of metaphor, particularly those with paradigmatic plurality.

This method of quantification is obviously very simple, but was able to account for the bulk of metaphorical processes in the texts examined. There remain several types of metaphor which cannot be accounted for with this analysis.

First, DEAD or FROZEN metaphors are excluded. Certain metaphorical expressions enter into the system of language, so that they become the typical or expected way of realizing that meaning. Take, for example, Process + Range configurations, such as *make a mistake* or *take a walk*. The process meaning embodied in the expression is metaphorically realized by the nominal group, and it would seem that this is now the typical way of realizing such meanings. Although we can still say *I was mistaken*, the probability attached to the congruent realization is so low as to be negligible. It would need a particular register (one with high formality, for example) to remotivate the choice. TECHNICAL terms (see Halliday 1985a: 329) and TAXONOMIZED terms are excluded for similar reasons.

Grammatical metaphors representing entities which are both abstract and general are a third type which were beyond the descriptive scope of the categorization as presented here. They constitute an important process in the language, where an abstract term such as *warfare*, *campaign* or *future* generalizes more than one action, forming a cover term for many different participants, activities and activity sequences.

As a final note on the quantification analysis, it should be remembered that the result is an average for a whole text: within a text, clause complexes may be found with no instances of metaphor, or with many more instances than the average. Further exploration at this level could present interesting results for genre analysis.

8.3 APPLYING

The above provides an initial approach to the study of grammatical metaphor, but does not really explain the motivation behind this option nor the functional explanation for its existence. What then, could be the reason for this choice which is available to us when expressing meanings?

Register theory in systemic linguistics provides the contextual background which is the key to an understanding of grammatical metaphor. It allows us to predict the likelihood of a particular choice—such as a congruent or metaphorical form—and provides the motivation for the choice. In the original study which led to this chapter, the key into a general exploration of grammatical metaphor was a study of metaphor and its relations with the register variable of mode. The hypothesis examined was that:

The factor that counts for most in determining the extent of metaphor in the grammar of a text is whether that text is spoken or written [because] speech and writing differ in the kind of complexity that they typically display. [Halliday 1985a: 329]

That is, the probability attached to the choice will be weighted according to the mode of the text. The direct implication of this is that grammatical metaphor contributes to the variation in complexity found between written and spoken texts.

The hypothesis was tested by taking a small set of texts which varied in mode and comparing the interrelationship of complexity and metaphor. The results confirmed the hypothesis. While there is not space here to discuss the full extent of this research, the relationship between mode, complexity and metaphor will be outlined. It should be noted that references to 'spoken' texts encompass only the monologic aspects of speech: features such as turn-taking were not considered.

Mode, as a connotative semiotic, is difficult to describe in a text unless the text is close to one of the idealized poles of the mode scale. Thus an academic treatise may be uncontroversially placed at the 'written' end, and a causal conversation placed at the 'spoken' end. Where, however, does the written article containing 'dialogue' belong? Or a formal, pre-prepared public speech? Gregory (1967) attempts to differentiate such texts on the mode scale. However, the only satisfactory description of texts for mode must look at the text from the plane of language, to measure the contribution of mode to the lexicogrammar.

Mode has been most closely linked with the textual metafunction in language (see, for example, Halliday 1978: 189), and it is in the ORGANIZATION of the message that mode largely makes its mark. Halliday (1985c) discusses this at length, and it is recapitulated here. The variation to be found in the lexicogrammar, coinciding with variation in mode, centres in the complexity of the text. Complexity is a composite of two features: GRAMMATICAL INTRICACY—the relationship of clauses within clause complexes—and LEXICAL DENSITY—the compacting of ideational information within the clause.

Lexical density is calculated by dividing the total number of lexical items over the total number of clauses. Grammatical intricacy is calculated on the basis of syntagmatic relations between clauses, within clause complexes. Clauses within a complex may enter into relations of recursion, interdependency (hypotaxis and parataxis), and logical–semantic relations (expansion and elaboration). Intricacy in a clause complex builds along two dimensions: the LENGTH, or the number of clauses in the complex, and the DEPTH, or number of ranking layers. Intricacy is a summation of the length and depth of the complex. Consider the following examples, divided into clauses, taken from Halliday (1985c: 12):

Ex. 1 — ||| Whenever I'd visited there before, || I'd ended up feeling || that other people might get hurt || if I tried to do anything more |||

Ex. 2 — ||| Every previous visit had left me with a sense of the risk to others in further attempts at action on my part. |||

It can be seen from these examples how similar semantic choices can be conveyed in different ways. The first carries its message via processes: *had visited*, *ended up feeling*, *might get hurt*, *tried to do*. This realization scatters the lexical items over several clauses, giving rise to syntactic complexity, while reducing its lexical density. In comparison, the only process in the second is *had left*. This example carries its message via participants: *every previous visit*, *a sense of the risk to others*, *further attempts at action on my part*, as well as the pronominal *me*. Although there is a similar ideational content as in the first, this realization via participants condenses the lexical information, increasing its density, while reducing the intricacy.

In the above examples, the text with the high lexical density and low grammatical intricacy is more likely to be characterized as 'written' than the text with low lexical density and high grammatical intricacy. This is not to say that one of these is more 'complex' than the other: the variation is not in LEVEL of complexity, but in TYPE. This variation in complexity reflects the essential difference between written and spoken texts. Although both are created dynamically, they are presented and processed in different ways. Speech is presented and processed dynamically, as an ongoing PROCESS, and must therefore organize its message in a different way to that of writing, which is presented and processed synoptically, as a finished PRODUCT. Hence the incongruity of the section headings in this chapter: they suggest that I am in the middle of doing something, whereas what is actually presented is a finished product.

It is possible to measure lexical density and grammatical intricacy in such a way that precise differentiation can be made between texts whose mode is otherwise difficult to distinguish (see also Halliday forthcoming; Ure 1971). However, density and intricacy are nothing more than a characterization of mode. The measures reflect the consequences of a choice which determines the type of information distribution in the clause, but they cannot explain this choice. A speaker does not choose, say, 'high density' in a text: the lexicogrammatical devices which result in such a density are chosen.

The ability to recognize, categorize and quantify grammatical metaphor, as outlined in the previous section, allowed Halliday's hypothesis regarding the link between metaphor and mode to be tested. It was found that texts typical of the 'spoken' end of the mode scale, with low lexical density and high grammatical intricacy, had relatively little grammatical metaphor. Those at the 'written' end, with a complementary complexity, had much more. That is, a predominantly congruent text is typical of the organization of spoken texts, where relationships are primarily between processes (within a clause complex), and a largely metaphorical text is typical of the organization of written texts, with relationships primarily between participants (within a clause). Not every instance of grammatical metaphor will have this effect; nor is this its only effect. However, the most prolific instance of grammatical metaphor, that of a process meaning being realized as a Thing, certainly brings about this change in relationships.

The way in which grammatical metaphor can create a switch from process relations to participant relations may be explained as follows. A ranking clause has only one process—it may be a complex verbal group, but there is still only one. If process meanings are to be related, it must be via a linking of the clauses, that is, via the resources of recursion, taxis and logical–semantic relations. However, if the process meaning is realized metaphorically as a Thing then it may function in the clause as a participant. In this way, two or more process meanings may be related within one clause, thus avoiding the clause complex systems. As a result, the ideational information of two or more clauses may be realized in one, with a correspondingly lower grammatical intricacy and higher lexical density.

This, then, is the primary link between metaphor, mode and complexity. A closer examination of 'reworded' versions of metaphorical or congruent examples highlights interesting effects in the constituents of the message: some differ between the two versions, or are backgrounded, or are irretrievable. Further, as each constituent contributes to the overall message, variation in the constituents leads to variation in the message. The departure point of the message, for example, is its Theme, realized in English by the first element of the clause. This element is typically a participant (nominal group), or a circumstance (adverbial group or prepositional phrase), but rarely a process. However, a process meaning can be the point of departure of the message if the resource of grammatical metaphor is deployed. When a process meaning is realized as a Thing, it may then function in the clause as a participant. Also, in terms of Given/New structure (see Halliday, 1985b), grammatical metaphor enables one to realize a process meaning in the unmarked focus of information: at the end of the clause. When metaphors are reworded (see, for example, Martin 1985: 5), it is often extremely difficult to retain the Thematic and information structure of the metaphorical version.

This demonstrates one of the functional explanations of grammatical metaphor: to achieve a particular organization in the text. Variation in the organization of a message gives rise to modifications of meaning: atypical parts of the message may be treated as given or may receive a focus which would not be possible through congruent realizations. Metaphor thus contributes to meaningful distinctions in the language. As the primary metaphorical resource used to achieve this message organization is that of category 1 (process meaning realized as Thing), the consequences in the lexicogrammar of using metaphor are the changes in density and intricacy characteristic of written or spoken texts. Figure 8.4 summarizes the interrelationship of the variables mentioned here.

Figure 8.4 Feature correlations

An understanding of the functional role and textual consequences of grammatical metaphor is thus essential for a full understanding of the meaning of any text which uses this option. An appreciation of both the positive functional aspects (such as the contribution to a particular text organization) and its possible negative aspects (such as the inability to retrieve certain information) is necessary for the comprehension and manipulation of written texts. This is particularly important in the context of teaching both children and foreign learners, who may have difficulty in mastering the resource. While this chapter is but a step towards explaining, classifying and quantifying the phenomenon, it is hoped that it will go some way towards articulating this understanding.

BIBLIOGRAPHY

Gregory, M. (1967), 'Aspects of varieties differentiation', *Journal of Linguistics*, 3, No. 2, 177–274.

Halliday, M. A. K. (1978), *Language as Social Semiotic: The Social Interpretation of Language and Meaning*, London, Edward Arnold.

—— (1985a), *An Introduction to Functional Grammar*, London, Edward Arnold.

—— (1985b), 'It's a fixed word order language is English', *ITL Review of Applied Linguistics*, **67–8**, 91–116.

—— (1985c), 'Spoken and written modes of meaning', in Horowitz, R. and Samuels, S. J. (eds), *Comprehending Oral and Written Language*. Academic Press (forthcoming).

—— (1987), *Spoken and Written Language*, Deakin University, Deakin University Press.

Martin, J. R. (1985), *Systemic Functional Linguistics and an Understanding of Written Text*, Department of Linguistics, University of Sydney.

Quirk, R., Greenbaum, S., Leech, G. and Svartik, J. (1972), *A Grammar of Contemporary English*, London, Longman.

Ravelli, L. J. (1985), 'Metaphor, mode, and complexity: an exploration of co-varying patterns', B.A. thesis, Department of Linguistics, University of Sydney.

Ure, J. (1971), 'Lexical density and register differentiation', in Perrin, G. E. and Trim, J. L. M. (eds), *Applications of Linguistics: Selected Papers of the Second International Congress of Applied Linguistics, Cambridge 1969*, Cambridge, Cambridge University Press, 443–52.

9 Cohesion in spoken Arabic texts

Yowell Y. Aziz
Mosul University, Iraq

9.0 INTRODUCTION

In recent years the focus of linguistic studies has increasingly shifted from language as a code—microlinguistics—to language as a means of communication—macrolinguistics. This change involves (a) studying language, not in its idealized form, but as used in a context, (b) looking for a unit larger than or beyond the sentence, and (c) stressing communicative competence rather than linguistic competence. Two units of analysis have gradually emerged within the field of macrolinguistics: text and discourse. Text analysis is concerned with the formal level of how sentences are built into larger suprasentential units or texts. Discourse analysis, on the other hand, deals with the functional level of how language is actually used in everyday life (James 1980: 102).

According to the linguistic system suggested by Halliday (1970), language fulfils three major functions: ideational, interpersonal and textual. The structure of language can be explained in terms of these three functional-semantic components. The ideational component expresses propositional relations and our experience of the outside world. The interpersonal component encodes speech roles and conveys the attitude of the speaker towards the 'content' of the message. The textual component is concerned with creating text, and cohesion is one of the methods of realizing this.

Cohesion addresses itself to the question of how sentences are tied up together to form a text. It studies such things as the nature of cohesive elements, whether they are semantic or syntactic, their direction, whether they point to what precedes (anaphoric) or to what follows (cataphoric), and the distance in terms of the number of the sentences intervening between the cohesive item and the element to which it refers.

Texts may be classified according to their medium of expression into oral and written. These may be further divided according to the purpose which they serve into various kinds, such as descriptive, narrative argumentative and expository.

This chapter studies cohesion in one type of oral Arabic texts which may be called narrative. It is based on the analysis of a one-hour, tape-recorded traditional (folklore) story related by a young woman residing in Mosul District (northern Iraq). Defining the boundary of an Arabic sentence is always fraught with problems. It is more so in oral texts than in written ones where the rules of orthography may offer some help out of the maze. In delimiting successive sentences in an utterance, my decision has been influenced by phonological and syntactic considerations. Long pauses, falling intonation in statements and open interrogatives, rising intonation in closed interrogatives, unrelatedness in syntactic structure and change of the speaker may be regarded as markers pointing to a new sentence.

Cohesion in English has been discussed by a number of linguists including Halliday and Hasan (1976), who mention five types of cohesive devices: Reference (a), Substitution (b), Ellipsis (c), Conjunction (d) and Lexical Cohesion (e).

(1) a. I met a man. HE was carrying a big bag.
   b. My shirt is too old. I must get a new ONE.
   c. What do you think of the poems?—A lot (OF THE POEMS) are excellent.
   d. He worked hard. He THEREFORE felt tired.
   e. There was a lot of smoke and noise. The SMOKE seemed to come from the direction of the village.

In analysing the text, I have mainly followed the method suggested by Halliday and Hasan (1976: Ch. 8), with slight modifications to suit Arabic texts. The main points taken into consideration are the types of devices used, their frequency in a sentence and in the text as a whole, and the direction to which they refer.

9.1 ANALYSIS OF MATERIAL

In applying the criteria stated above, I have found that the text comprises 328 sentences. The total number of the devices attested is 1,135, giving an average number of 3.460 ties per sentence. Eight main types of ties have been attested. These are: Reference, Lexical Cohesion, Conjunction, Repetition, Question–Response, Ellipsis, Substitution and Parallel Cohesion. Table 9.1 shows the number and percentage of each of these types.

9.2 REFERENCE

As a cohesive element, Reference has a semantic basis; it functions as a proform which identifies anaphorically or cataphorically a person or a thing stated somewhere in the text. Within Reference four subtypes of cohesive ties have been attested: Personal pronouns, Demonstratives, the Definite Article and Comparison.

Pronominal Reference is by far the most frequent among the subtypes of Reference, totalling 479 instances. Typically, third-person pronouns may act

Table 9.1 Type of Cohesive Devices

Cohesive Device	Number	%
Reference	587	51.718
Lexical	460	41.528
Conjunction	32	2.819
Repetition	21	1.850
Question–Response	17	1.497
Ellipsis	10	0.882
Substitution	4	0.353
Parallel	4	0.353
Total	1,135	100

as cohesive ties. First- and second-person pronouns do not, for they normally identify persons or things in the outside world; their reference is (in Halliday's terminology) exophoric. This is confirmed by the present study: all the pronominal ties are third-person pronouns, including what may be termed implicit or ellipted pronouns. In Arabic, a pronoun is understood but not explicitly expressed, when it is fully given information. In (2)

(2) We are waiting for the train. IT is already late.

train is given information in the second sentence. In English it is normally replaced by a pronoun (*it* in this case). In Arabic, if the event is expressed by means of a verb, then its subject is usually left out both in written and oral texts, as in (3).

(3) ʿanuntidhir lqitār. tʾakhar.

In (4) *rijjāl* the subject of the verb *ja*, being given information, has been deleted. (The number after S refers to the number of the sentence in the text.)

(4) marrat l-ayyām. w ja. (S20) (Several days passed by; then (he) came.)

This may be compared with (5) where the pronoun, usually carrying a heavy stress, expresses new information.

(5) ja ʿAli ?—la, HUWA ma ja. akhu ja. (Did Ali come? No, he didn't, but his brother did.)

In such instances, the pronoun is explicitly expressed in Arabic. This is also illustrated in (6):

(6) ma aʿrif, gallu, lazim nidhbaḥḥa HUWA bala ḥis abu ṭalaʿ barra. (He said, "All the same, we must kill her." HE (the son) went out unseen by his father.)

Although the Definite Article comes second in frequency, it accounts for only sixty-one instances (6.984 per cent). Normally, the Definite Article, functioning as a cohesive tie, introduces given information, a person or a thing which has already been mentioned in the text. Its direction is usually anaphoric. In (7) the new information is first introduced by the Indefinite Article; in the second sentence the information has become given and is expressed by the Definite Article.

(7) I saw A MAN and A WOMAN coming. THE WOMAN was tall and blonde.

This is also true of Arabic, as illustrated by (8).

(8) hādha damma hiyanu B-SHUSHA. hādha za'aṭu L-SHUSHA. (S24–5) (Here is her blood in a bottle. They gave him the bottle.)

In Arabic, as in English, Demonstratives may function as determiners (9a) or as independent pronouns (9b). Unlike English Demonstratives, Arabic Demonstrative determiners are always used with definite nouns.

(9) a. chan aku farid rijāl. HĀDHA l-rijāl kilma tijinu binit yedhbaḥa. (S1, 2) (Once upon a time, there was a man. This man used to . . .)
   b. HĀDHA farid yūm, huwa ra'iḥ 'ala safar. (S3) (One day, this (man) intended to go on a trip.)

Moreover, Demonstratives in Arabic are sensitive to number and gender, and may refer to a person or thing far or near in time or space. Forty-one instances of Demonstratives have been attested in the text; all except one have near reference. Pronominal Demonstratives are slightly more frequent, accounting for twenty-three instances (56.098 per cent) as against eighteen (43.902 per cent) instances of Demonstratives used as determiners. All the examples have anaphoric reference.

Comparative reference may express identity, similarity or difference between two things. Only six instances (1.023 per cent) of Comparison were attested in the text, five of which belong to difference and six to similarity. Table 9.2 shows the number and percentage of the subtypes within Reference.

Table 9.2 Subtypes of Reference

Subtype	Number	%
Pronouns	479	81.601
Article	61	10.392
Demonstrative	41	6.984
Comparison	6	1.023
Total	587	100

9.3 LEXICAL COHESION

Lexical Cohesion may be achieved through reiteration of the same item (10a), its synonym (10b), superordinate (10c), general item (10d), or collocation (10e).

(10) a. We saw an abandoned car. THE CAR looked old.
    b. The AUTOMOBILE looked old.
    c. The FORD looked old.
    d. The old THING was in good condition.
    e. There was no trace of the DRIVER.

Four subtypes of Lexical Cohesion have been attested: reiteration of the same item, collocation, synonym and general item.

Reiteration of the same word accounts for the highest number of ties within Lexical Cohesion, totalling 393 (85.969 per cent). This is hardly surprising since a narrative text belongs to an institutionalized style which relies heavily on a limited vocabulary. Such a style is easier to transmit orally from one generation to another than one which depends on a larger repertoire of words.

Collocation represents a looser type of link between two items, which may not be related with regard to their reference (cf. 10e). The relationship is based on the probability of items occurring together in a text. The total number of instances in the text is thirty-nine (8.478 per cent).

The third subtype in terms of frequency is reiteration in the form of a synonym. This relation is based on identical reference of items. In the text, it accounts for twenty-one instances (4.566 per cent).

Items governed by a general relation have also identical reference. They are of infrequent occurrence in the text, totalling only five (1.087 per cent), probably because this device belongs to a higher rhetorical style. Table 9.3 summarizes the number and percentage of the subtypes within Lexical Cohesion.

Table 9.3 Subtypes of Lexical Cohesion

Subtype	Number	%
Same	395	85.869
Collocation	39	8.478
Synonym	21	4.566
General	5	1.087
Total	460	100

9.4 CONJUNCTION

Conjunctions are explicit markers which link two successive sentences. They may express various meanings including additive (11a), temporal (11b), adversitive (11c), causal (11d), or continuative relation (11e) between two sentences.

(11) a. He has always worked hard. FURTHER, he never complains.
    b. The girl explained everything about the accident. THEN she sat down and burst into tears.
    c. From morning till night they looked everywhere for the missing animal. BUT there was no trace of it.
    d. They THEREFORE abandoned the search early the next morning.
    e. WELL, nobody knew what happened to it.

Four subtypes of Conjunction have been attested in the text: additive, temporal, continuative and adversative.

The additive conjunction represented in the text by *wa* (and) often contracted to *w* merely adds to what has been said in the previous sentence. It normally joins two successive sentences. Temporal conjunctions represented by *ba'da* (after) and *lamma* (when) express a sequence in time between two sentences. Continuative conjunctions, here exemplified by *mut'akid* (of course), *maynshid* (all the same) and *'ajal* (well) convey the idea of continuation between successive sentences. The relation expressed by adversative conjunctions, represented in the text by *'ajal* (then), expresses the idea of something happening contrary to expectation. The number and percentage of the subtypes of Conjunction in the text are shown in Table 9.4.

Table 9.4 Subtypes of Conjunction

Subtype	Number	%
Additive	17	53.125
Temporal	10	31.250
Continuative	3	9.375
Adversative	2	6.250
Total	32	100

The devices already discussed may be described as major in terms of frequency, to be distinguished from the ties which will be mentioned below and may be termed minor.

9.5 REPETITION

In order to achieve cohesion, the narrator sometimes repeats part of the preceding sentence (cf. Wonderly 1968).

(12) fatat l-bnaya, bintim, ṭitlib minim gharaḍ. LIMMA ṭilbit ḥay, daḥag ʿalihā. (S27, 28) (The girl, their daughter, came to them to ask for some object. When she asked he looked at her.)

This is in contrast with English, which often uses conjunctions to mark logical connections between sentences (Quirk 1972: 661). Repetition sometimes links in a loose way as in (13).

(13) minū gaʿid? l-hārūn. limma gaʿid l-hārūn, nhaḍam w-ziʿil. (Who was sitting? The tom-cat. When the tom-cat was sitting he became very angry.)

Repetition is the most frequent of the minor devices and accounts for twenty-one instances (1.855 per cent).

9.6 QUESTION–RESPONSE

A cohesive device which is probably a characteristic of oral texts and is not attested in written texts (cf. Aziz forthcoming) is what I term Question–Response technique. The narrator asks a question, which he usually answers in the following sentence.

(14) thani yum minu ja? ja l-shaikh. (S118, 119) (The next day, who came? The Shaikh came.)

Among the minor devices, this technique is relatively frequent, accounting for seventeen instances (1.502 per cent). The response may involve either repetition as in (14) or ellipsis as in (15).

(15) minu aku wara l-bāb? akhuha Mḥammad. (S162, 163) (Who was behind the door? Her brother Mohammed.)

Often the response immediately follows the question, but this is not necessary as in (16).

(16) minu shāf l-ṣindūg w l-dābba? aku jamaʿa jaīn min l-chūl. rajʿīn min l-ḥaṣād. shāfu l-ṣindūg. (S200, 202) (Who saw the box and the donkey? A group of men were coming home from harvest. They saw the box.)

This type of cohesion may be regarded as cataphoric since the first sentence (question) points forward to the second (response).

9.7 ELLIPSIS

Ellipsis means deleting from a sentence certain elements which can be uniquely recovered. This device is used to avoid repetition or focus attention on new information. As a cohesive tie, Ellipsis usually functions anaphorically and may involve omitting one element or more, ranging from the subject of a clause (17a) to the whole clause except the item expressing polarity (17b).

(17) a. lakin hiya shlūn binit! nūr tiḍwi. (S250, 251) (What a girl she was! Very beautiful.)
b. inta ṭamām shiltu?—lā walla. (S268, 269) (Did you really take it?—No, honestly.)

Ten instances of Ellipsis have been attested in the text; the ellipted elements are: subject (one instance), predicate (two instances), prepositional phrase (one instance), object (one instance), subject of a nominal sentence (two instances), the whole clause (two instances), the verb of existence and adverb (one instance).

9.8 SUBSTITUTION

The last two devices attested in the text are Substitution and Parallel. Only four instances of each were found. They may therefore be regarded as infrequent ties.

Substitutive devices found in the text are stereotyped expressions which are used to avoid repeating certain parts of the story which have already been mentioned.

(18) galulū tara ibni l-salfa HĪCHI w HĪCHI. (S255) (They said: "O son, the story is such and such.")

9.9 PARALLEL

Parallel cohesion is a rhetorical device based on producing and placing together similar structures. Brutus's oration in *Julius Caesar* and the first page in Dickens's *A Tale of Two Cities* are well-known examples in English. The examples attested in the text are less involved as one can judge from (19).

(19) baʿad ayām martu wildit. wildit binit. (S9, 10) (A few days later, his wife gave birth (to a child). She gave birth to a girl.)

It should be acknowledged, however, that identifying parallel structures in oral texts is not easy: many utterances show some kind of similarity in their construction. For these structures to be considered parallel is a matter of degree; in other words, parallel cohesion forms a cline here.

9.10 CONCLUSION

Sentences in oral narrative texts use certain cohesive ties including referring items, lexical relationships, explicit logical connections, ellipsis, repetition, question–response, substitution and parallel structures. It has been noted by a number of linguists that certain languages, when achieving cohesion, tend to avoid repetition through using substitution, ellipsis or proforms. English may be considered one of these languages (cf. Wonderly 1968). Other languages go in the opposite direction; they prefer to realize cohesion by repeating certain items of the preceding sentence. A quick look at Table 9.1 and Table 9.3 shows that Arabic belongs to the second group of languages. Ellipsis and substitution are not frequent; whereas repetition of the same word or part of the preceding sentence has a high frequency among the cohesive devices. If this is confirmed by further investigation using larger and more varied data, it will have interesting pedagogical implications. Arabic learners of English will have to get rid of some of their acquired habits of preferring repetition. English learners of Arabic, on the other hand, will have to learn to do the opposite. However, further investigation of other types of oral texts is required before a full account of cohesion in oral Arab texts becomes available. As I have already said, such knowledge would be useful pedagogically and for people interested in translation. It will also contribute to the general theory of contrastive analysis.

KEY TO THE TRANSLITERATION OF ARABIC WORDS

Consonants

‘ : glottal stop similar to the sound which replaces 't' in some dialects of Glasgow.
th : voiceless inter-dental sound pronounced like the first consonant in the English word *three*.
ḥ : voiceless pharyngeal fricative.
kh : voiceless velar fricative.
dh : voiced dental fricative pronounced like the first consonant of the English word *the*.
ṣ : voiceless velarized fricative.
ḍ : voiced dental velarized stop.
ṭ : voiceless dental velarized stop.
ẓ : voiced velarized inter-dental fricative.
c : voiced pharyngeal fricative.
gh : voiced velar fricative.
q : voiceless unaspirated uvular stop.

Vowels

ā : long vowel pronounced like the English vowel in *cat*.
ī : long vowel pronounced like the English vowel in *beat*.
ū : long vowel pronounced like the English vowel in *boot*.

BIBLIOGRAPHY

Aziz, Y. Y. (1986), 'Textual Cohesion in Written Arabic', *Adab Al-Mustansiriya*,
Halliday, M. A. K. and Hasan, R. (1976), *Cohesion in English*, London, Longman.
James, K. (1980), *Contrastive Analysis*, London, Longman.
Quirk, R., Greenbaum, S., Leech, G. and Svartvik, J. (1972), *A Grammar of Contemporary English*, London, Longman.
Wonderly, W. L. (1968), *Bible Translation For Popular Use*, London, United Bible Societies.

10 Text structure and text semantics

J. L. Lemke
City University of New York, New York, USA

10.1 TEXT STRUCTURE AND ACTIVITY STRUCTURE

The structure of a text is the result of the structured social practices that create that text. In this sense we may consider a text structure to be a special case of an ACTIVITY STRUCTURE (Lemke 1984, 1985a). Such a notion of text structure then applies equally to the structure of spoken and written language because we formulate the structural relations as relations among actions, rather than among spoken or written text units.

Activity structures are characteristic of a community. They are regular, repeatable and repeated, sequences of context-dependent options for the organization of meaningful actions into socially recognizable events or situation types. The social meaning of an action is determined to a large extent by the activity structure context in which it is performed. Each action takes its meaning from a context which it itself helps to create. More precisely, the DYNAMIC meaning of an action is its meaning in the context-up-to-now (the time created by its performance), at which point it has a further MEANING POTENTIAL contingent on the possible actions that may follow it within the same activity structure. When an activity structure has been, at least potentially, completed, all its constituent actions are RETROACTIVELY assignable their SYNOPTIC meanings in the completed structure (cf. Bourdieu 1972; Martin 1985; Lemke 1984, 1985a). The tendency to regard all meanings as synoptic derives from the overemphasis in text study on written texts. It neglects some essential aspects of meaning, and structuration, that are clearer if we consider the dynamic flow of spoken language or even the moment-to-moment meaning-making processes of reading an 'object-text' (Lemke, in press, c).

The object-text belongs to the order of 'things' rather than that of meanings *per se*. It is the physical text, the printed marks on paper, the illuminated pixels on the screen, the magnetized domains on tape or disk. The social conventions of reading practices, enacted in the activity structure of reading, WRITES a 'meaning-text' WITH the object-text. There are as many meaning-texts as there are readings, and it is only the commonality of the social conventions concerning reading that lets us speak even approximately of a 'meaning of the text'. It is a dangerous approximation, mainly used by those in authority to demand limits on the meaning-texts made in a community.

Consider the text of an episode of classroom discourse (see transcript in the Appendix.) The activity structure of this episode can only be described in terms of an analysis of many episodes and lessons (Lemke 1983b). The episode presents an instance of an optional element, STUDENT INITIATED DIALOGUE, within the activity structure of CLASSROOM LESSON. CLASSROOM LESSON is an obligatory element within a larger structure we might call SCHOOL ROUTINE, the activities of a day at school. This subtype of STUDENT INITIATED DIALOGUE has a regular pattern with obligatory elements Student Question and Teacher Answer and optional Teacher Check-up and Student Response, all in that order. The optional elements have the teacher ask the student if he or she is satisfied with the answer, and the student reply. In this case two other optional elements precede the Student Question: a Student Bid, realized by Cheryl's raising her hand, and a Teacher Nomination, 'Cheryl' at the end of line (1). The Question is asked in lines (2–3); the Answer is realized by an extended rhetorical structure of Triad Dialogue (see below and Lemke 1983b), covering lines (4–27). The Check-up is line (28), and the Response is an implied Negative, realized by an uncompleted structure beginning with a Student Challenge in line (29). The episode concludes with the obligatory Teacher Reply to a Negative Response, lines (30–33, 34–37), and a new Student Question (line 38), starting another STUDENT INITIATED DIALOGUE.

Dynamically, we do not know at the end of line (1) that the synoptically definable activity structure just described has indeed begun. Cheryl might have raised her hand to signal a Bid in any one of a number of activity structures (e.g. GETTING THE PASS, or Bid to Answer in relation to the Question on line (1), etc.). Note, moreover, that her utterance is not initially in the form of a direct question, nor is the Answer immediately recognizable as an answer. In fact it proceeds almost immediately to a question, line (5). Members of this community, or any community that uses these activity structures, will not be unsure for long, however, what is happening. When line (28) is reached, even the novice analyst has no doubts about the synoptic structure. We will continue to analyse this episode throughout the chapter. First, however, we need to consider more carefully a fundamental notion.

What do we mean by 'structure'? Following Halliday's (1985) notion of MULTIVARIATE STRUCTURE, and neglecting infinite recursion, we can define the notion of 'a structure' as a set of relations on a linear sequence of units, such that criteria can be defined for when the structure (a higher-level unit in a constituency hierarchy) has been completed (instanced, realized). Nominal groups, clauses, folktales, soccer matches, concerts, Catholic masses and washing-up are all structures in this sense. To define a completed, or at least a possibly completed structure, we need to use a FUNCTIONAL rather than strictly a formal set of relations and units. Neither the units nor the relations need take priority. What is a 'process' but whatever can stand in a 'process–participant relation' to a 'participant'? We tend to give priority to units only because of the habit of reification. Functional relations define functional units, and vice versa. More importantly, the relations must be (at least in part) relations between the HETEROGENEOUS units. If all units are of the same functional type (class), and all relations are, say, 'participant–participant' relations, completable structures can be defined only formally (e.g. a three-participant homogeneous 'structure' or a five-participant one). A true multivariate structure must contain at least two functional types of unit (or equivalently at least one heterogeneous relation) to be functionally, and generally completable. We know that we have a (possibly) complete structure of a given kind when we have a specific number of units in specific relations to one another. Otherwise, as in Halliday's UNIVARIATE structures, recursion dominates and there is never any reason to expect an end (cf. a cohesion chain, a recursive verbal-complex or clause-complex). These are not properly structures at all in the sense I am using the term now. My own COVARIATE STRUCTURE (Lemke 1985a), which includes Halliday's univariate type, covers the case of homogeneous relations of co-classed units, and should perhaps be called a 'structuring principle' rather than a kind of structure.

It does not matter to the notion of completability that it is possible to go on extending an actual realization of a structure indefinitely in principle. What matters is rather that it is possible to stop at some points, but not at others, and have the cumulative sequence count in a community as complete. Special cases, such as acceptable ellipsis, also do not matter to the principle, since each structure is defined as a set of 'context-dependent options' and these must take into account WHEN ellipsis is or is not acceptable. If it is not clear from the definition and examples, we should note explicitly that an activity structure may realize an action within a larger (higher-order, or rank) structure. Context-dependence refers not only to the occurrence of units at the same rank, within a structure, but also to dependence on details of the higher structure.

In our classroom episode, if we look at line (10), we clearly need the full hierarchical structural context to make sense of it. The initial *The S* is a confirmation, a Positive Evaluation of Cheryl's own *S* in line (9). It is followed by a Teacher Elaboration on that answer, which presumes the whole exchange from line (5), and the rhetorical structure of TRIAD DIALOGUE, whose typical extended pattern is: Teacher Preparation, Teacher Question, Student Bid, Teacher Nomination, Student Answer, Teacher Evaluation, Teacher Elaboration. The semantic structural relations of these units are implied by their names, and can be formalized further (see Lemke 1983b).

At the next higher rank, all of this TRIAD DIALOGUE is realizing the element Teacher Answer in the classroom activity structure of STUDENT INITIATED DIALOGUE, which is itself an optional element in the larger activity structure of the CLASSROOM LESSON. The elements in all these structures are defined functionally, and completability is ensured once the final obligatory element has occurred, even though recursive options might continue indefinitely.

10.2 ACTIVITY STRUCTURE AND GENRE

GENRE in the sense of 'generic structure potential' (Halliday and Hasan 1985: Ch. 4; Hasan 1984, forthcoming) corresponds exactly to a specification of a completable activity structure, though there are differences of perspective. The notion of the obligatory elements shows both the feature of heterogeneity and of completeness despite optional recursion. The specification of options, and of ordering, complete this picture. What is less considered are the RELATIONS that must be construed between elements (pairwise or otherwise) for them to count as being those elements. That is, in what SEMANTIC relation must we construe the realizations of two elements in order for us to be able to make them fit the pattern of the structural formula of elements? In a GSP, each element has a functional label, but a great deal more is implied by these labels about the semantic relations of the elements, and this needs to be specified. Specifying the semantic features of ELEMENTS and their typical realizations is only a very indirect, and incomplete, way of specifying the semantics of their relationships. By and large it is only the FORMAL RELATIONSHIPS (e.g. ordering) that are specified directly in the GSP approach.

Another, and perhaps more important, aspect of the activity structure specification which is not foregrounded in the notion of the GSP is context-dependence. Whether or not something can count as an element within a particular GSP will in part depend on whether or not some other element has occurred. This point has recently received more emphasis in Hasan's (forthcoming) discussion of genre in terms of OUTLINE.

When we consider the dependence of the structural meaning of an element on one structure's place in a larger structure, things become even more complex. It is only a rough approximation to take a genre of GSP as being autonomous, i.e. being itself definable independent of its wider context. For some very ritualized genres, the approximation will work, and naturally it is a wise choice to study these genres first to develop a model of genre structure. But, in general, a sequence of acts may be construed, apart from context, as fitting many possible genres or subgenres.

The SYNOPTIC meaning of an element derives from our construing it as a particular functional unit in a particular structure. This assumes that we have a completed structure of reference (even if itself ambiguous), i.e. that we know WHICH GSP is relevant. But DYNAMIC meanings occur on the way to a completed structure. Since structures of many ranks may be involved, there is always a degree of incompletion, and the meaning of an action (or bit of text) depends in part on these wider, still indeterminate contexts. Real life and its texts are full of surprises. In literature it takes consummate artistry to shape later events so as to compel wholesale reinterpretation of what has gone before. In life it happens all the time, and dynamic meanings are correspondingly important. If a text from life turns out in a certain way, the path it took to get where it did depends on the moment-to-moment dynamic meanings that its creators, and we, responded to. We do not follow finished scripts. We branch, diverge and realize options in ways not predictable before the events we respond to occurred. We respond to the dynamic meanings of those events, as they seem at the time—times, always, when the longer-term synoptic picture is not yet available to us; when the meanings of the moment depend on still uncompleted and unpredictable larger structures of action in which we find ourselves immersed. To give an adequate account of the structural organization of meanings in a text, we must be able to follow the continuous recontextualizations of meaning as it emerges moment to moment, and so our notions of the context-dependence of GSP assignments, or equivalently of the GSP definition of a functional genre, must be adequate to this important task.

The last major difference between the ACTIVITY STRUCTURE perspective and that of GENRE defined through a GSP are their answers to the question of WHAT it is that is structured. Neither really makes the mistake of claiming that 'text' is structured. In a GSP it is the relations of the functional elements that are structured, i.e. it is the genre itself that is structured. A text is construed as having a particular genre structure when we read a GSP 'onto' it. The alternative view is that it is the social activities that give rise to the text which are structured. We can read a structure onto a text by interpreting its meanings (making the meaning-text) as if the abstract text had been produced by the actions of a familiar activity structure. Or, more simply, we 'write' the meaning-text using some particular activity structure of reading practices. The activity structure perspective forces us to consider genre structure as both more contingent, and more the product of social practices, than a view which tends to reify genres as givens. Of course, the same dangers exist with respect to the activity structures themselves, but hopefully the overall emphasis on social practices rather than texts as fundamental will help us avoid this. From here on, I will use the term GENRE to refer to an activity structure in which language is used in such a way as to produce a specific, context-dependent set of semantic relations among the elements defined and ordered by a GSP. This use of GENRE will refer equally to speech genres and written genres.

Finally, it seems appropriate to comment on Martin's (1985) suggestion that GENRE be set up as a connotative semiotic above REGISTER, with registers as its realizations. This proposal has the advantage that apparent pre-selections in REGISTER can be attributed to selections at the level of GENRE. It is certainly true that once we find ourselves in a particular framework of an institutionalized activity of the community, only particular selections from Field, Mode and Tenor will regularly co-occur. It is also true that this should be explained in terms of activity structures, and that activity structures do form a social semiotic system. However, that system is not best regarded, I think, as being in a connotative semiotic relation to the semiotic system of REGISTER. The reason is that the 'stacked semiotics' approach leaves out a flexible account of context-dependencies. We need to specify which selections from Field, Tenor and Mode will have which social meanings, in relation to which activity structures, according to which GSP genre assignments. A semiotic system is a system of resources. It ought not also to be asked to describe the patterns in which those resources are actually co-deployed to make the regular meanings of a community. We need to distinguish carefully between semiotic resource systems, like REGISTER and LEXICO-GRAMMAR, and typical patterns of use of those systems in a given community (GENRES, ACTIVITY STRUCTURES and the THEMATIC and DISCOURSE FORMATIONS discussed below).

10.3 THE SEMANTICS OF STRUCTURAL MEANING

The meanings we assign to any stretch of text, or to any action, are, of course, a function of many contexts. The analysis of those contexts and how a community assigns meanings differently according to them is the province of SOCIAL SEMIOTICS. In the particular case of meanings made with the resources of the linguistic semiotic system, we can speak of the study of SEMANTICS. Some of these contexts are paradigmatic ones, as with the meaning of one lexico-grammatical selection from a system *vs.* another. Others are syntagmatic, as in the case of the meanings we assign according to the functional role of a unit in a group, clause or genre structure. Some are textual, in the sense that the context lies in some sense within what we take to be the same overall text. Others are intertextual, and may belong to the same activity structure (but not the same text), or to other texts of the same genre, or of the same thematic or discourse formation (see below and Lemke 1985a). I want first to consider here the nature of structural meaning, i.e. of the semantic contribution of functional role in a genre (and more generally in an activity structure).

In any genre or activity structure the assignment of a portion of text or an action to a functional role contributes to the meaning we make with them. The same statement may function as both a Thesis (in an initial position) and as a Conclusion (in a final position) in a genre of Argument-from-Evidence (cf. Lemke, in press, b). But its synoptic meanings are quite different depending on whether, in the one case, it precedes or, in the other, follows Evidence. Likewise, a potential Thesis is synoptically different in structural meaning depending on whether it was followed by Evidence or by its Consequences (in which case we might label it Cause, rather than Thesis, synoptically, i.e. after the fact). A Teacher Question carries a very different meaning interactively when part of a REVIEW, in which students are expected to know the Answer, than in a DEVELOPMENT episode, where they are not necessarily expected to; similarly for a Negative Evaluation in the two cases (Lemke 1983b). The meaning of any action is a function of the relations we construct for it to other actions, thereby making them its contexts. Typical contextualizations are made in a community by means of its typical activity structures for contextualizing (cf. meta-contextualization relations in Lemke 1984). Structural meanings arise from connections we make, the structural semantic relations we construe, between an element and other elements within the same (including hierarchically higher-level, embedding) structure. The organization of structural meaning in a text is one of the fundamental constituents of text semantics (an other being the interlocking organization of thematic meaning, discussed below).

The organization of structural meaning is segmental, multivariate and hierarchical. It is segmental in the sense that elements of a structure tend to be realized by one or more discrete linear segments of a text (or linear sequences of actions in general). It is multivariate in the senses we have already discussed: completable sequences of functional elements interrelated semantically in a heterogeneous fashion. It is hierarchical in the sense of constituency hierarchies and rank-realization hierarchies. Each element of a structure may in turn be itself a substructure (constituency). Or its realization may be a structure of a different kind. Hasan (1984, forthcoming) has argued convincingly that EXCHANGE STRUCTURES, defined as sequences of speech acts, are not constituent substructures of genre structure, but are rather possible realizations of its elements. For similar reasons I have been led to define RHETORICAL STRUCTURES as multivariate, regular functional sequences of speech acts, which can realize elements of more than one genre structure (Lemke in press, b). Frequently, a genre structure element can also be realized by more than one possible rhetorical structure. The notion of 'speech act' itself is not a fundamental or privileged level in the analysis. It is merely a placeholder name for the elements of a rhetorical structure, or, when no ambiguity arises, for units at still lower ranks. Which 'speech act' a given portion of text is cannot be determined from that bit of text alone, but only from a contextualization of it, in at least the next higher-rank structure. Rhetorical structures, while not by this definition genres, are still, of course, activity structures. The classroom TRIAD DIALOGUE pattern referred to above (Teacher Question, Student Answer, Teacher Evaluation and optional elements) is thus a RHETORICAL STRUCTURE, while REVIEW or DEVELOPMENT, whose elements may be realized by TRIAD DIALOGUE sequences, are speech GENRES. In our classroom episode we have seen the TRIAD DIALOGUE rhetorical structure used to realize a Teacher Answer, an element of the STUDENT-INITIATED DIALOGUE classroom genre. The Thesis–Evidence–Conclusion pattern is also a rhetorical structure, as is the Cause–Consequence pattern (see Lemke in press, b; in press, c).

With rhetorical structures, as with activity structures at all ranks, and no matter how realized (i.e. by resources of whatever semiotic system, including non-linguistic systems), assignment to a structural element entails structural semantic relations (e.g. the thesis–evidence relation, the cause–consequence relation, the question–answer relation) that contribute to text-semantic meaning.

10.4 THEMATIC ORGANIZATION OF MEANING

Multivariate structures are not the only means by which meaning is organized in texts. Nor, of course, is structural meaning the only kind of meaning a text element can be given. We are accustomed to talking in terms of the semantic meanings of words and other text units, and even to thinking of these as relatively fixed meanings that are properties of the words or phrases themselves. But all meaning is made by contextualization; the actual occurrence-meaning, use-meaning or text-meaning of a word or phrase depends entirely on its contextualization (Lemke in press, b). This is not to deny that in addition to text-meaning, it is also useful to speak of the MEANING POTENTIAL of a lexical item: the sets of semantic options that are regularly realized by it within the systems of lexicogrammar (cf. Hasan 1985, 1986). But a lexical item does not HAVE to be used only in its typical ways; by creating text and action contexts around it, we can use it in new ways (see Lemke 1983a on semantic novelty). Indeed, its typical meanings, its meaning potential, in any community must be dynamically reconstituted through its actual uses. What is most often missing in contextual models of semantics is reference to inter-textual contextualization (Lemke 1985a). It is not just by construing semantic relations to the immediate textual, or even situational, context that we make a word or phrase mean. It is also by construing relations to other texts and situations in which that word or phrase has been used. This kind of contextualization would be hopelessly under-determined, of course, were it not for the fundamental fact that patterns of semantic relations among the same or closely related words and phrases are regularly repeated over and over again in many texts in a given community. These patterns I have called THEMATIC FORMATIONS (Lemke 1983a, 1985a, in press, a, in press, b). The use-meaning of a word or phrase tends to be established mainly by contextualizing it with co-thematic texts, those that share the same thematic formation. We can, therefore, speak of thematic contextualization, in which each text element is construed as being in particular semantic relations to other elements according to the pattern of a thematic formation abstracted from the set of co-thematic texts.

If, in reading a text, we come across the lexical item *electron*, and also *atom*, *orbital* and *valence*, then we can construct semantic relations among these items (thereby also specifying semantic features for each, as relevant), according to a pattern we have encountered in many other texts. That pattern is a characteristic of the community, much as an activity structure is (both are semiotic formations; see Lemke forthcoming). There may, of course, be more than one thematic formation in which the constituent thematic items are realizable by these lexical items. In each there could be different semantic relations among the items. But wider contextualizations of situational and actional contexts (cf. REGISTER) are usually sufficient to make only one match probable, at least in a particular subcommunity. Thus the relation of [*electron*] to [*atom*]—as thematic items now, realized by the lexical items—in typical thematic formations for the discourse of chemistry and physics, may be that of part to whole (meronymic). Or [*atom*] may be the regular locative circumstantial attribute whose carrier is [*electron*], i.e. *electrons are in atoms* (see Halliday 1985 for the categories; Lemke 1983b, 1985b for the formation).

In the classroom episode, the first formation that is instanced is one having to do with <School Homework>, but as we pass into the STUDENT-INITIATED DIALOGUE we find thematic items from <Electron Configurations> which include here: *1s2, orbital, energy*. A semantic relation of the formation is that *orbitals have energies*, which is in fact a grammatical metaphor realizing the underlying intertextual semantic relation [Carrier: orbital / Attribute: energy] (see Ravelli's discussion of grammatical metaphor in this volume.)

A thematic formation may be represented as a web-like, non-linear diagram (mathematically, a directed graph), whose nodes are thematic items (realizable by a set of formation-specific, near synonyms), connected, perhaps multiply, to one or more other nodes by lines which specify the thematic relation between them. A thematic relation may either be a semantic category relation of the kind used in traditional lexical semantics (synonym, antonym, meronym, hyponym, etc.), or it may be the regular GRAMMATICAL semantic relationship in which the items are typically found (e.g. carrier/attribute, classifier/thing, process/goal, etc.). 'Typically' here simply means that it is possible to define a set of co-thematic texts where the specified thematic–semantic relations of the items obtain. Entire formations may be glossed by lexical items and have thematic relations to items or other formations. They may also have metadiscursive relations, such as heteroglossic relations to one another (Lemke in press, a, in press, b).

Use-meanings depend on thematic contextualization as well as structural contextualization. We make sense of a word or phrase, both in terms of an assignment to a functional role in a grammatical, rhetorical or genre structure, and in terms of an assignment to a thematic item with specific thematic relations to other items (both those that occur in our particular text and those that may only occur in other co-thematic texts). This view of semantics not only allows for intertextual contextualization, complete context-dependence of use-meanings, and analysis of the discourse formations actually in use in a community; it also provides the basis for understanding the THEMATIC organization of meanings in a text, a non-structural pattern of organization.

As we move through the linear sequence of a text, at first dynamically, and eventually synoptically as well, first one and then the other thematic formations are instantiated in the text. Of course, it is possible for a text to be a pure instance of one formation, but in general texts interweave several formations, or subformations, in complex but analysable ways. One formation might continue to be relevant to the thematic meanings all through a text (CARRIER formation), while other formations appear only over shorter stretches. Within a given structurally defined unit, we might have many formations 'active' in the sense of being instantiated (i.e. being used to make sense of the semantic relations in that stretch of text). We can imagine a representation of a text like an orchestration for a line of sung lyrics. The text line has below it other lines on which we indicate whether or not a given formation (instrument, voice) is active. This enables us to define a PROSODIC THEMATIC ORGANIZATION for the text. Units of linear text can be defined by specifying which overlapping formations are active in them. A prosodic boundary between units will then always be characterized by the entry or exit of one or more thematic 'voices' (i.e. active formations). Major boundaries are then either (1) those where many formations either all enter or all cease to be active at once, or (2) those where formations which are active over long stretches of text enter or (perhaps temporarily) become 'silent'.

These thematic strands (like cohesion chains, cf. Lemke in press b; Aziz's discussion in this volume) do not merely run parallel to one another. Texts make explicit semantic connections between them. It should be clear that this can only be done by establishing STRUCTURAL semantic relations between thematic items of different formations (cf. interacting chains, Halliday and Hasan 1985: Ch. 5). So, for example, an item of one formation may be introduced in a rhetorical structure as a Cause for a Consequence realized by an item from another formation. Or a grammatical structural link, such as Actor/Process, or Classifer/Thing may be forged. Similarly, genre structure relations may be used in the same way. Particularly important prosodic segments of texts may be those where the maximum number of locally active formations are all linked by the relations of a single, lower-rank structure (e.g. clause or clause-complex: cf. the notion of a THEMATIC NEXUS in Lemke in press, b).

In the classroom episode, at line (15) the <Electron Configurations> formation is joined to one we can call <Hotel>. The link is forged by <*electron* . . . *go into* . . . *hotel*>, where the grammatical semantic relations of the elements of this abstract clause bridge between two otherwise quite disjoint formations. Of course, we recognize here a rhetorical strategy of Conceit, based on an implied correspondence (itself a metadiscursive relation of the formations) in which:

Electron	→	Traveller
Atom	→	Town
Orbital	→	Hotel
Energy	→	Cost

The stretch of text where both these formations are active, lines (15–17), can be defined as a prosodic thematic segment, independently of any purely structural segmentation of the text here.

The thematic relations of a formation are as they are because such structural connections among their constituents have been made in the past, and continue to be made in the same ways. Structural relations create new thematic relations as they become 'institutionalized' in a community. Conversely, of course, our ability to 'parse' structures, i.e. to assign lexical items and strings to functional roles in particular structures, often depends on our recognizing familiar THEMATIC relations among the items.

10.5 TEXT STRUCTURE AND THEMATIC ORGANIZATION

We have just seen how it is possible to define two segmentations of a text. One is based on the hierarchy of genre, rhetorical and grammatical structures. The other is a prosodic segmentation based on changing constellations of active thematic formations. These two aspects of text organization work together. As I have shown elsewhere (Lemke in press, b), there is a strong tendency for there to be an inverse correlation between the rank of a structural boundary and the number of formations that are continuous across that boundary. This means that for major boundaries, e.g. between GENRE ELEMENTS, there will be a few (often only one) thematic formation in common on both sides of the boundary, but that for minor boundaries, e.g. between elements within a rhetorical structure, there will be a maximum continuity of formations (and their interactions).

Thematic and structural organization in a text are complementary in the interests of maintaining its coherence (and, *a fortiori*, its cohesiveness). When thematic continuity is at a minimum, e.g. when there is total change of topic, coherence is maintained by rhetorical and genre structure, so that the new topic may be seen as a digression, a new case, or example of a specific sort which will later be synoptically reintegrated somehow into the structure of the text. Conversely, when structural continuity is at a minimum, e.g. when we are at a transition from one major genre or activity structure to another, thematic continuity maintains the unity of the text or event.

In our classroom episode, the major structural boundary is between lines (1) and (2), where a major thematic shift also occurs (from <Homework> to <Electron Configurations>). Two lesser boundaries occur at lines (27–29), between elements within the Student-Initiated Dialogue genre structure, and lines (37–38) between the first and second such episode in a series. The <Electron Configuration> formation is continuous across these boundaries, as is its interaction with a related subformation <Order of Orbitals>. What changes at the minor boundaries is only whether this subformation is linked semantically to <Energy Order>, before and after, or to <Chart Order> in between. A brief intrusion of the formation <Nature Order> is in fact challenged by a student, line (34), as a violation of the norms of classroom science discourse (see Lemke 1983b). This moment, dynamically pregnant, but synoptically isolated by the teacher's failure either to respond to the potential challenge or to use further the <Nature> formation, also illustrates the role of contextualization relations in the use of an activity structure or thematic formation. In the context of CLASSROOM LESSON, and the immediate context of a Teacher Answer to a question using a Science formation, the use of an anthropomorphizing formation <Nature> can be interpreted as incompetence or disrespect for the addressees. Without such an analytical framework, there is no discursive regularity to the occurrence of line (34), whereas in fact it is a highly regular and probable response in this context.

The organization of meaning in a text can thus be seen to be a complex function of the hierarchy of structures and the interconnection of thematic formations instantiated in it. Every stretch of text is made sense of in terms of its functions in these structures and its semantic relations in these formations. The elaboration of hierarchical structures in a text and the interplay of its thematic formations allow meanings to be made at the level of whole texts that cannot be made in single clauses, or even clause complexes, no matter how long. That is why these resources have been developed historically in our community and its predecessors. Since construal of a structure, or of a thematic formation, ultimately relies on relations a text may have to other (co-thematic or co-generic) texts, these resources are properly intertextual ones. It is ultimately the resources of intertextual contextualization that underlie text structure and text semantics.

APPENDIX

Episode transcript

(DRS: 12L23–14L4. Cheryl's question)

1.	T:	[Pause] OK. Do I have all the homework papers? . . . CHERYL.
2.	Ch:	What I don't understand . . . I don't understand is WHY do
3.		they come this way: 1s2, 2s2, 2p, then, um, 2p6, 3s—
4	T:	All right. [8 secs, T draws at board]
5.		This is ENERGY. [Pause] What orbital has the lowest ENERGY?
6.		. . . Cheryl.
7.	Ch:	K
8.	T:	That's a, that's a SHELL. What ORBITAL has—
9.	Ch:	S
10.	T:	The S . . . and that would be, the lowest one would be, 1s.
11.		OK? Which one has the NEXT lowest energy?
12.	Ch:	2s
13.	T:	Which one has the NEXT lowest energy?
14.	Ch:	2p
15.	T:	OK? . . . Electron comes to town, wants to go into the cheapest
16.		hotel. It goes into the cheapest one that's available. If the
17.		2s is there, if it's empty, fine, 2p? great. What's the
18.		NEXT lowest? Josephine?
19.	Jo:	4s
20.	T:	Thank YOU . . . What happened to 4d? [means 3d]
21.	Jo:	It has less, it has less energy than . . . I mean . . . I don't
22.		know how to explain it.
23.	T:	Yes you do.
24.	Jo:	It has less energy than 4d, uh, 3d.
25.	T:	Which has less energy?
26.	Jo:	4s
27.	T:	Yes. 4s is lower energy level than the . . . 3d.
28.		Does that answer your question, Cheryl?
29.	Ch:	But in here it has the 3d first. [Pause] On the chart—
30.	T:	On the chart it—because the chart was put together by a
31.		PRINTER, who likes to go in numerical order, if it was put
32.		together by a chemist, or if it was put together by NATURE
33.		. . . it would go THIS way.
34.	St:	Mother Nature, right?
35.	T:	And I—I as—as a matter of fact, when I tend to write
36.		these down, and think about 'em, this is the order I think
37.		about. And I would write down 4s before I'd write down 3d.
38.	St:	What's after 3d?

BIBLIOGRAPHY

Bourdieu, P. (1972), *Outline of a Theory of Practice*, Cambridge, Cambridge University Press.
Halliday, M. A. K. (1985), *An Introduction to Functional Grammar*, London, Edward Arnold.
Halliday, M. A. K. and Hasan, R. (1985), *Language, Context and Text*, Geelong, VIC (Australia), Deakin University Press.
Hasan, R. (1984), 'The structure of the nursery tale', in Coveri, L. (ed.), *Linguistica Testuale*, Rome, Bulzoni.
—— (1985), 'Lending and borrowing: from grammar to lexis', *Beitrage zur Phonetik und Linguistik* (Special Issue: Essays for Arthur Delbridge, Clarke, J. E. (ed.))
—— (1986), 'The grammarian's dream: lexis as most delicate grammar', in Halliday, M. A. K. and Fawcett, R. (eds), *New Developments in Systemic Linguistics*, London, Pinter.
—— (forthcoming), 'Situation and the definition of genres', in Grimshaw, D. (ed.), *Perspectives on Discourse: Multidisciplinary Study of a Naturally Occurring Conversation*, Norwood, NJ, Ablex Publishing.
Lemke, J. L. (1983a), 'Thematic analysis: systems, structures, and strategies', *Recherches semiotiques/Semiotic Inquiry* (Toronto), 3, 159–87.
—— (1983b), *Classroom Communication of Science*, Arlington, VA, ERIC Documents Service (ED 222 346) (Final Report to the US National Science Foundation).
—— (1984), *Semiotics and Education*, Toronto, Victoria College/Toronto Semiotic Circle Monographs.
—— (1985a), 'Ideology, intertextuality, and the notion of register', in Benson, J. D. and Greaves, W. S. (eds), *Systemic Perspectives on Discourse, Volume I*, Norwood, NJ, Ablex Publishing.
—— (1985b), *Using Language in the Classroom*, Geelong, VIC (Australia), Deakin University Press.
—— (in press, a), 'Discourses in conflict: heteroglossia and text semantics', in Benson, J. D. and Greaves W. S. (eds), *Functional Perspectives on Discourse*, Norwood, NJ, Ablex Publishing.
—— (in press, b) 'Intertextuality and text semantics', in Gregory, M. and Fries, P. (eds), *Discourse in Society: Functional Perspectives*, Norwood, NJ, Ablex Publishing.
—— (in press, c), 'Social semiotics: a new model for literacy education', in Bloome, D. (ed.), *Learning to Use Literacy in Educational Settings*, Norwood, NJ, Ablex Publishing.
—— (forthcoming), 'Heteroglossia and social theory', in New York Bakhtin Circle (eds), *M. M. Bakhtin: Radical Perspectives*, Minneapolis, University of Minnesota Press.
Martin, J. R. (1985), 'Process and text', in Benson, J. D. and Greaves W. S. (eds), *Systemic Perspectives on Discourse, Vol. I*, Norwood, NJ, Ablex Publishing.

11 Cognitive process in context: a systemic approach to problems in oral language use*

Jonathan Fine
Department of English, Bar-Ilan University, Ramat-Gan, Israel

11.0 INTRODUCTION

The basic question of this chapter is: why does cognition have to be considered along with social–contextual facts in the study of language use? The answer to the question is in two parts: (1) cognition has a direct influence on language use, and (2) the influence of the cognition combines with social and contextual influences on language use.

The structure of the chapter is as follows. First, there is a brief introduction to the approach of looking at cognitive and social–contextual facts simultaneously, including the strategy of looking at 'problems in oral language use'. Second, data will be presented on the referencing patterns of some psychiatric patients. Attention will be paid to changes in referencing patterns over time and the association of these referencing patterns with clinical states and cognitive ability. This section will thus deal with the combination of cognitive and social factors. The third section presents data on sentence stress from two subjects: one autistic, the other schizophrenic, to show how they compare to each other and how the choices these subjects make from the stress and cohesion systems compare with other speakers. Again, the point of the comparisons will be to show the operation and interaction of cognitive and social forces in the USER's selection of options and the social effects of this USE of language. Finally, the conclusion places the role of cognition in a functional approach to language that also takes social and contextual factors seriously.

The following discussion is based on the theoretical framework of systemic linguistics. In usual systemic terms, language is taken to be a resource with series of more or less interdependent options (Halliday 1973, 1985). That is, language provides the resources to accomplish different ends in social interaction. Systemic theory adopts the position that language is created and used for

---

* The data reported here were gathered in collaboration with Giampiero Bartolucci and Peter Szatmari, psychiatrists at McMaster University Hospitals, Hamilton, Canada. Support was received from the Medical Research Council of Canada Grant MA5685 to Giampiero Bartolucci. Without these colleagues this chapter could not have been written. However, they bear no responsibility for the use I have made of the data.

social functions. The social functions derive from the culture (Halliday 1973, 1978; cf. Hasan 1985). The focus here will be on the reasons for choosing one option or another in actual language use. There is ample evidence for the role of social settings in influencing the choice of options. See Martin (1983) for examples from children's language, Rochester and Martin (1979) for schizophrenics, Fine (1985) for the reading disabled, and Gumperz (1982a, 1982b) for detailed analysis of a wide range of cases.

To the social effect of language, however, this chapter adds a consideration of cognitive influences and the combination of social and cognitive influences. The goal is to include the USER and his cognitive processes as an influence on the USE of language and then to consider the communicative effect of the particular selection of language options. The social and cognitive realms influence the choices from the systems of language resources. In turn, the particular realization of those choices then constitute the ongoing communication as a social act.

On different occasions one or other of the social or cognitive influences may be predominant. To take transparent examples: aphasics have a clear cognitive (and neurologically based) impairment that strongly influences their selection of options. On the other hand, a speaker addressing a supreme court in session or a head of state is subject to strong, socially based constraints. Thus, although the basic resources of language remain constant, the use of these resources can be highly constrained by either cognitive or social factors. In less extreme examples than those mentioned above, there is usually an interplay of a range of typical cognitive and social influences. These examples are not typical of language in use. However, they are meant to clarify the role of cognitive and social forces in shaping language output. The objective of this study is to characterize both the typical and atypical USES of language and to supply explanations for the uses in terms of the social and cognitive factors contributing to the language event. These factors come together in the speaker who is both an organism with cognitive processes and a social entity for whom language is the chief means of realizing social interaction.

Before completing this introduction and turning to the data, the strategy of studying atypical uses of language will be discussed. The linguist's ultimate goal may be to characterize typical uses of language and explain those uses in terms of cognitive and social factors. However, at an early stage, the investigation of atypical uses of language (from speakers with language or communicative disorders, children or second-language learners) can show how the systems operate when there is a strain somewhere in the process of language use. It is inappropriate to make direct inferences about typical language processing from the cases of atypical processing; however, from these cases we start to specify the requirements of a theory that will explain both the typical and atypical uses of language. The more typical uses of language can be understood as involving different values of some parameters compared to the clearly atypical uses that were the first objects of investigation. Heuristically, though, it is simpler to start with the atypical uses so that the parameters can be identified.

To support the above arguments about the contributions of both social and cognitive factors to language use, two sets of data will be presented. The first concerns the patterning of reference in schizophrenic patients. Two ways of characterizing referencing in conversation will be presented and then related to changes in clinical state and standardized measures of psychological functioning. The second set of data is drawn from a study of sentence stress and referencing in the language of two teenage subjects: one autistic, the other schizophrenic. The data will be used to show the cognitive sources of some aspects of language use and to chart the social effect of other aspects.

11.1 STUDIES

To turn now to the first set of data, Rochester and Martin (1979 and elsewhere), Bartolucci and Fine (1987) and others have studied cohesion (Halliday and Hasan 1976) in various psychiatric populations. Aside from the particular findings, these studies have shown that only specific kinds of cohesive analysis show the relationship of language use to either diagnosis or to hearers' judgements. For example, Rochester and Martin (1979, especially Ch. 7) show that some referencing categories (e.g. generics, bridging) discriminate among groups of speakers (normals, thought-disordered, and non-thought-disordered schizophrenics) but that the patterning and power of discrimination of the referencing categories are dependent on contexts in which the samples of language were gathered (e.g. narratives, interviews or describing and interpreting cartoons). The use of linguistic systems, then, must be studied with respect to specific contexts.

Four psychiatric patients with a variety of diagnoses were each interviewed twice to study longitudinal changes in their language. The measure of language use in this study is called the index of self-referencing. It was constructed as follows: for each endophorically referring nominal group (see Rochester and Martin 1979) the antecedent was identified. The antecedent was then noted as either being in the speaker's own (earlier) speech or in the interlocutor's speech. That is, endophoric links were classified as being tied to either the speaker or to the interlocutor. The following constructed conversation illustrates how the endophoric links were identified. In utterance (1) speaker A sets up an endophoric link between *Mary* and *she*. That is, *she* refers back to an antecedent that is within the speaker's (A's) own speech. Similarly in utterance (3), speaker A uses *she* to refer back to an antecedent spoken by A, (*Mary* in utterance (1)). The use of *there* in utterance (3) is also endophoric, but instead of linking back to an antecedent spoken by A, *there* sets up a link to the speech of B. The antecedent of *there* is *in town* in utterance (2) spoken by B. In this fragment of conversation, speaker A refers back to his own speech twice (*she* in (1) and in (3)) and to his interlocutor's speech once (*there* in (3)).

(1) A: I saw Mary yesterday and she was cheerful.
(2) B: Were you in town?
(3) A: Yes, and she seems happiest there.

The more language a speaker produces relative to the interlocutor, the greater is the chance that the speaker will create links to his own speech—there is simply more to link back to. In order to control this factor, the number of links established by endophoric references was proportionalized by the number of words the subject and the interviewer spoke. The formula is as follows: where $L-S$ is the number of endophoric links to the subject's own language, $L-O$ is the number of endophoric links to the interviewer's (other's) language, $W-O$ is the number of words spoken by the interviewer, and $W-S$ is the number of words spoken by the subject:

$$\frac{L-S}{L-O} \times \frac{W-O}{W-S}$$

This index thus measures how the speaker constructs semantic continuity in an interactive situation. A higher value for the index signifies that the speaker is drawing relatively more on his own speech to signal the continuity of meaning—chiefly the continued identity of participants.

The subjects for the study were four psychiatric patients: one manic, one Wernicke-Korsakoff syndrome (which led to a permanent amnestic syndrome), and two acute schizophrenics. Each subject was interviewed for about ten minutes by a psychiatrist associated with their cases. In addition they were tested on the Wechsler Adult Intelligence Scale (WAIS—Wechsler 1944). The verbal score was based on the comprehension, similarities and vocabulary subtests. The performance score was based on the digit span, picture completion, block design and picture arrangement subsets. Two to four weeks later all subjects had shown clinical change as assessed by the attending psychiatrists. See Table 11.1 for details of the subjects' characteristics and changes from the test to retest periods. As the table shows, clinically the manic and one schizophrenic improved while the Korsakoff-Wernicke and the other schizophrenic showed a deteriorated psychiatric state.

The results (see Table 11.1) show that the index of self-referencing moved in the direction of the clinical change. Clinical improvement was associated with greater referencing to the speaker's own language. Clinical deterioration was associated with less referencing to one's own language and relatively more referencing to the speech of the interlocutor. This relationship between clinical state and self-referencing is difficult to interpret without further data. However, there is independent evidence of self-referencing. The amount of self-referencing compared to other-referencing increases between the ages of five and nine in the conversational language of school children (Fine 1978). Furthermore, the teachers in these conversations show the highest levels of self-referencing. That is, increasing self-referencing in conversations seems to be an aspect of developing language use.

Self-referencing in psychiatric patients is related, then, to general psychiatric state when the patient's language is studied longitudinally. However, this is not the only relationship that self-referencing enters into. For these four subjects there is a direct relationship between self-referencing and verbal (but

Table 11.1 Subject characteristics and scores for the index of self-referencing and the percentage of unclear referencing

Patient				Period between tests (weeks)	Index of self-referencing		% unclear referencing	
Sex	Age	Diagnosis	Clinical change		Tests		Tests	
					1	2	1	2
F	49	schizophrenic	deterioration	4	2.52	1.69	17	11
M	24	schizophrenic	improvement	3	4.49	1.51	22	16
M	20	manic	improvement	2	0.35	2.02	9	4
F	51	Korsakoff-Wernicke	improvement	4	0.35	1.68	4	8

not performance) IQ. This relationship was also found (unpublished data by Bartolucci and Fine) in a larger sample of psychiatric patients with mixed diagnoses including schizophrenias, manias and depressions [$r = .60$, $t = 3.125$, $p < .01$ two-tailed, $df = 17$]. There thus seems to be a connection between general cognitive abilities involving language and the specific pattern of using and presenting information in conversation. These relations of cognitive processing to language use also may affect social interaction. A listener may have to readjust listening strategies to fit the management of information required by a speaker's pattern of self-referencing. At this stage, however, there is no direct evidence of the adjustment by the listener.

The above relationship between cognition and self-referencing can now be usefully compared to the findings of unclear referencing found in schizophrenics and especially thought-disordered schizophrenics. Unclear referencing is referencing that explicitly specifies that some further information is needed to interpret a reference item, but the listener is then not given the necessary information. The failure may lie either in not providing any suitable information as in (4) (called additioning) below, or in providing two likely pieces of information such that the reference item is ambiguous as in (5) below (see Rochester and Martin 1979; Bartolucci and Fine 1987).

(4) The donkey was crossing THE OTHER river (when no prior river has been mentioned or is inferable).
(5) A commuter and skier are on a ski lift and HE looks completely unconcerned.

Unclear referencing as defined by these two specific language patterns is not correlated with verbal IQ in the larger sample of psychiatric patients [$r = .25$, $p > 1$]; nor does unclear referencing change in the same direction over time as the index of self-referencing (see Table 11.1). In both the synchronic and longitudinal data, self-referencing and unclear referencing are independent of each other. These two measures of referencing, which signal the continuity of meaning in conversation, seem each to have a cognitive underpinning but, it must be argued, the cognitive processes involved differ for each kind of referencing.

Unclear referencing and self-referencing are thus seen as emerging from the cognitive processes of the speaker. However, language is used for communication and the social impact of the two measures of referencing must also be considered. Unclear referencing is noticeable and disturbing to social interaction. However, the amount of self-referencing seems to be below a threshold of recognition of participants in a conversation. Self-referencing involves how a speaker encodes semantic continuity with respect to what both speaker and interlocutors are saying. However, differences in how this semantic continuity is established are not noticeable even to those who must follow those various patterns of continuity. These studies of referencing, then, show that choices from the same system of cohesion and the retrieval of information are sometimes socially important and sometimes more indicative of specific cognitive processes than of the resulting social impact of the utterances. To take a wider perspective, we can see choices from semantically defined systems in language as being based on cognitive ability and having social impact. The speaker is a cognitive and social being at the same time and the linguistic system is subject to variation implicating these two aspects of the speaker.

A second set of data that points to social and cognitive involvement in specific language choices will now be presented. Primarily this study involves sentence stress in the language of two teenage subjects: one autistic, the other schizophrenic. The account of sentence stress follows a more or less standard description: in the unmarked case, sentence stress falls on what the speaker is coding for the hearer as new. By the choice of the location of sentence stress the speaker can display his understanding of the hearer's information state. The following utterances (where capitals indicate the sentence stress) encode as new different items and amounts of information.

(6) John gave Mary the BOOK.
(7) John gave MARY the book.
(8) John GAVE Mary the book.
(9) JOHN gave Mary the book.
(10) The BOOK, John gave Mary.
(11) To MARY, John gave the book.
(12) John gave Mary THE book.

In (6) *the book* is certainly new information and some undetermined amount of information to the left of *book* is also new. Utterance (6) can answer the questions: What did John give to Mary? (the narrowest interpretation of what is encoded as new), What did John give? What did John do? or What happened? (the broadest interpretation). Sentence (6) has the unmarked location of sentence stress and is appropriate in a range of contexts since the amount of information encoded as new is not fully determined. In comparison, sentence (7) is reasonably only an answer to Whom did John give the book to? sentence (8) is an answer to What did John do to get the book to Mary? and sentence (9) is only an answer to Who gave the book to Mary? The above description and examples of sentence stress are of the most standard cases only. A speaker may choose to be sarcastic, ironic or insulting by manipulating sentence stress to, for example, code as new what is known to be obvious to the hearer.

Sentence (6) above represents the unmarked case for which sentence stress falls on the last lexical item in the tone group. In sentences (7)–(12) there is an atypical association of sentence stress with the lexico-grammatical structure of the sentence. Frequently, the meaning of these marked uses of sentence stress is contrastive (see Gunter 1974). The speaker is signalling that the presumed information state of the hearer is correct except for the information receiving the marked sentence stress. The hearer should then correct his information state by including the stressed information. It should be noted that the speaker's assessment of the information state of the hearer may largely be derived from what the hearer has himself said earlier. Frequently, then, contrastive stress can be interpreted as 'What you have said is correct if the information under contrastive sentence stress is substituted for the corresponding information in your earlier utterance(s)' (Gunter 1974).

Given this background on sentence stress, the subjects and specific focus of study will be presented. The schizophrenic subject was a fourteen-year-old male with typical defining characteristics of schizophrenia including emotional withdrawal, hallucinations and flattening of effect. The autistic subject was also a young male, eighteen years old at the time of testing. Autism is defined by onset before thirty months, lack of response to others, deficit in language development, evidence of history of echolalia and pronominal reversals, bizarre behaviour and absence of childhood schizophrenia (that is, schizophrenics typically have hallucinations and delusions that are by definition not found in austistics). The data, as in the first study, consist of ten-minute conversations with a familiar clinician.

To compare the language of our subjects to the established findings on schizophrenic speakers, the frequency of unclear nominal groups was tabulated. The schizophrenic subject used unclear referencing (additioning and ambiguity as in (4) and (5) above) in 8 per cent of his nominal groups. This level of unclear reference is consistent with other studies of the language of schizophrenics in interviews (Rochester and Martin 1979; Bartolucci and Fine 1987). In contrast, the autistic subject used unclear reference in only 3 per cent of his nominal groups. These findings established one predictable difference between the subjects in terms of the ease of decoding the references made in nominal groups: the autistic subject is easier to understand than the schizophrenic subject.

The focus of the study, however, is on sentence stress. Sentence stress was investigated by coding intonation focus in major and minor clauses spoken by the subjects. These foci were then further coded as unmarked (on the last lexical item of the tone unit) or marked (all others) (see Halliday 1967; Crystal 1975 for details). For the autistic subject there were thirty-five marked intonation foci in ten minutes, while for the schizophrenic subject there were just four. The autistic subject had an additional unusual intonation pattern. He put the sentence stress on the main finite verb and used a secondary stress later in the clause. This pattern was found four times in the austistic's speech but not at all in the schizophrenic's speech. Passages (13) and (14) are examples of the autistic's speech. In (14), note the stress on PEOPLE given the verbal context presented. Slashes (/) indicate tone group boundaries, small capitals indicate tonic focus.

(13) Well / my MOTHER said / that she LOVED my father and still does and I (tonic focus) / do BELIEVE that my father does look AFTER my mother (interviewer: um hm)
as well / my father seems to be a good father to my SISTERS / our BELIEFS our STANDPOINTS are widely VARIED / as my father HIMSELF said / HIMSELF and I (no tonic focus) / are about as DIFFERENT as we can POSSIBLY BE /

(14) However, I understand the basic principles of how such equipment works and I know how to adjust the mechanisms, the switches and such

(interviewer: um hm)
of such equipment so that I can get maximum use out of it
(interviewer: I see)
Some PEOPLE are afraid to adjust the controls on let's say a VCR.

Given that our autistic subject speaks with unusual sentence stress, how should such a pattern of use be understood? Again the social impact and cognitive influence on language use will be considered. First the social perspective: the autistic's frequent use of marked intonation focus sends the following message to the listener: 'Your expectations that this piece of information can be taken as given are incorrect—this information is new and/or contrastive given what we suppose each other shares about the verbal context and the non-verbal situation'. Such a message, sent repeatedly, leads the hearer to doubt the presumed sharing of information by hearer and speaker. The hearer is led to this doubt as follows: as a speaker/hearer of English the hearer knows the marked and unmarked uses of intonation focus. In particular, he knows that marked intonation focus is only used if there is a particular reason for it, including, for example, contrastive stress. Contrastive stress, and in fact other uses of marked intonation, send special messages to the hearer. The hearer of a large number of such special messages must determine why the speaker is sending such messages, given the verbal and non-verbal contexts which suggest certain shared information between speaker and hearer. The hearer must conclude that either the speaker is not following the normal rules for using English or that the speaker has a different view of the world and especially of the information state of the hearer. Although the hearer may feel that the speaker's language is somehow unusual, the data collected reveal few if any overt indications from hearers that there is a communication problem. This lack of overt dissatisfaction is in contrast to the unclear referencing discussed above. Unclear referencing leads to clear and explicit breakdowns of communication such that the hearer overtly asks for clarification.

We have looked at the social effect of a pattern of unusual linguistic choices. However, a short background of the syndromes involved can lead to statements about how social factors shape language use. Autism involves a severe developmental problem in interaction, including specifically delayed language acquisition and lack of attachment to caretakers and others. These early indications of autism help to explain the linguistic patterning found in this study. At an early age, these children do not have the practice nor are in situations which will demonstrate to them how talk is mutually constructed. The placement of intonation focus is connected to the expression of socially relevant meanings. Such meanings and the devices for their expression must develop from interactions the child has with others. If those interactions cannot take place because of either delayed language or social withdrawal (the two are probably complexly related, but that relationship is irrelevant for the present argument), then it would be difficult for the child to acquire the required appropriate uses of language.

Leaving the above predominantly social view of the austistic subject's language, there are some tentative remarks to be made about the cognitive side of language use. One possibility that must be explored in explaining the autistic subject's use of language is a difficulty in the cognitive processes used to understand social facts. The subject may not be able properly to parse the relevant social facts (including, for example, what information the hearer can be assumed to have available) that are necessary for the construction of socially appropriate messages. There is a possibility here of blurring the distinction between cognitive processes and the social use of language. Specific studies are needed to separate these concepts. For example, aphasias involve predominantly cognitive processes (with underlying neurological sources), but the use of language by different kinds of aphasics has clear social effects. In cases where there is less clearly a specific problem in cognitive processes (and an identifiable neurological source) such as autism or schizophrenia, the involvement and interaction of cognitive and social processes is less clear. In terms of autism the account of the interaction of cognitive and social processes may be as follows: if there exists a cognitive (or even physiological) cause for the unusual intonation pattern, the social miscommunication resulting from the mismatch of speaker and hearer expectations for linguistic patterns can lead to problems in social interaction. To some extent, interaction will be hampered. This difficulty with interaction can then itself hinder the learning of facts, including facts about social concepts, and the development of the cognitive structures needed to cope with social interaction. The meaning potentials available to the speaker will be restricted. Thus the difficulties in cognitive processes affect social processes and vice versa. It is the task of linguistic analysis in a broad sense to show carefully the interactions of social and cognitive processes with respect to specific classes of speakers and for language use in general.

11.2 CONCLUSION

This chapter has presented the position that language use is a creation of cognitive forces as well as social forces. Cognition, unlike social structure and interaction, is not a source of meaning or a source of systems of meanings. Cognition is inherently individual, whereas meanings must come out of negotiated interactions for which individuals must agree with each other what and how language means. However, to predict and explain language use better, we must take into account the cognitive processes of individuals and the interaction of cognitive and social processes. Although cognition may be inherently individual, this does not foreclose the possibility of generalizing about cognition and its effect on language use. Four specific points are to be made in this connection:
1. Minds to some extent work alike. One task of linguistics conceived of broadly is to discover what is common among minds and what is specific to particular minds.
2. Groups of minds certainly work alike. As studies of cognitive disabilities (from any theoretical perspective) show, it is possible to generalize about

syndromes and even to generalize about the language produced by speakers having specific syndromes.
3. Minds work alike when processing social artefacts. Speakers of a language interpret language and other semiotic systems similarly.
4. Even phylogenetically, cognition must have been formed and shaped by the social and communicative character of man.

Our goal is to specify the limits of influence that cognition has on the social use of language. To advance towards this goal, we must focus on specific language systems and how cognition influences specific choices within the system. The use of specific choices, then, has consequences in terms of the social effect of language. These social consequences should be predictable from a functional theory of language. Just as the social consequences are predictable from an appropriate theory of language, so we should work towards a compatible cognitive theory that will predict more of language use than is predictable from social and contextual considerations alone.

The abstract systems of language are actualized in specific situations for specific social purposes. Generalizations are thus derivable from how groups of speakers have agreed to interact. Cognition initially would seem to involve states and processes of individuals. However, a strictly individual focus is illusionary in two ways: firstly, minds do work alike for biological reasons; secondly, minds must necessarily be similar to allow for social interaction and the social nature of man. For example, minds must be similar in the amount of information they can store for specific periods of time, the rate at which new information can be processed. The social–cognitive approach presented can exploit the social and functional theories of language as first steps in investigating how minds must process language to achieve the shared meanings of successful communication (see Fawcett 1980). The strategy of this study has been to take systemic functional descriptions of language as hypotheses of the cognitive processes of individuals communicating in social contexts.

The goal of predicting more about language use will involve THE USER and THE USE of language with generalizations at the level of the code, generic situations (Gregory 1985) and cognitive processes. The cognitive part of the theory will involve an active processing model rather than a static view of the individual or groups of individuals having knowledge of language. Rather, people have cognitive abilities which act on language systems and contribute to specific linguistic productions. The goal then remains to predict more about language use within a functional framework but at the same time trying in specific formal terms to chart the contribution of cognition to language use.

BIBLIOGRAPHY

Bartolucci, G. and Fine, J. (1987), 'The frequency of cohesion weakness in psychiatric syndromes', *Applied Psycholinguistics*, **8**, 67–74.
Benson, J. D. and Greaves, W. S. (eds) (1985), *Systemic Perspectives on Discourse, Vol. 1: Selected Theoretical Papers from the 9th International Systemic Workshop*, Norwood, NJ, Ablex.

Crystal, D. (1975), *The English Tone of Voice*, London, Edward Arnold.
Fawcett, R. P. (1980), *Cognitive Linguistics and Social Interaction*, Heidelberg, Julius Groos.
Fine, J. (1978), 'Conversation, cohesive and thematic patterning in children's dialogues', *Discourse Processes*, **1**, 247–66.
—— (1985), 'Cohesion as an index of social-cognitive factors: oral language of the reading disabled, *Discourse Processes*, **8**, 91–112.
Fine, J. and Freedle, R. O. (eds) (1983), *Developmental Issues in Discourse*, Norwood, NJ, Ablex.
Gregory, M. (1985), 'Towards "Communication" Linguistics: a framework', in Benson and Greaves (eds) (1985).
Gumperz, J. J. (1982a), *Discourse Strategies*, Cambridge, Cambridge University Press.
—— (ed.) (1982b), *Language and Social Identity*, Cambridge, Cambridge University Press.
Gunter, R. (1974), *Sentences in Dialog*, Columbia, SC, Hornbeam.
Halliday, M. A. K. (1967), 'Notes on transitivity and theme in English, II', *Journal of Linguistics*, **3**, 199–244.
—— (1973), *Explorations in the Function of Language*, London, Edward Arnold.
—— (1978), *Language as Social Semiotic: The Social Interpretation of Language and Meaning*, London, Edward Arnold.
—— (1985), *An Introduction to Functional Grammar*, London, Edward Arnold.
Hasan, R. (1985), 'Meaning, context and text: fifty years after Malinowski', in Benson and Greaves (eds) (1985).
Martin, J. R. (1983), 'The development of register', in Fine and Freedle (eds) (1983).
Rochester, S. and Martin, J. R. (1979), *Crazy Talk: A Study of the Discourse of Schizophrenic Speakers*, New York, Plenum.
Wechsler, D. (1944), *The Measurement of Adult Intelligence*, Baltimore, MD, Williams and Wilkins.

Index

activity structure
  and genre
  and text structure 158–60
agnation 141
Akindele, Femi *99–119*
Arabic
  demonstratives 151
  and ellipsis 155, 156
  and parallel 155
  and reference 149–51
  repetition 154
artificial intelligence 5
Aziz, Yowell, Y. *148-57*

Bentham, J. 91–4
Bever, T. 51
Bolinger, D. 33, 53
Bowers, Frederick *90–8*
Brazil, D. 101–3
Burton, D. 109
Butler, Christopher S. *13–27*

Chafe, W. 52, 63
Chomsky, N. 49–50
clinical applications 4
cohesion
  and conjunction 153
  and ellipsis 155, 156
  in English 149
  lexical 152
  nature of 148
  and parallel 155
  in psychiatric populations 173–81
  and question response 154
  and reference 149–51
  and repetition 154
  and substitution 155, 156
cognition
  and autism 179–80
  nature of 180–1

  and self-reference 174–7
  and social use of language 181
cognitive
  ability 176–7
  influences 172–3
  processing 176, 180–1
combination rules (CRs) 37–8
communicative dynaminism 77–81
computational linguistics 5
congruence 135
conjunction 153
context
  and semantic specifications 34–6
  and text structure 160, 161, 165, 166
  and utterance 120–3
contextual
  features 31–2, 34–8, 122
  specification (COS) 34–42
conversational structure
  and breakdown 111–13
  and exchange 102–14
  and systemic linguistics 23
  of Yoruba families 114–18
Coode, G. 91, 94–6
Coulthard, M. 101–3, 105

Davies, Eirian C. *28-45*
deixis 22–3
derivation 141
directive 102–3
discourse
  analysis 148
  definition of 2–3

elicitation 102–3
exchange
  analysis of 102–4
  bound 109–14
  boundary 105
  classification of 105
  informatory 108–10

INDEX

exchange (*cont.*)
  prefatory 106–8
  repeat 113–14
  structures 164

factive verbs 21–2
Fawcett, R. P. 18–19
Fine, Jonathan *171–82*
functional grammar (FG)
  and theme 90–1, 97, 98
functional sentence perspective (FSP)
  and communicative dynamism 77–81
  realization operands 88
  and relevance 79–81
  and textual analysis 81–3
  and theme and rheme 76–9, 80, 81–7

generic structure potential (GSP) *see* genre
genre 161, 163
grammatical metaphor
  choice motivation 143–6
  and complexity 143–6
  detection of 141
  Halliday's framework for 133, 134–5
  as lexicogrammatical realization 136–8
  and mode 143–6
  model of 135–6
  and paradigmatic plurality 140–3
  quantification of 141–3
  and syntagmatic plurality 1
  types of 138–43
Green, G. 56–7
Gundel, J. 55–6

Halliday, M. A. K. 4, 6, 13–19, 55–6, 72–3n, 76–7, 97, 110–11, 129, 133–5, 145

illocutionary force 17–19, 28, 121, 129
implicature 19–20
informative 102–3
initiation 114–18
institutional discourse
  in non-native English 99, 114–18
inter-organism 14
intonation focus 179–80
intra-organism 14

Kies, Daniel *47–75*, 90

Leech, G. 14–19, 23–4
Lemke, J. *158–70*
lexical
  cohesion 152
  density 144
literary criticism 5
Lyons, J. 56–7

macrolinguistics 148
marked themes (pronominally reinforced and unreinforced)
  connective function of 61–2
  contrastive function of 62
  definition of 47–9, 72–3n
  frequency of 56–7
  and new and old information 53–5, 61, 63–71
  and pragmatic functions 50–2, 60–2
  presentational function of 60–1
  and presupposition 57–60
  and semantic studies 52–6
  and stylistic reordering 49–50
  syntactic analysis of 57–60, 71–2
  and word order 71–2, 73–4n
Martin, J. R. 162–3
meaning
  definition of 30, 32–3
  multiple, hypothesis 29–30, 32
  options 120, 131, 133
  organization of structural 164
  potential 133–4, 165, 180
  semantics of 163–4
  single, hypothesis 29–30, 32, 33–44
  textual 133
  thematic organization of 164–7
metafunctional hypothesis 16–17
metalinguistic markers 48–9
metaphor *see also* grammatical metaphor
  dead (frozen) 142–3
  ideational 138–43
mode 143–6
mood 125
moves
  following 103–4
  informatory 102–4, 115
  initiating 102–3, 106, 107–10, 114
  opening 109
  response 103–4
microlinguistics 148
multiple meanings hypothesis (MMH) *see* meaning

nominalization 134–5, 140
nuclear disarmament 138–43

paradigmatic
  phenomena 16
  plurality 138–43
  relations 24
perspective 2–3
polar interrogatives 28, 30–1, 125, 126–7
pragmatic(s)
  ambiguity 29–30, 32
  functions of marked themes 50–2

INDEX

general 24–5
intro 2, 13–14
multivalency 28–9
socio- 24–5
presupposition 20–1
process 2–3
product 2–3
propositional attitudes 36
prosody 128–30
prototypical categories 16

Ravelli, L. J. *133–47*
realization
  congruent 18, 135, 136–8, 141–3
  lexicogrammatical 121, 134, 136
  metaphorical 137
  prosodic 121
  and register 162–3
recursion *see* paradigmatic plurality
reference 149–51, 176–8 *see also* self-reference
register 162–3
repetition 154
requests
  acceptability of 124–6
  form of 123–8
  incomplete 125–6
  nature of 123–5
  success of 124–6
  and tone 128–30
rheme 76–9, 80, 81–7
rhetoric 3
rhetorical structures 164
Ross, J. 53

self-reference
  and cognition 174–7
  and psychiatric patients 173–81
  and psychiatric improvement 174–6
semantic
  ambiguity 29–30, 32
  specifications (SeSs) 34–42
sentence stress 177–9
SHRDLU program 5
significance 31–2, 34–6
Sinclair, J. McH. 101–3, 105
single meaning hypothesis (SMH) *see* meaning
social semiotics 163, 172

stylistic reordering 49–50
syntactic form 31–2
syntagmatic plurality 141
systemic functional grammar (SFG) 3–4, 7, 24–5
systemic linguistics 13–14, 16, 171–2

text 3, 148
text structure
  and activity structure 158–60
  covariate 160
  definition of 158
  and meaning 163–4
  multivariate 159–60, 164
  and thematic organization 167–9
  univariate 160
theme
  and functional grammar 90–1
  and functional sentence perspective 76–9, 80, 81–7
  iconic functions of 94, 97–8
  and metaphor 145
  and meaning 164–7
  and principal object 92–3, 95
  and speech-act force 94–5
  and text structure 167–9
thematic
  contextualization 166–7
  formation 165–7
  fronting 47, 90–8
  organization 166–9
  relations 166–7
tonality 17–18
tone 128–30
tonicity 17–18
topicalizations 47, 53
Tucker, G. *120–31*

unclear reference 176–8

Williams M. P. *76–89*

Yoruba English
  concept of 100
  data analysis 101
  data collection 101
  and initiation 114–18